About the Author

ANNETTE KOLB [1870-1967] was born and grew up in Munich, the daughter of a German garden architect and a French pianist. Her first novel, *Das Exemplar*, was published in 1913, followed in 1928 by a second, *Daphne Herbst* and in 1934 by a third and final novel, *Die Schaukel*. She also wrote two volumes of short stories and a number of biographies: Schubert, Mozart, Wagner and King Ludwig II.

During the First World War she became an outspoken and active pacifist, just escaping arrest by fleeing to Switzerland. During the period of the Weimar republic she was at the centre of literary life in Germany and a prominent supporter of the League of Nations. Her political articles were published in the leading newspapers and magazines in which she warned constantly of the dangers of the growing power of the National Socialists. She was a friend of Thomas Mann, who used her as a model for one of the characters in *Dr Faustus*; her publisher, Gottfried Fischer, said of her, 'she towers like a monument over the chaos of our times'. In 1933 she emigrated to Paris and in 1941 to the USA where she continued to alert the world to the danger of the Nazis. She issued appeals to the German resistance to 'bring the tyrants before the tribunals before it is too late'.

She returned to Europe after the end of the War, in 1945, living in Ireland, Switzerland, France and Germany, spending her last years in Munich.

Prion Lost Treasures
Other titles in the series

The Bourbons of Naples
Harold Acton

Disraeli
Robert Blake

The Marquis of Montrose
John Buchan

The River War
Winston S Churchill

The Dilessi Murders
Romilly Jenkins

Napoleon and his Marshals
A G Macdonell

The Atrocities of the Pirates
Aaron Smith

Conversations with Wellington
Earl Stanhope

Napoleon's Letters
J M Thompson

by

ANNETTE KOLB

With an Introduction
by
Jean Giraudoux

This edition published in 1998 in Great Britain by
Prion Books Limited
32-34 Gordon House Road,
London NW5 1LP

First English edition published in 1939 by Victor Gollancz
Translated by Phyllis and Trevor Hewitt

ISBN 1-85375-285-1

Cover design by Bob Eames
Cover image *Mozart* by J. Lange courtesy of The Mozart
Museum, Salzburg

Printed and bound in Great Britain
by Creative Print & Design, Wales

Contents

List of illustrations

Prion would like to thank Dr Gabriele Ramsauer of The Mozart Museum in Salzburg for her help with the photographs.

Introduction [1]

WERE WE NOT PROFOUNDLY CONVINCED THAT THE world's lack of understanding is ultimately dearer to genius than its applause, the life of Mozart would be one of the greatest burdens of guilt handed down to us by our grand-parents, an original sin, as it were, which I should find far harder to bear than that of the Garden of Eden. While not being so unfortunate as to be descended from that Count Arco who kicked him out of the room, or from that Duchesse de Chabot who refused, one icy day, to allow him to warm his fingers before playing, neither I nor any of you, on the other hand, can claim descent from him who lent him support when he found his mother dead in their room in Paris, for at that hour he was alone, nor from those who followed his corpse to the cemetery of St. Marx, for, owing to the inclemency of the weather, not a single one of the mourners had the courage to go on to the end. The

[1] Translation from the introduction to the French edition.

inestimable privilege, the hereditary patent of nobility, that would have been conferred by the simple fact of having closed the eyes of Frau Leopold Mozart, of having lent Mozart one's best suit of clothes, of having shoed his carriage-horses free of charge, of having stopped him in the street to tell him that he was to be one of the world's most precious possessions, and then when, polite and flattered, he had turned to go, of having run after him and assured him that what one had just said was but a fraction of the truth—and when he had again thanked one, bestowing one of those twittering nicknames on one which he gave to his friends and which made the birds flock to him, of having followed him in silence, as though struck dumb and as though one could never in all one's life utter a word again—these privileges we rejected in the persons of our great-grandparents. So much the worse for us. It is we who are the losers. The important thing is that it was Mozart who most fully appreciated Mozart. No poet, no musician, ever wrote so much for himself as he. In every poem, in every symphony, a large number of concessions are made by the author, not to *those* who are not himself, but to *that* which is not himself. Or again, there are parts of himself which do not participate in the miracle. Take Goethe. His work is all Goethe, and yet I am not sure that everything in his being is completely Goethe. I know all that in Goethe which is not for Goethe and is for us, the passages in Goethe which did not afford him complete satisfaction, owing either to a certain human imperfection, or, on the other hand, to an excess of human sublimity. In Mozart all is for Mozart. Goethe would have been happy, ennobled, contented, admired, loved, even had a poet called Goethe not existed at the same time as he. What an admirable chamberlain, what a perfect doyen, what an amazing lover

Goethe would have made even without Goethe! But I cannot conceive without a shudder of the passage of Mozart through this world, of his indigence, his poverty, his anguish of soul, of what a tatterdemalion, what a blind, blundering creature he would have been, had *Mozart* never existed. And that might well have been. Those men are much rarer than one would suppose who bring with them into this world their own sustenance, and the demands of whose souls, whose inner urges, are in exact proportion to their genius. I do not think, therefore, that, faced with the blindness and obtuseness of Salzburg and Vienna, Mozart experienced real suffering, for he never knew doubt. One feels convinced that his impatience was due, rather, to his feeling for humanity, his desire to see the best in it, to find brothers amongst his fellow-men. As to the women, let us pass them over; if they do not understand genius, they bear it company, they understand its lesser attributes, the honour and glory, the merry prattle, the gaiety, some the riches, others the poverty. Elated for the wrong reasons, provoked for the wrong reasons, eager, with or without reason, to sacrifice themselves, they at least are unrivalled at filling in the lesser, but not necessarily trivial, moments of creation and inspiration—the donkey-rides and the duets on the piano. All the same, it is pretty disheartening, very disheartening when a man is at the point of death, to have to entrust a legacy such as the music of Mozart to a world of which he is no longer sure. An archbishop's rage, a fire in the archiepiscopal grate, a fit of spite on the part of Constanze, and all is over; no more *Magic Flute*, no more *Requiem* . . . One has only to remember how Mozart, feeling death upon him, hid that *Requiem* from his wife, moving it from cupboard to cupboard. Humanity having failed him, he would have been content with an ordinary safe. Everything in human form was a menace to his *Requiem*: the unknown purchaser, his wife, death also . . . And yet to what other order of beings was he to entrust it?

These are some of the reflections to which you will be led by Mlle. Annette Kolb's *Mozart*. Mlle. Kolb—who, in a series of delightful novels, the equals of which we shall seek in our own literature until such time as they too have become French, has depicted all the doubts, joys and sorrows of the souls touched by Mozart, those Mozartian souls who are still to be found wandering about here and there on this earth, in big ships, in little English hotels, in Munich drawing-rooms—has been unable to evade the duty of giving us the 'novel' of Mozart himself. That it should be Mozart who has introduced her to the French public, is a piece of good fortune which is her due, and we shall all be moved by her presentation, the most sensitive we have ever had, of the composer's life. An emotion which, as we read her, deepens our conviction that Mozart was German through and through, that the Germany he created began to disappear with him, and that it is idle to play Mozart in a country where that which is Mozart, that is to say, liberty, candour and joy, is lost. May I tell her that if Mozart bears witness to Germany's lost happiness, if for his other countries he is no longer anything but the memory of a golden age, I have nevertheless a feeling that he is becoming one of our French contemporaries. I know she will forgive me for thus, in this introduction written in her praise, sounding the praises of my own country.

JEAN GIRAUDOUX
1938

Fanfare

THERE HAVE BEEN HAPPENINGS IN THE CASE OF WHICH there has been no final settlement, no passing over to the order of the day, no closing of a chapter. They live on as echoes, caught in the clefts of the rocks or in the far corners of the forests, and their reverberation does not die away.

The interment of the thirty-five year-old Mozart in a pauper's grave in a Viennese cemetery was one of these happenings. On December 6th, 1791, he was borne thither in a blinding snowstorm, unattended by a single mourner. Owing to the inclemency of the weather the handful of friends who had followed the bier decided, when there was still another mile to go, not to proceed as far as the cemetery. And so it came about that when the coffin was lowered into the grave, and a mass grave at that, there was no one to pay it his last respects.

Soon after this, on October 21st, 1793, Queen Marie Antoinette, Mozart's one-time patroness, also found herself, although, it is true, still alive, on her last journey. Her arms were so tightly bound behind her back that the cords cut into her hands. Thus yielded up to the gaze of the mob, she passed by the Louvre, and looked up at its windows with eyes out of which all expression had faded. Then the tumbril rattled along down the rue St. Honoré towards the place of execution. An aura of mystic dignity, we may be sure, enveloped her features. And yet we possess a drawing by one eye-witness, Louis David, in which, appropriately enough, we can perceive the artist's homage to the rulers of the day. For a certain peevishness, nay commonplaceness—if you please!—is introduced into the profile, which reflects the baseness of the portraitist himself; it is as though he were savouring, not without satisfaction, the moment when the severed head of this Queen, tortured to her last breath, would be hurled at her feet.

As a child she had played with Mozart at Schönbrunn. When, on one occasion, he had fallen on the slippery parquet floor of the palace, the little Archduchess had picked him up with that charming grace which she was to display throughout her life. From that moment the child prodigy had adored her.

In later years there were to be no more meetings between them. Life ordained otherwise. Only in death, in the desolate circumstances of their despatch from this world, whereby the corpses of both are to this day undiscoverable, were the destinies of these two victims of the barbarity of our hearts united. And was he any less regal perchance, poor Mozart, whom they gave so ignominious a burial that no arrangements, even, were made for a cross to mark the place where he lay? A grave, it is true, was no fitting lodging for him—and therein, too, was he distinguished from the run of mankind. But how significant, nevertheless, was that farewell of his from a world in which all things are ever and again possible! A world that, caught up in time, yet labours under the delusion that it changes, and claims to be a different world simply because to-day it makes pilgrimages to Mozart's house, because the most sorry orchestras rattle out the overture to Figaro and the veriest tyros assault our ears with his most difficult airs. The lack of recognition accorded to him in his own day, then manifested in repudiation of him, has its counterpart in the profanation of his works to-day. The services, it is true, of the societies and institutes which grow up round a great cultural heritage are in the highest degree praiseworthy. It is to their pious efforts that we owe the fact that so many treasures have been unearthed or preserved. In this connection, too, *Les études mozartiennes* in Paris are doing magnificent work, whereas an entire library of superb old Italian compositions is hoarded up as so much dead material in the museum of Naples.

It is, however, a dangerous and mischievous piece of folly to set out to popularise great and noble music. We know what the Bach vogue, the Beethoven vogue, the Wagner craze brought upon us. Even Mozart can only have a small circle of devotees, just as during his lifetime only isolated admirers and friends stood by him. And even these did not remain loyal to him. How was it that the rich Lodge to which he belonged did not champion his interests? And the noble and princely patrons by whom but a few years before he had found himself so assiduously courted—what had they against him? The Esterhazys, the Lichnowskys, the Countess Thun, of whom so much has been heard? Who can tell us that?

Perhaps the banality of the following sentences from a letter written by a certain Herr Foster of Berlin while on a visit to Vienna will put us on the right track. "You will scarcely credit," he writes enthusiastically, "how condescending, how friendly the people are here. One is scarcely conscious of being among people of rank, and at every moment one is like to forget it and to treat them on familiar terms, as friends and equals . . ." Mozart's self-assurance was proportionate to his greatness. We find scathing, contemptuous, even despairing tones in his letters, but never a hint of fawning. And he anticipated—ahead of his time in this respect too—that sublime conception of freedom which was to sweep Europe from France like a roaring wind. True, he was *a priori* raised above such things as groups, parties, ideologies and illusions. It is because his intellectual qualities never obtruded that we so rarely mention his intelligence. He had, however, seen through the hollow mechanism of our earthly existence, which denied him all opportunity of self-fulfilment. The fact that he was to leave it so rich a legacy, the world did not take into account. In everyday life only the petty problems of the moment count. Whereas the most precious instrument that perhaps the world has ever known was allowed to fall to pieces, and not a voice was raised in protest. Mozart saw more and more clearly that effective help would come either not at all or too late—which is much the same thing—and that he would be yielded up to defeat, to early death. His intuition in the last years of his life was like a dark shadow that walked ever before him.

Yet with a devotion as selfless as though he fancied he could shake to its foundations a world in which he no longer believed, he remained true to himself. An irresistible force drew him on to where ultimate isolation awaited him.

The eternally beautiful utterance: "Ye are gods!" was addressed to mortals in whom the divine spark was as unquenchable as in him.

❧

Mozart's Portraits

LET US RETURN TO EARTH. IT WAS, IT IS TRUE, WITH AN ineffably heavy heart that Mozart parted from it. Yet the completeness with which he vanished from the earth is symbolical. He did in very truth bid it farewell.

Mozart's portraits are for the most part lacking in authenticity; the few authentic ones preserved are in almost all cases copies or even copies of copies, and there is no connecting link between them. They contradict each other as flatly as do the extremely meagre utterances of his contemporaries about him. Clementi took him, because of his elegant appearance, for a gentleman-in-waiting; the actor Backhaus, on the other hand, who refused to admit him to one of his own rehearsals in the Concert Hall in Frankfurt, for a journeyman tailor. There were those who extolled the marvellous beauty of his large eyes. On May 27th, 1789, some time before the beginning of a concert, Tieck, then a lad of sixteen, entered the dimly-lit, still empty auditorium of the Berlin National Theatre and saw in the orchestra a man unknown to him. He was short, brisk, restless, and dull-eyed, an insignificant figure in a grey top-coat. Bustling from one music-stand to another, he seemed to be eagerly scanning the music placed upon them. It was Mozart.

"This, then, was the impression he created when he was not inspired and his gaze was not kindled."

There exists in a private Viennese collection a spirited portrait of him as a boy, painted by Cignaroli in Verona during his first Italian tour in 1770.

From the year 1774 dates a portrait of a sixteen-year-old Mozart in a suit of dark silk, with lace jabot and lace cuffs turned back to display an almost ethereal hand. The figure is well-proportioned, the nose unusually large; the brow, the large deep-set eyes, which betray signs of ill-health, are aglow with the inward rapture, the exaltation, of first love. Here before us is a noble youth of great distinction.

Completely different is an oil painting, executed three years later, before the journey to Mannheim. The bearing is perfect, but the proportions are no longer so happy, the eyes are a trifle prominent and their gaze is curiously sombre; the expression indubitably bespeaks the musician. His father called it an "incomparable likeness". We do not know, however, how far this copy, sent as a present to Padre Martini at Bologna, does justice to the original, which has been lost.

We should not, of course, pass over the Salzburg family portrait; the father already somewhat crabbed, but of superior breeding to the now deceased mother, who gazes down in effigy at her children as they play a duet; the daughter, Nannerl, somewhat passé, fussily-dressed in provincial style, with headdress and lace embroidery, takes the treble, Wolfgang, with completely expressionless mien, the bass.

The most popular portrait at the present time is the unfinished oil by Lange, the husband of the once so ardently loved Aloysia Weber. The half-lowered profile is gazing down on invisible keys and Mozart is lost in a reverie. The contours of the head, the form, the setting and the size of the wide-open eye might be extremely impressive, were the effect not spoiled by the dilettante holding of a chance, fleeting expression. For here we have a woeful, not to say sentimental, Mozart. And who was less so than he? But this conception is in keeping with the way in which certain conductors—unfortunately very famous ones amongst them—conduct his adagios to-day, with incursions into sickly sweetness. And who was less sugary than Mozart?

We find the wide-open eye also in the life-size, very handsome and very inadequate silver-point by Dora Stock, which is so frequently reproduced. Executed at Leipzig in the year 1789, it shows him even more in profile than the oil by Lange, and reveals obvious signs of ill-health. The head is almost fragile.

An engraving of the same year, however, presents him as almost a dwarf and a hydrocephalic.

As a child he was beautiful, sturdy, fearless, and of a merry disposition; there seemed to be every prospect of his living to seventy or more. Of the youthful Mozart we know, too, that he captivated both young and old. "Some took him for a German nobleman, others for a Prince, and I was taken for his tutor," his father proudly and gladly writes home from Rome on April 14th, 1770. We also hear of two summer suits, one of "rose-coloured silk, yet of such an unusual shade that in Italy it is called *colore di fuoco*, with silver lace and sky-blue facings"; another is an apple-green watered silk, with silver buttons and rose-coloured taffeta facings". "If Wolfgang continues to grow at this pace," runs his father's letter of July 21st, "he will be quite tall by the time he arrives home."

But his growth shortly afterwards met with a setback: the inevitable consequence of the inordinate quantity of work which the child, the boy, had to get through as clavierplayer, violinist, improviser, and contrapuntist: all the sonatinas, sonatas, fugues, church-music, cantatas, and other compositions, including two operas; there was a great deal, it is true, that was immature among them, but even at this age he had written such arias as those from *Il Re Pastore* and *Bastien and Bastienne*, and the magnificent antiphon, *Quaerite primum regnum Dei*, composed in Bologna in 1770—works, that is to say, produced long before the age of eighteen. The only breaks that we know of in an incessant round of composing and performing were those necessitated by one or two serious childish illnesses. The father mentions in one of his letters, it is true, that he takes good care to see that Wolfgang shall have a rest after meals, but of a real holiday we never hear.

There is no doubt that Mozart felt the need of a fine setting in which to shine, and that even at home he set great store by clothes. Fully conscious of his own worth, arrogant, if at all, only at Court, he was for the rest kindness and consideration itself, one of the most lovable and approachable, though reticent, of natures. We find mention of his large head, his profusion of fair hair, his enormous nose; on the one hand of emaciation, and on the other of corpulence. He was also short. What further do we know?

Without unduly straining our imagination we can visualise the figure of a Goethe, a Beethoven, a Wagner. Most of the great men of the last few centuries—even J.S. Bach—we should recognise if they stood before us. But the veil of night that obscures the figure of Mozart has never been lifted. The way in which he walked or stood, his gaze, his gestures—let him who can conjure up a picture of them come forward. Dead are all grandchildren of grandchildren who saw him, dried up all our sources of information, exhausted all the material at our disposal, burned, torn up, indiscoverable, all letters that make further mention of him and might give us something upon which to build.[1] We do not know what he looked like.

It is significant that we cannot picture Mozart to ourselves. Either in life or in death, for his death mask, which would have been so revealing, crumbled to dust, was swept away with the rubbish. His features have eluded us, they are beyond all knowing; all trace of them, as also of his grave, has vanished.

[1] It has recently been reported that a number of Mozart's letters exist in America and are awaiting publication.

❧

Early Years

LET US TAKE THE DATES OF MOZART'S LIFE AT A CANTER, so to speak; to do more than that would only be to recapitulate what has been said over and over again, whereas we are here more concerned with what can be read between the lines.

The fullest accounts are those that date from his childhood. For at this period we find his father writing fully to his friends in Salzburg of the concert tours which he undertakes with his family. Later on we find the son less communicative in comparison.

Like Gluck the Bavarian and Beethoven the Rhinelander, Mozart lived and died in Vienna; he was a true Austrian only on his mother's side.

His father, Leopold Mozart, a native of Augsburg, where his relatives, one-time masons who had risen to be bookbinders, still lived, was the first of his family to make a name. Intended, because of his talents, for the priesthood, he became instead a violinist and composer. He studied for two years at the University of Salzburg; all serious-minded and ambitious musicians of that period, among whom he was undoubtedly to be numbered, endeavoured to obtain an academic as well as a musical education. And yet how poor he must have been to have lauded so gratefully as his saviour a certain Count Thun whose service he entered as musician and valet—this combination of functions being also in keeping with the custom of the period. The Count had, averred Leopold Mozart in the dedication to a sonata engraved by himself—for he was granted complete freedom for his musical preoccupations—"*ad un tratto cavato dalle dure tenebre d'ogni mio bisogno e stradato ver l'orizonte della mia fortuna.*"[1]

This fortune took him on to the court of the Archbishop of Salzburg, the kindly and well-meaning Count Schrattenbach, in whose service he was promoted from fourth to second violin and finally to assistant *Kapellmeister*, becoming very soon not only a very busy but also a highly respected man. Besides training the choir, he had to teach fifteen choir-boys the violin, and later also the clavier. In addition to this he had private pupils. A number of his compositions have been preserved. His masses have been criticised on the score that there is far too much of a booming *allegro con brio* about them, but, after all, the churches of that period were inclined to be gay and a trifle theatrical. A treatise on the violin was considered to be his chief success. Even before its appearance the Leipzig Society of Musical Studies had made him a member.

In the bringing up and education of his famous son, therefore, it was he who was the decisive factor and not his

[1] "Snatched me from the grim shadows of my need and set me on the road to where fortune loomed for me on the horizon."

wife, Anna Maria Pertl, daughter of a deceased court official of St. Gilgen, whom he married in Aigen in the year 1747. Of seven children, who were brought up on water instead of milk, only two survived: a daughter, Maria Anna, called Nannerl, born on June 30th, 1751, and Wolfgang, who was born on January 27th, 1756, at eight o'clock in the evening. Nannerl revealed herself at the age of eight as a brilliant pianist, and Wolfgang as early as the age of four as a musical prodigy who was the talk of Salzburg. The father, therefore, resolved to present his daughter and his little son, whom he idolised and in whom he recognised a budding genius, to the courts of Europe, and to seize the opportunity of making capital of such unusual talents.

In January, 1762, he set out with his family. Their first objective was the court of the Elector of Bavaria in Munich. In September of the same year the four of them went by boat to Vienna. Among rulers with a fondness for music at this period the Habsburgs were pre-eminent, and it was fashionable for members of the nobility to maintain their own private orchestras. In Passau the travellers were detained for five days by the Archbishop. In the monastery of Ips the Franciscans rose from the table at which they had just seated themselves to hasten to the church and cluster round the little Wolfgang as he played the organ. Even customs barriers fell when he produced his miniature violin and played a minuet to the officials, and the Mozarts were allowed to pass without the usual formalities. People "of the highest nobility", as the father was fond of expressing himself from now on, smoothed their path for them, placed travelling coaches at their disposal, blazoned ahead the fame of the children, especially that of Wolfgang.

To us, however, this blaze of glory that was shed on Mozart's early life remains a consoling thought, a source of gratification. He had little time for play, but as a child he thoroughly enjoyed life; occasional over-strain could not quench his gaiety. Wonderlands they were that the wonder-child visited on his travels. Life glided towards him like a gaily beflagged galleon. There is no one, probably, who has ever gazed upon the world with such assurance. And he had every reason to do so, for at this period it lay at his feet. It seemed to harbour no grudge against him. Only the anxious father, knowing its perfidies, planned ahead, deliberated, calculated and weighed up their chances. The times were favourable. Even the Imperial family was unwilling to miss the sensation and there ensued the famous invitation to Schönbrunn. We know the rest: how little Wolfgang jumped on to the Empress's lap and how she allowed him to remain there. Who, we may wonder, was the more innocent, the trusting child, who as yet knew so little of the ways of this topsy-turvy world, or the great and noble Maria Theresa, who, when he grew up, was first of all to withdraw from him her special favour, and finally to lose all interest in him, to spurn him, to fail completely to recognise his greatness?

Although at this tender age he was already versed in the differences of rank, "Ugh! that's all wrong!" he shouted into the little closet where the Emperor was engaged in playing the violin. He had no liking for such stagey effects as playing on an instrument covered with a cloth, which his father, in his capacity of impresario, interspersed freely among his tricks of stage-management. He beckoned to Wagenseil, the famous composer, pianist and Imperial music-teacher, to come and turn over the pages for him. "I'm going to play a sonata of his," he announced. "He knows something about music."

The bright groundwork of his nature gained its colour

from the brilliance of those first few years. Only now and again did painful and dangerous illnesses, which attacked him, his sister and his father, intrude into the fairy-world in which he lived. Nevertheless it was a fairy-world. And how many children must have gazed wide-eyed in wonderment at the wonder-child, who, in all the magic of his gold-embroidered court-dress—a present from the Empress—performed so unconcernedly before the world.

It was only for a brief period that the Mozarts stayed in Salzburg after their return from Vienna. On July 9th they set off again, to be away for more than three years—and this time their main objective was Paris. After months of travelling, of course. En route the children gave performances in Munich, Augsburg, Ludwigsburg, Schwetzingen, Heidelberg, Mainz, Coblenz, Aix, Frankfurt-on-Main. It was there that the fourteen-year-old Goethe saw the eight-year-old Mozart "in powdered wig and sword". It was an impression that he was never to forget for the rest of his life. At all the German courts, in all the concert halls, honours, presents and ducats were showered upon them. Many people admired Wolfgang at the organ even more than at the clavier. For some time now he had also taken delight in composing. In Brussels he wrote an allegro in C major which was later to be included in his complete works.

On November 18th the Mozarts reached Paris, where they stayed at the house of Van Eyk, the Bavarian ambassador, whose wife was a daughter of Count Arco of Salzburg. But the many letters of recommendation that they had brought with them did not help them forward here; their countrymen Grimm, secretary to the Duke of Orleans, was the only one who received them, and in return for this courtesy Leopold Mozart retained for him exaggerated feelings of gratitude, trusting him blindly and lauding his kindness and philanthropy to the skies.

And by Christmas things had progressed so far that they were presented at the Court of Versailles and to the Marquise de Pompadour, who, to Wolfgang's chagrin, was not so willing to be kissed by him as had been the Empress Maria Theresa. On the other hand, Louis XV's daughter made much of him. And from now on the family's success was assured in Paris also. Wolfgang played the organ in the court chapel in the king's presence, two big concerts were arranged, Nannerl's performance called forth the usual applause, while Wolfgang enjoyed a triumph both as violinist and pianist, accompanied arias at sight and was for the first time heard to improvise on the clavier.

Grimm might well be proud of his protégés, and he referred, indeed, with intense satisfaction to his discovery "du prodige." He himself wrote the dedication to the sonata for violin and piano which Wolfgang had composed in honour of the King's second daughter and his father had had engraved. Gold pieces came pouring in, and a host of costly presents for the children, the value of which the father noted down meticulously. Highly satisfied with the visit to Paris, he set out with his family for England, reaching London on April 22nd, 1764. By the 25th an invitation had come from King George III and Queen Charlotte. The royal pair's favourite pieces were put before the little Mozart, and he played them at sight. The invitation was repeated on May 19th. On June 5th the children gave a public performance, to the great delight of a vast audience. The takings were enormous. The reception in England exceeded all expectations. Life might well have continued like this. The imagination of the little Wolfgang, the pet of kings and royal personages, now dwelt in a kingdom of his own, a realm round which he travelled, issuing orders, giving directions, enforcing his will, and among the subjects of which he distributed rewards and presents. "Rücken" he called it, the Kingdom of Rücken, and it belonged to him. He had leisure, moreover, to devote himself to it, for his father fell ill, and the happy course of their sojourn in London received a rude setback. The family moved out of the town to enable the father to recuperate. He was unable to endure music of any kind; and during this period Wolfgang for the first time tried his hand at composition without his father's help; at composing orchestral music, moreover, for two symphonies date from this time. Thus the summer passed. Not until October 25th did the children play again at court. The father had six new sonatas for piano and violin or flute by Wolfgang engraved at his own expense; they were dedicated to Queen Charlotte, of whom Joseph Haydn was yet to say that for a queen she was a tolerably good pianist. Fifty guineas was the remuneration received for this. The next concert, however, had repeatedly to be postponed. The times were no longer so propitious. New sensations exerted their attraction. Repeated announcements and hints as to the imminent departure of the two "Wonders of Nature", as the children were described in showmen's language, were necessary before they could appear before the public on February 21st. From that date onwards they gave private performances daily from twelve o'clock and the trick of playing with covered keys was once more resorted to. Wolfgang composed for himself and Nannerl his first piano sonata for four hands. On July 25th, 1765, they set out on fresh travels; and there ensued a period of astounding successes in Holland, of new sonatas, piano variations on an air and a new orchestral piece by the little Wolfgang, but also of new and dangerous illnesses for the two children. Yet in January and February two big concerts took place, at which only orchestral compositions by Wolfgang were performed. In Ghent, in Antwerp, he gave organ recitals in the churches and here, as in London, he was acclaimed even more as an organist than as a pianist. At the Hague the children were given a most flattering reception by the Prince of Orange and his sister the Princess Weilburg. They played duets for four hands, and were everywhere petted and overwhelmed with presents. Everyone was quite crazy about Wolfgang. The Hague orchestra performed symphonies composed by him. Then in October Nannerl was struck down by such a severe illness that her parents despaired of her recovery. Scarcely had she recovered than Wolfgang fell sick. Months went by. Not until the end of January could the concerts be resumed. In March the Mozarts were due to be present at the coming-of-age celebrations of the Prince of Orange. Fresh compositions, concerts, further performances at court, in Amsterdam, in Utrecht. Finally, on May 19th, the little family was back again in Paris. This time friend Grimm had arranged accommodation for them. The musical pundits marvelled at Wolfgang's progress, but the initial curiosity of the "wider circles" had here, too, died down. In Versailles, however, the children performed several times and there the Crown Prince of Brunswick, the hero of the Seven Year's War, himself a competent violinist, was enthusiastic in his praise of Wolfgang and acknowledged his genius. From this period dates a small liturgy for a choir of four voices with orchestral accompaniment.

On July 10th the return journey began. This, too, dragged out for many weeks. First of all they stayed in Dijon on the invitation of Prince Condé, then in Lyons, Geneva, Lausanne, Berne, and Zurich, where a concert was given and where the Mozarts spent such a happy time with Salomon Gessner and his family that they were loath to part from them. In Donaueschingen Prince Wenceslas von Fürstenberg detained them for two weeks; on their departure he loaded them with presents and was "moved to tears". By November 8th they were in Munich at the court of the Elector of Bavaria. Not until the 30th of the same month do we find them back in Salzburg after an absence of three and a half years.

They were still heart and soul united, the child prodigy and his radiantly happy father; still Leopold was Wolfgang's chosen guardian, teacher, guide and impresario; still it fell to him to sort out and select and give "popular" form to the fascinating, jostling, tangled throng of ideas in Wolfgang's brain. Thanks to a quite uncommon degree of adaptability the boy composed in Paris in the manner of the highly talented Schobert, whilst in London his style was determined by the influence of Johann Christian Bach and of Handel.

The "popular" remained for Leopold Mozart, excellent musician though he was in general, the final criterion. Music was to a great extent a business, and the public appeared to him in the light of a clientele whose favour must be retained at all costs. But what could a little boy, caught up as he was, on the one hand, in the brilliance of his career, on the other overworked and overproduced, understand of such practical considerations, even when he was not actually riding at full tilt round his imaginary kingdom, which was so unlike reality? He had blind faith in his father, who in his opinion came "next after God" and how can one expect him to have been scandalised at the publicity, at the cataloguing and valuing of the presents, at his father's hopes of remuneration for a sonata that he had had engraved at his own expense "as a token of gratitude" for Queen Charlotte? And how could he have grasped the meaning of all these mercenary proceedings which he was one day to face with such complete ineffectiveness and lack of comprehension? Cruel enough was the revenge that everyday life was to take on him. Meanwhile, from one generation to the next, this free spirit forged his way upwards; it was not the Pope who dubbed him knight; nature itself was to make him one. The ideas of the French Revolution, as we have already said, found their torchbearer in him. Fully conscious of his rank, he was to cast aside the gold-laced coat that his father still complacently accepted as part of the bargain. But as yet there was no sign of the rift that was one day to open between the two of them—no hint of the bitterness that was to mar their personal relations, of the painful estrangement of father from son, of the revelation of Mozart's fundamentally different spiritual heritage. Those days were still in the dim future.

For the moment we behold the little family happy on its return to Salzburg. The long journey has been crowned with monetary rewards, success and fame. The father, who has planned and been responsible for it all, may justly look back upon it with pride and boast of it to his friends.

❧

Vienna I

THE EMPRESS WAS NOT ALTOGETHER WRONG IN principle when she referred disparagingly to wanderings of this nature as "begging tours". How wrong she was, nevertheless, in this quite exceptional case! For these tours were of the greatest importance in building up and fostering Mozart's developing genius. All that he heard and saw, noted and observed, served to strengthen that innate mental freedom, to nurture in him that *desinvoltura* of the spirit, that sophisticated assurance which, however poor he remained, were increasingly to signalise both his character and his work—were, indeed, positively to become fundamental characteristics of his art.

The mass of accumulative impressions, the heavy and constant demands made both on his receptiveness and his capacities, had meanwhile weakened a constitution that was naturally delicate and vulnerable. And this at a time when he was still such a child that he would run off and leave Madame Music and all her paraphernalia if a favourite kitten came scampering along; yet a child with a very heightened sense of self-esteem. “I do not recall, Sir, to have seen you elsewhere than in Salzburg.” In such words did he rebuff a fine gentleman who ventured to address him patronisingly as “we”.

He had not yet renounced his fairy kingdom, and he got their servant to draw a map of it for him. He gave the various places in it all kinds of fantastic names. And his subjects were still children, on whom he bestowed the most marvellous presents.

And what of his education? What did Wolfgang learn, what did he read? And did he go to school? As always when the Mozarts are at home our information with regard to them is meagre in the extreme, because the communicative father no longer writes letters. Most likely he took upon himself the role of teacher in other subjects as well as music, for he permitted no idling. An exercise book filled with problems to be solved bears witness to the fact that Wolfgang had to master the intricacies of counterpoint, and this study was not discontinued until the first Italian tour.

This tour was already under consideration, but a protracted stay in Vienna was to intervene which brought in its train the first illnesses and disappointments and was rich in incidents and experiences. By September 11th, 1767, Leopold Mozart and his family were on their way. Approaching wedding celebrations at the Imperial court provided the excuse. But the family journeyed this time under an unlucky star. The Emperor Joseph, it is true, did not fail to display interest in them, but smallpox was raging in the city; the epidemic carried off the bride and pitiably disfigured the features of Maria Theresa’s most beautiful and most high-spirited daughter. All else but mourning was out of place. And Leopold Mozart delayed too long. They fled to Olmütz—but too late for the children's safety. Scarcely had they arrived there when Wolfgang fell so severely ill that for nine days he was blind. Once more we can speak of Providence. Listen to the father's cry of triumph in a letter of November 10th, 1767: "*Te Deum laudamus!* Wolfgangerl has safely survived the smallpox." And where? In Olmütz. And where? At the residence of His Excellency Count von Podstatsky. This estimable man, who, unlike almost everyone else, had no fear of the epidemic, took the whole family into his house, and nowhere, probably, could the small patient have received more tender and careful treatment. The doctor was presented with an aria as a fee. Nannerl, too, caught the disease, but only very slightly; the Mozarts celebrated Christmas happily in Brünn, and by the New Year were back in Vienna. And now at last, on January 10th, came the long deferred audience at court, during which the Empress displayed quite extraordinary graciousness and interest. The net result, however, was only a medal of no particular value. And even the patronage of the highest nobility, extended though it was now as ever to the children, yielded little financial gain, for the Emperor Joseph II was setting an example of deliberate parsimony and a new era had been inaugurated. Joseph II was not fickle by nature. We find him taking a lifelong interest in Mozart's career, but his understanding for him is only partial, his sympathy but scanty. To the last he failed to recognise the importance, the greatness, of this star in his country's firmament. Owing, apparently, to the importunacy of his ambitious father, Wolfgang now received a commission from the Emperor to write a great *opera buffa,* and he applied himself to the task with a will. *La Finta Semplice* was the title of the prosy libretto. But very soon the experts got on their hind legs. He was too old for a prodigy, too raw for the composer of an opera; and were they to obey the baton of a twelve-year-old youngster? The opposition both on the part of the singers as well as of the director of the theatre hardened. Leopold Mozart upbraided the whole world, harboured suspicions of Gluck, and endeavoured in vain to get the opera through; but before ever it was put on, it was set aside.

Meanwhile many months had elapsed. The 7,000 lovely florins brought back from the grand tour were gradually being used up, while many a snuff-box, trinket, and ring had been disposed of to finance the unsuccessful stay in Vienna. Fortunately it yielded at least some moral satisfaction. Dr. Mesmer, later to become so famous, commissioned Wolfgang with the agreeable task of composing a German operetta, and this was performed for the first time in October, 1768, in the open-air theatre in Mesmer's garden. This early work of Mozart's, redolent of the first green freshness of Spring, was *Bastien and Bastienne*.

There was yet another great compensation in store for Wolfgang. He was invited to conduct a Mass composed by himself at a church concert, given on the occasion of the dedication of an orphanage. Honour was saved. The Mozarts could show their faces again to the townsfolk of Salzburg and the Archbishop, and by January 5th, 1769, they were back at home.

Materially this trip had been anything but successful. The profit derived from it was of a purely spiritual nature, and that for Wolfgang alone. Even the ill-fated *Finta Semplice* had meant for him practice, progress, experiment. And Vienna, the musical centre of the world, what profoundly stimulating impressions had it not provided! If in

Paris he had followed French, in England English, models, it was now the turn of the German masters. In the opera he heard works by Piccini, Gassman, Scarlatti, Hasse, and above all, Gluck's *Alceste*, which was performed in January, 1768. Instrumental music, which borrowed extensively from the opera, had at that time its chief exponents in Joseph Haydn, Starzer, Gassman and others; a ripple of the literary *Sturm und Drang* had reached Vienna from Germany and left its mark, in particular, on Gluck, that pioneer amongst musicians and dramatists. Gluck's *Alceste*, of which Leopold Mozart could make neither head nor tail, provided Wolfgang with his most powerful and enduring impression of Vienna.

For more than his father could teach him, more, indeed than he himself knew, the boy now learned from other sources than his father. In Paris Schobert, whom Leopold Mozart spurned, and in London Händel, whom he despised, had exerted an influence on Wolfgang, in Salzburg he had refused to be turned against Michael Haydn, in Vienna the *Alceste* swept him off his feet. And so during this visit the independence of his judgment became clearly marked.

How happily is this inner freedom reflected a year later in the portrait of him as a boy painted by Cignaroli in Verona!

He is still a handsome child.

"He is handsome," writes Hasse from Vienna in 1769, "lively, charming, and behaves so becomingly in every way that it is impossible to help loving him. One thing is certain: if he continues to develop thus as he grows older, he will be a marvel. But his father must not spoil him too much and turn his head with exaggerated praise. That is the only danger that I fear . . ."

Yet things are apt to turn out differently from what one fears.

❧

First Italian Tour

(December 13th, 1769, to Maunday Thursday of the year 1771)

LEOPOLD MOZART HAS A CLAIM ON OUR GRATITUDE, indeed he is worthy of our profound respect, in so far as he fostered—and with what devotion, with what self-effacement—the developing genius of his son. True, he had planned things differenty from the way in which they were to turn out. He had envisaged a brilliant career, worldly happiness, a great and assured position for his son, and for himself a quiet old age in the shadow of Wolfgang's successes. Nothing came of all this, but he was to a great extent responsible for the richness of Mozart's development, and our consequent enrichment.

In order to find himself completely it was essential for Mozart to assimilate the spirit of Italian as well as of German music, and we cannot but admire the forethought of his father in arranging these educational tours. And nothing but the study of Italian music was allowed to decide what towns, what places they should visit. We do not know what impression the plastic arts or the beauties of nature, the alps or the seas, made on Mozart. We may assume that chains of mountains meant less to him than the winding paths in the baroque gardens the fragrance of whose flowers his arias, his symphonic phrases waft to our senses. Nothing Faustian about his muse, no horrors, no spiritual torments! No self-communings, but unquestioning surrender to the promptings of his genius. We cannot help being astonished at his lack of communicativeness, at what little inclination he shows consciously to think things out. In his case all experimentation, deduction, cogitation, is expressed in notes and syncopations. Music is the very air he breathes, is to him an element. He is the most unliterary of all composers.

Mozart paid three visits to Italy under Leopold's tutelage. His mother and sister remained behind in Salzburg. It was no longer profitable to take Nannerl with them. Wolfgang, on the other hand, was now able to set out on his journey with the title of Archiepiscopal *Konzertmeister*.

Everywhere they went the travellers were accorded a splendid reception. In Innsbruck they got into touch with a number of musicians, in Rovereto a festive Christmas dinner and a private concert were arranged in their honour, and the church was thronged when Wolfgang played the organ there. In Verona an enthusiastic music-lover commissioned the portrait by Cignaroli which is one of the few portraits to have been preserved.

One of their main objectives was Milan, where Count Firmian, the Governor-General of Lombardy, a native of Salzburg, stood sponsor for his two interesting compatriots. Wolfgang played at concerts there and received the *scrittura* for the first opera of the Carnival of 1771, being promised the usual fee of 100 ducats. Here, as everywhere, he met well-known singers and musicians such as Piccini, and also many other great figures of the day, almost all of whom are now forgotten. The most important of all their encounters for Wolfgang was that with the great teacher of music, Padre Martini, in Bologna, who took a genuine and sympathetic interest in the boy, and under whom he studied with the greatest seriousness and enthusiasm.

From Bologna the two Mozarts went to Florence, where Wolfgang accompanied the famous Nardini at a court concert and was received by the Grand Duke Leopold. Count Firmian had given them an introduction to Count Pallavacini, who in his turn gave them an *entrée* to the houses of a number of the nobility. In Holy Week they were in Rome, where they hob-nobbed with cardinals, princes, and great figures in the world of music. Wolfgang was interested only in the latter. Of the Sistine Chapel all that seems to have held his attention was the Miserere by Allegri, and that so thoroughly, moreover, that he wrote it down from memory. His senses seem to have been stirred by the music, the opera, the singers, of Italy, not by the country itself. He passed through the most beautiful Italian cities. In the short postscripts he wrote to his father's letters or in his letters to his sister, he either cracks jokes or mentions operas and singers. "The orchestra good . . . *prima donna* not bad," he writes from Cremona. "I cannot really write much to you from Milan, we have not yet been to the opera . . . At Parma we made the acquaintance of a singer . . . the famous Bastardella." "Every post-day," he writes from Bologna, " when the German letters come, I enjoy my food and drink far more." Rome and Naples seemed to him " two sleepy cities." For he was tired and worn-out; before his departure from Salzburg he had had another illness. From the middle of May to June 25th he was in Naples.

Leopold Mozart was worth far more as a cicerone than an impresario. It was not merely that he was not sparing enough of the boy's flagging energies; he also jeopardised his reputation by the crudity of his publicity methods and his pompous manner. It was precisely the fastidious and critical in whom he aroused scepticism. "I have already told you," writes the Abbé Galiani, who was bored to death in Naples, to Madame d'Epinay in Paris, "that the little Mozart is here; no longer so wonderful, although still the same little prodigy but he will always be a prodigy and nothing else." But Padre Martini, more perceptive than the clever salon cleric, refused to let his judgment of Wolfgang be affected by Leopold's bragging. And if this first Italian tour was not the triumphal progress the father painted it, it was pervaded with an extraordinary brilliance.

On June 25th they left Naples and travelled to Rome in twenty-seven hours without a halt. And here Wolfgang was received in audience by Pope Clement XIV, who conferred on him the Order of the Golden Spur. "The same order as Gluck," his father wrote home jubilantly and with pardonable pride. Later on he was to have his portrait painted wearing the order. But whereas the wary Gluck never relinquished the title and the advantages that went with this order, Mozart, so feckless in such matters, was never to wear it in later years in Germany, and only once, in a letter from Rome to his sister, did he sign himself: "*votre frère chevalier de Mozart*."

It was at this time that Wolfgang struck up a romantic friendship with Thomas Linley, a young English boy of his own age and a highly gifted musician; a meeting in Lucca however, planned by the two of them, never took place, for during the headlong journey from Naples, from which Mozart arrived in Rome half-dead, his father sustained an injury to his leg which compelled him to travel by a direct route to Bologna and spend three months there. Meanwhile Wolfgang had perforce been listening to Italian opera, for his own opera was to be composed in that style. The bulky libretto of *Mitridate, Re di Ponto* had duly arrived, and he set to work eagerly on the composition of the opera at Count Pallavicini's country seat near Bologna, where he stayed as a guest from August 10th to September 27th. In Bologna itself he once more enjoyed the benefit of Padre Martini's invaluable tuition, and encouraged by him passed with flying colours the examination which preceded election to the Philharmonic Academy. And thus it was not only as a knight but as a member of a learned society that he attended the first performance of his opera on December 26th. The audience received him with cries of: *Evviva il maestro, il maestrino!* And if the success of this youthful composition was not enduring and was purely local, it yet brought him a commission for an opera for the autumn of 1771 and the *scrittura* for a further opera for the Carnival of 1773.

"My dear Mamma, I cannot write much for my fingers ache very much from writing so many recitatives: I beg Mamma to pray that the opera goes well, and that we may then be happily reunited," Wolfgang writes home on October 20th.

We can well believe that he was exhausted. On January 4th he gave another concert. Then at last he was free to abandon himself to distractions. He made an expedition with his father to Turin, where they met the famous Pugnani and visited the opera. They were in Venice for the Carnival.

In Venice lived the Abbate Giovanni Ortes, a rich man and a passionate lover of music. In Vienna, in the autumn of 1769, Leopold Mozart had asked the famous Hasse, who had willingly complied with his request, for a recommendation to him, as to many other famous Italians.

> "The young Mozart is assuredly a marvel for his age," wrote Hasse to the Abbate from Milan in the spring of 1771, "and I truly love him with all my heart. The father, so far as I can see, is eternally discontented with everything. Here too complaints are being made about this. He idolises his son a thought too much, and does everything possible to spoil him. But I have so good an opinion of the natural good sense of the young man that I hope that despite the flattery of his father he will not let himself be spoiled but will grow up into a fine man."

And, indeed, it was impossible to spoil him. It was extraordinary how rapidly he dismissed all the externals of life, absorbing only the essentials. We find him even as a small child refusing to lose himself in worldly vanities. True, he jumps on the Empress's lap. But he gives the pianist Wagenseil pride of place. "He must come over here, he knows something about music." And thus the decisive factor in his development was not the blaze of glory in which he was bathed, not the success of his operas, the homage and the flattery, but his intimate relationship with the tranquil old Padre Martini, the greatest theorist of the science of music of his day, who helped him forward in his studies. Such seriousness on the part of a fourteen-year-old lad, the old man probably realised, spelled genius.

In Venice, meanwhile, Mozart came in contact once more with social and musical notabilities. A gondola was placed at his disposal, and he revelled in the pleasure of trips on the lagoons: the father was accepted for the sake of the son. In the evenings they usually went to the opera. Hasse, the old representative of the classical school, still ranked first; Piccini and Paesiello represented the new trend. From the Spirit of the Italian buffa style, its mannerisms and all its basic ideas, Wolfgang took and adapted to his own uses all that suited him. On the whole the tour had been a great success, as witness the honours—the town of Verona had also elected him a member of its academy—the fresh commissions, an oratorio in Padua, an opera for Milan, and so forth, all the work accomplished, the innumerable successes . . . It was only for a brief interval that our two travellers, their minds set on fresh tasks for the future, returned home on March 31st, 1771.

This interval in Salzburg was taken up with studies work, adolescent love affairs, four symphonies, which reveal partly Italian, partly German, influences. Saint Foix and others maintain that Mozart's first contact with Joseph Haydn is to be ascribed to this period. From it also date a number of organ sonatas, and in these the spirit of Padre Martini is plainly discernible. Amidst all these varying influences Mozart's compositions were now to become more and more "Mozartian".

❧

Second Italian Tour

ON AUGUST 31ST MOZART ONCE MORE SET OUT WITH his father. And with this journey were associated very concrete hopes; for after all *Ascanio in Alba,* a *serenata* combined with a ballet—the score of only the former is extant—was composed specially for the betrothal celebrations of the Archduke Ferdinand, the son of the Empress Maria Theresa, who was scarcely a year and a half older than Wolfgang, and who, it was thought, might take him into his service. We know that the Archduke really did contemplate fulfilling this desire of Wolfgang's and Leopold's, and that he applied to his mother for her opinion with regard to this plan. We shall give her answer in the original: "*Vous me demandez de prendre à votre service le jeune Salzburger. Je ne sais comme quoi ne croyant pas que vous avez besoin d'un compositeur ou de gens inutiles. Si cela pourtant vous ferait plaisir je ne veux vous empêcher. Ce que je dis, est pour ne pas vous charger de gens inutiles, et jamais des titres à ces sortes de gens comme à votre service. Cela avilit le service, quand ces gens courent le monde comme des gueux, il a en outre une grande famille.*" Whereupon the appointment fell through.

Ascanio, on the other hand, was a very notable success and was performed even more often than Hasse's *Ruggiero*. In addition to his fee, Wolfgang received a costly diamond-studded watch.

Somewhat lightheartedly he also agreed to compose an opera for the Carnival in Venice by the same date. And now once more he was in direct contact with the leading composers and singers of Italy. New interests came to the fore, and inspired by the thought of all his plans and the thirst for musical creation, he returned to Salzburg with his father for a short breathing-space.

The day of his return, however, December 16th, 1771, happened to coincide with the death of his patron, Archbishop Sigismund, and in March his successor, Count Hieronymus of Colloredo, took over his office both as Count Palatine and Bishop.

There was no sign as yet of the dissensions that were to come. Wolfgang wrote the opera that was to celebrate the Bishop's formal installation; this was *Il Sogno di Scipione,* a one-act dramatic *serenata*. This work does not rise to the level of the other works which date from his Salzburg period, so rich in compositions. Such genuine Mozartian symphonies as the A major Symphony (K.134[1]) were produced at this early date; as a symphonic composer Mozart had attained the stature of a master and he could match Haydn's great symphonies of the same period. The new Archbishop now took him formally into his service at a

[1] The letter K refers to the Köchel index of Mozart's works.

yearly salary of 150 florins, and he and his father were given leave of absence to enable him to fulfil his commission to write an opera for Milan. Nevertheless they set out in low spirits. None of the advancements hoped for by Leopold had materialised, and the Salzburg sky had clouded over when, on October 24th, the couple set out for the third and last time for Italy. And it is from this time on that we find the numerous passages in cipher in the family letters.

Wolfgang's letters to his sister, it is true, are still full of jocularities and witticisms—expressed as brilliantly, tersely and plastically as though he had in him the makings of a great writer. Of inner turmoil they betray no sign at all.

The new opera was an *opera seria* and bore the title *Lucio Silla*. Partly "popular", as his father always urged that his works should be, its passionate and sombre accents are so inherent a part of it that biographers have assumed the existence of a romantic episode in his life at this period. But it was precisely those accents—and they interest us most keenly in the work to-day—that had such a disquieting effect on the Italian audience.

Wolfgang did not receive the *scrittura* for a fresh opera, and, bound as he was by the contact with Milan, he was unable to carry out the obligation he had entered into with Venice. The father's letters express profound discouragement. True, they were still filled with accounts of their reception by the nobility of the first, second and third rank, but his hopes of obtaining a post for his son in Italy had come to nothing. He took refuge in illness: an attack of rheumatism was to provide an excuse for postponing their return to Salzburg. He admitted in cipher that it was only simulated. "I find it hard to leave Italy," are his concluding words in a letter to his wife.

What Wolfgang's feelings were we can only conjecture. For Italy was now exerting all its fascination on him, and his native town appeared to him in all its provincial narrowness. The loves he had left behind there had faded from his mind. He was in the toils of another spell, that of the Italian countryside, which he had formerly overlooked, and the magic, too, of Italian music. He had come into close contact with the musician Sammartini; Marcello, Corelli, and above all Tartini were exerting their influence upon him.

Nevertheless *Silla* proved a failure. Mozart had fallen out of favour with the Italians. He found himself directed along other paths; fate had marked him out to become, not an Italian, but a German, composer—yet with what untender hands was that fate to lay hold of him!

❧

The Salzburg Years

MOZART WAS NOW SEVENTEEN—HALF OF HIS EXISTENCE had almost slipped away. His health was impaired, it may be owing to the excessive amount of work that he had already accomplished, it may be owing to the illnesses to which he once again fell a prey. From 1773 to 1777, except for two short trips to Vienna and Munich, he had to possess himself in patience in Salzburg almost without a break and he became thoroughly acquainted with its oppressive, restricted atmosphere. The "good friends", so loyally greeted from afar, did not suffice to chase away the moods of depression, which from now on his father shared, so much so that he was untiring in his efforts to free his son from the new Archbishop's yoke. We know but little of this period. But nothing that was once drawn into the orbit of Mozart's life, was touched by it, has been overlaid with dust; all has remained vivid and alive. Yet what a contrast between the past and the present, what a fall from the heights for the spoiled and hypersensitive Wolfgang, who had written such exuberant letters and postscripts from Italy! Here is one to his sister:

"Naples, June 5th, 1770.

"Vesuvius is smoking furiously to-day. Hell, fire and brimstone! *Haid homa gfresa beym Herr Doll. Dos is a deutscha Compositör und a brawa Mo.*[1] And now I shall begin to give an account of my life. *Alle 9 ore, qualche volta anche alle dieci mi sveglio, e poi andiamo, fuor di casa, e poi pranziamo da un trattore, e dopo pranzo scriviamo, e poi sortiamo, e indi ceniamo, ma che cosa? Al giorno di grasso, un mezzo pollo ovvero un piccolo boccone d'arrosto; al giorno di magro, un piccolo pesce; e di poi andiamo a dormire.*[2] *Est-ce que vous avez compris? Redma dafir soisburgarisch, don as is gschaida. Wir sand Gottlob gesund, da Voda und i.*[3] I hope you too are well, and also Mamma. Naples and Rome are two sleepy cities. *A scheni Schrift! Net wor?*[4] Write to me and don't be so lazy. *Altrimente avrete qualche bastonate di me.*[5] *Quel plaisir! Je te casserai la tête . . . Mädli, las Da saga, wo bist dan gwesa, he?*[6] The opera here is by Jomelli; it is beautiful, but too pompous and old-fashioned for the theatre. De Amicis sings incomparably . . . The King has rough Neapolitan manners and always stands on a stool at the opera in order to look a little taller than the queen. The queen is beautiful and gracious, for she has bowed to me at least six times on the Molo (that is a public promenade) in the most friendly manner."

Postscript to his mother and sister:

[1] Dialect for: "To-day we dined with Herr Doll. He is a good composer and a fine fellow."

[2] "I wake up every morning at nine o'clock, but sometimes not till ten, when we go out. We dine at an inn; after dinner we write, and then we go out again, and afterwards sup. But on what? On *jours gras* half a fowl, or a small slice of roast meat; on *jours maigres* a little fish; and then we go to bed."

[3] "Let us talk Salzburgisch, for that is more sensible. My father and I are well, thank God."

[4] "Fine writing, is it not?"

[5] "Otherwise I shall give you a good beating."

[6] "Fair maiden, tell me where have you been, eh?"

"I am well and merry and cheerful as ever, and enjoy travelling . . . and am your son Stefferl and your brother Hansl . . ."

Were they not as free as birds!

"We have," writes Leopold from a country estate near Bologna on August 11th, 1770, where they spent several weeks as the guests of Count Pallavicini, "a footman and a valet at our disposal, that is to say, two menservants, and the footman sleeps in our antechamber in order to be available at any moment; it is the valet's duty to dress Wolfgang's hair . . . His Excellency has put us in the best room. The young Count, who is Wolfgang's age, and the only son and heir . . . You can well imagine that this young gentleman and Wolfgang are the best of friends . . . We are offered the choicest figs, melons and peaches! And I am delighted to be able to tell you that all is, God be eternally thanked, well with us. Wolfgang has just gone out walking with the Countess."

And on September 1st:

"Not only are we staying with His Excellency Count Pallavicini . . . it looks as though we shall remain here for some time longer . . . Wolfgang is unable to write, as he has gone out with Her Excellency the Countess . . ."

On September 22nd they are still there. And from Rome, moreover, Leopold writes on July 4th, 1770: "When we went the other day to see the Cardinal, he addressed Wolfgang several times as Signor Cavaliere . . ."

"Rome, July 7th, 1770.

"What I wrote you the other day about the cross of an order in my last letter is perfectly true . . . He will have to wear a splendid golden cross, and you can imagine how I laugh at hearing him called *Signor Cavaliere* all the time. We are to have an audience tomorrow with the Pope."

"Milan, October 20th, 1770.

"We remained in Bologna a few days longer than we had intended because the *Accademia Filarmonica* unanimously elected Wolfgang a member of their society and presented him with the patent of *Accademico*. This took place, however, with all the requisite formalities and preliminary tests. On October 9th, at four o'clock in the afternoon, he was obliged to present himself at the hall of the Academy. There the *Princeps Accademiae* and the two *Censores* (all former *Kapellmeister*) gave him, in the presence of all the members, an *antiphona* from an *antiphonarium*, which he was to set in four parts in an adjoining chamber, whither he was conducted by the beadle, who locked the door on him. As soon as he had completed the work it was examined by the *Censores* and all the *Kapellmeister* and composers, who thereupon voted with white and black balls. All the balls being white, he was called in, and on his entrance everyone clapped and congratulated him, the Princeps having already informed him, in the name of the Society, of his election. He returned thanks and that brought the proceedings to a close."

"January 12th, 1771.

"I must tell you that yesterday I received news from Signor Pietro Luggiati that the *Accademia Filarmonica* of Verona have made our son a member, and the Board of the Academy is preparing the diploma for him."

"Venice, March 1st, 1771.

"We are . . . invited here, there, and everywhere, and in consequence the gondolas of the quality are constantly outside our house, and we go out daily on the Grand Canal. . ."

But of all the honours, titles and marks of distinction that had come the way of his young *Kapellmeister*, Archbishop Colloredo took not the slightest notice. For him the young man was first and foremost a retainer of his, and no more. The Archbishop was accustomed to address everyone who did not happen to belong to the highest nobility in the third person, as though he were a lackey. Such was the attitude adopted by the man whose alleged enlightenment many still champion to this day.

The Archbishop was a far from stupid man, but woe to the entourage, no matter at what period, of a despot such as he. For a sullen proletarian heart beat within him, and such a heart is always moved by class hatred. And it was precisely Wolfgang's obvious nobility that exasperated Colloredo most of all. His resentment went to such lengths that he pooh-poohed the verdict of the greatest connoisseurs and declared categorically that Mozart knew nothing at all about music and would have to take a course of study at the Naples Conservatoire. Mozart's indignation when this came to his ears may be imagined.

"That was in those days", many, perhaps, will protest, who allow their vision to be dimmed by the present Mozart boom. But it is precisely in our own times—as though to epitomise the eternal whirligig here below, to the subject of which we shall return later—that so many people have rushed forward to whitewash the character of Archbishop Colloredo, whose record should be allowed to remain a closed chapter. In such a penetrating and important biography as that by Abert we come across the following: "True, Hieronymus shared the standpoint of the enlightened despots of the period (why enlightened, may one ask?) that the life of every subordinate must conform absolutely to the ideas of his Prince, and that the subject must in all circumstances look upon him as his benefactor. But at that time all artists who were in princely employ had to bow to that dictum, and most of them managed to get along quite nicely."

What artists they must have been! It was precisely because of their inner freedom that there existed between them and princes worthy of the name that affinity, that mutual attraction, that silent spell, exerted by the one upon the other, which impelled the one to make concessions to the nature of the other and released in the other the springs of affectionate devotion. We have the example of Leonardo at the court of Lorenzo di Medici, of the great sculptors of the Cinquecento at Rome and Florence, of the poets at Louis XIV's court, of the Margrave of Bayreuth and Voltaire, of Marie Antoinette's relationship with Gluck, of Goethe at Weimar, of Richard Wagner at Munich. The secret threads that bound them one to the other, as though they had been equals, were woven of that instinctive and unerring sense of the fitness of things that the philistine mind is bound utterly to misinterpret.

We know that Mozart was somewhat free in his utterances and not always discreet. In this connection we find in a life of Mozart, published in 1926 by the firm of Patel, Berlin and Leipzig, and described as being "compiled from the most recent available sources" a reference to his "garrulity". The biographer could not characterise himself more aptly, and since this pronouncement serves as his visiting-card, to mention his name would be superfluous.

It was, of course, in the very nature of Mozart's life that his relationships towards the people whom he loved could only in quite rare cases become crystallised. Either he struck up mere travelling acquaintanceships, as in France, England or Italy, or he was geographically separated from his friends, as in the case of Joseph Haydn, the Irishman Kelly, and the young English virtuoso, Linley, who met an early death; or, again, death snatched his friends from before his very eyes, as in the case of Doctor Barisani and of the young Count Hatzfield, or sheer privation relegated all else to the background. Moreover, lack of time, and the inherent reserve of his music-drenched soul played an increasingly important rôle in Mozart's life. More vividly than all his portraits do the shrewd words of his sister-in-law, Sophie Haibl, conjure up a picture of him for us:

> "He was always in a good humour, but even in his best moods very contemplative, looking one straight in the eyes and answering all questions, cheerful or sad, after due consideration, and yet seeming to be profoundly occupied in turning over something quite different in his mind. Even when he washed his hands in the morning he would pace up and down his room, never still for a moment, knocking his heels one against the other, lost in thought the whole time. At table he would often take the corner of a napkin, screw it up, and absentmindedly draw it back and forth under his nose, apparently unaware of what he was doing, and often grimacing the while. He always displayed enthusiasm for every new diversion, such as riding or billiards. In order to keep him from doubtful company his wife patiently tried everything herself. His hands and feet, moreover, were never still, he was always playing with something, with his hat, for instance, pockets, watch-chain, tables, chairs, as though on the clavier."

But let us return to Mozart's early years in Salzburg. The restricted life there was not all desert. During the four and a half years which were now beginning he ripened into a master of his art. A vast number of works were produced during this period. In the sonatas, quartets, *divertimenti,* symphonies, the German element has gained the upper hand, the Italian rhythm has died down; stilled, too, the "storm and stress", the agonised outbursts of *Lucio Silla*. Mozart had leisure in which to gather his forces. A first break occurred, moreover, as early as July, 1773. His father, bent as ever on freeing him from the Archbishop's yoke, took advantage of the latter's absence to travel with his son to Vienna. Their stay lasted six weeks; it was rich in exhilarating experiences, but did not bring the eagerly sought appointment. In the opera Gluck had at last triumphantly established himself and ousted Italian supremacy. In the sphere of instrumental music Joseph Haydn had taken the lead, and the so-called Viennese school, whose harmonic resources were to be decisive for Wolfgang up to the year 1774, was flourishing. We know how easily he changed from one style to another. It has been said of him that it was with him in the realm of music as with Don Juan in life. He turned constantly from one beauty to another. In 1774 the "gallant" style had come into vogue, and occasioned an astonishing and complete *volte face* on the part of Joseph Haydn. Rococo became the unchallenged mode. The fundamentally different character of Mozart's church compositions, in particular, at this time bears witness to his hesitation to acknowledge this fashion, to the struggle within him. But in the end he surrendered to the force of the current, finally even vied with it, outstripped it and left it far behind. Moreover, the Archbishop would tolerate none but the "gallant" at his court. And so pathos and depth of feeling gave place in Mozart's work to sweetness, to elegance; and, too, those magnificent, though hardly substantial, effects, those sonorous, somewhat schematic *finales* that we find in his work, came into favour with him. Richard Wagner, whose profound understanding and love for Mozart were expressed in terms hitherto unsurpassed, speaks somewhat sternly on the subject of these in the following words:

"And so Mozart . . . had fallen back into the banality of expression which frequently presents his symphonic phrases to us in the light of so-called table music, that is to say, music which, apart from attractive melodies, also provides an attractive noise as a background for conversation. To me, at least, the constantly recurring and noisily ostentatious half-closes of the Mozart symphony are suggestive of the din and clatter of the plates and dishes at a princely table set to music."

Today, however, the more we become acquainted with the works of Mozart's early youth, the greater the surprises they have in store for us. Side by side with works of a more indifferent nature blossomed forth the ravishing Symphony in A major (K.201), written in 1774.

The monotony of life in Salzburg was broken in upon that same year, as though by a message from heaven, by a commission from the Elector Maximilian for Mozart to write a comic opera. This was *La Finta giardiniera*, the first performance of which was held on January 13th, 1775, in Munich. Wolfgang was able to write home to his mother of "a tremendous uproar and clapping and shouts of '*Vivat maestro*'". An account in Schubart's "Deutsche Chronik" reads: "I also attended a performance of an *opera buffa* by the wonderful genius Mozart. It is called *La Finta giardiniera*. There are flickers of genius here and there, but it is not yet the still, peaceful altar fire ascending in clouds of incense smoke to heaven. If Mozart is not a hot-house plant he must surely become one of the greatest composers that ever lived." One sees that there is already a nimbus surrounding his name. Yet it is a matter of no more than the recognition of a select few, of splendid half-successes. Even his later triumphs are sporadic and do not succeed in establishing him, and Mozart refuses to lay himself out to secure the favour of Providence by pandering to the public. Hell holds no fury like a public scorned. Archbishop Colloredo happened to be in Munich at the moment when it was reverberating with the praises of Wolfgang and his *Finta giardiniera*. The feelings of benevolence that he harboured towards his young *Kapellmeister* were so meagre, although he was glad enough to boast of having him in his service, that some days before the opera was to be performed for the first time he took his departure from the town. He got him, however, to write an opera to celebrate the visit to Salzburg of the youngest son of the Empress Maria Theresa. This was composed after a libretto by Metastasio, *Il Re Pastore.*

La Finta giardiniera was soon relegated to oblivion. The bravura aria *Aer tranquillo* from *Il Re Pastore* still charms us to-day in concert halls or on gramophone records, and the six sonatas which a certain Baron Dürnitz of Munich commissioned and neglected to pay for are included in all collections of Mozart's works for the piano. They are K.279 to 284. Saint Foix professes to detect in them both leanings towards the French style and the influence of Schobert, whose works are unfortunately as good as inaccessible to us. And in them, too, we find concessions to the gallant style; in them, too, there are passages of unmistakable baroque, sometimes carried to the point of stiffness, and in K.284 we are conscious even of pedantry. But what mature craftsmanship there is in the twelve variations, what grace, what poetry of ideas in those tenderly beautiful adagios, those dreamlike andantes, which only await the touch of practised and chosen hands to come to life! They live all the more, these sonatas, for not being hammered out—for how sensitive they are!—and murdered by unskilled, harsh fingers, in rooms, moreover, with windows opened wide on to the streets. Mozart is still, unfortunately, the mode, but strumming on the piano, fortunately, no longer so. And for this we cannot be too grateful to that often most heinous of offenders, the wireless.

Mozart was back in Salzburg and was now in his twentieth year. His fame as a composer was partial and did not extend very far beyond Munich and Salzburg, yet wherever he went his name was on all lips and his popularity was considerable. To the Archbishop this, as also Mozart's successes, which he completely ignored, was yet another reason for keeping the young man down. This fellow Mozart wanted to rise in the world, he must be put in his place.

The tone obtaining amongst the members of the orchestra was coarse, and not even between Mozart and Michael Haydn, whom he admired so much and with whom he had so many points of contact as an artist, did there exist a really lively friendship. Hitherto his circle had been composed of friends of the family, the Hagenauers, Haffners, and Maiers, and the von Barisanis, von Robinigs, and von Mölks, members of the so-called second-rate aristocracy. Next in his regard came the Abbé Bullinger, a product of the Munich Jesuit seminary, in whom parents and children alike confided and who often mediated between them and alluded to Wolfgang as his best friend. Salzburg under Hieronymus—one must give him due credit for this—was a pretty gay town; there were masked balls and performances by troupes of strolling players. Sunday was the day for archery practice, and there was no doubt general delight if Wolfgang, in a good humour and ready for a lark, joined in. When he left Salzburg, there was profound and general regret.

The year 1776 brought in its wake both a turning-point and a crisis; here again we have to rely largely on conjecture.

❧

1776

THE YEAR THAT WAS JUST BEGINNING AWAKENED IN Mozart a spring-time of the emotions, and caused such a rich fount of musical inspiration to well up within him that in his years of full maturity he was still to draw from it. Its murmurs were still to reach the ears of the master and revive in him all the imperishable splendour of his fleeting summer.

The unique position which Mozart occupied in Salzburg was no insignificant matter. We should not, simply because certain social conditions have undergone radical changes, become inverted snobs and ignore its importance at that time. The European nobility, to-day either threatened by or actually involved in the collapse of all around them, at that time still held a lease of dignity and power, of the treasures of culture, of a lavish and exquisite mode of life. No one who was not of the nobility could afford to disregard it; renunciation all too easily resulted in the harbouring of resentment, or at the best in a sense of incompleteness. In Mozart's case there was the additional fact that, in order to be able to create his Almaviva, his Don Giovanni in all their verisimilitude, it was essential for him to have the "cavalier" type at his finger-tips. The circles which now admitted him into their ranks and courted him, appealed to the man-of-the-world vein which had, from childhood up, in the course of all his many travels, developed in him. Prince Zeyll, who had an estate on the near-by Cliemsee, had long since been an enthusiastic patron of Mozart's, and his example was followed by Counts Firmian, Wolfegg and Kühnburg, Leopold and Sebastian Lodron, and Countess Lützow, the wife of the Commandant of Holensalzburg, for whom Mozart composed a symphony. But first and foremost among all these was the Countess Antonia Lodron. She lived in grand style and had two daughters, Louise and Josefa. Mozart gave lessons to the two of them, and they became firm friends. He felt, not flattered, but *at home* in the mirrored halls of palaces. They provided a setting that became him, and gave his native charm full scope for development. The air that blew there was the natural element for the *grand seigneur* which existed in him side by side with so many other attributes. True, he was short, thin and pale, but to offset that there was his luxuriant fair hair and, too, those hands, of which he was so vain. What a spell they must have exerted when he was playing, when those eyes of his, with their deep sea-blue, were opened wide in the candle-light!

He wrote a concerto for three pianos. The part for Josefa, the youngest, was very easy; she had practically nothing to do; and he wrote the "*Lodronsche Nachtmusiken*",[1] wrote music, now as ever, in the gallant style,

[1] *Divertimento* in F major (K.247) and *Divertimento* in B flat major (K287).

but more free of external influences, less *derivative*, and from this period date those marvellous adagios, borne along on their own flame. For his sister too, perhaps to make up to her for some slight, he wrote a serenade, with a violin concerto, which he himself performed, for once again he was playing the violin a great deal. He also wrote a concerto for the flute; and, no doubt more or less incidentally, *divertimenti* for the Archbishop. July witnessed the birth of the *Haffner Serenade*.

Life in Salzburg was considerably enlivened by troupes of travelling players, and at masked balls Mozart indulged in all sorts of buffoonery. For a long time yet Nannerl was to call him "Pantaloon" in her letters. She had no more idea than the Robinigs, the Hagenauers, or Katharina Gilowsky, of the double life to which he was secretly abandoning himself. They had no opportunity of observing him. All the invitations, the favours, were for him alone. Nannerl was regarded as an excellent teacher of the clavier, nothing more. Leopold bore the Countess Lodron a grudge. He was in the future frequently to refer to her as a deceitful character and to expatiate in his letters to his son on the falsity of her friendship. She was, nevertheless, an intelligent and, it would seem, determined lady. Wolfgang was always in and out of her house. Always concerned for his outward appearance, he now took twice the pains with his lace jabots, his embroidered cuffs, the colour of his coats, always backed up by his mother, who stuck to him through thick and thin. We may assume that this period was for him a May-time of the bitter-sweet pangs of love; and also that Louise Lodron—Josefa was as yet a child—was the chosen of his heart. We do not know. For there is nothing to give him away but the new fresh inspiration apparent in his music, its intensified light.

Just imagine the relief it must have been to him to find himself fêted in the very neighbourhood of the Archbishop to whose humiliations he was daily subjected. It was inevitable, indeed, that Archbishop Colloredo, being what he was, should, out of secret mortification at Mozart's success, have made him realise all the more the subordinate position he occupied in his service—assessed at twelve florins a month. Mozart was later on to record for our benefit specimens of the tone employed by the Archbishop; that is, in so far as he ever honoured him with a word.

The sharpest contrasts were invariably to form the setting for Mozart's life. His path, which was continually leading towards fair prospects, always turned off just before the point of happiness was reached, leading, instead of over laughing slopes, over the mountains of disappointment. One has only to think of how, again and again, his triumphs were short-lived, never enabling him to put his affairs on a sound basis. His name, it is true, stood high amongst the cognoscenti, but he found himself slighted; considered, it is true, when a post fell vacant, but always passed over in favour of someone else.

For great figures of Mozart's stamp are never taken seriously by their age. And so such men, unless they happen to have been born rich, remain poverty-stricken. In the last years of his life Mozart was to write out-and-out begging letters, at first for fairly large sums, then later for a mere five florins, even for three. We know that he used to dance with Constance in their lodgings to keep himself warm because they had no fuel. And then at length he scored a magnificent success with his *Zauberflöte* and at last took the Viennese by storm. But too late! He was to leave his wife and children entirely destitute.

He was by nature gay, with a keen sense of fun and a

zest for the good things of this world. Beethoven was a more colossal, but a more one-sided, figure. No one has expressed the seriousness of ultimate things in such dread accents as Mozart. The magnificent *Qui Tollis* from the Mass in C minor is a monument of dread. So is the churchyard scene in *Don Giovanni*. Mozart's demonic power, which is so often mentioned, did not lie in this or that demonic characteristic, but in the vast range of his personality.

See him now, in an elegant coat, giving Louise Lodron a lesson, his gaze resting upon her. Watch him walking through the garden, conversing with her and Josefa. It is summer: the light is sultry, as so often.

But what is this other coat, the fateful colour of which is one day to provoke Aloysia Weber's scorn? Is it its red colour or ultimately the amount of gold lace that distinguishes it from the archi-episcopal livery? The father dons the coat without a murmur, but it sears the body of the son. He has no theories about it, it is true, but inwardly he seethes with a welter of conflicting feelings. For his consciousness of class, his ideas of honour, are different from those of Leopold; and here are to be found the many doors through which he slips from kith and kin.

Let us linger a while longer on the days which in his memory perhaps seemed to him the happiest of all. His dreams—who is there to forbid him them? The magic of youth has lifted him out of his humdrum existence. He is Tamino! The golden notes of the aria *Dies Bildnis ist bezaubernd schön* is an echo of the pulsing of his own heart at this time. For whom, does it beat, if not for Louise? What maiden else? Who else is there whose memory could have endured so wondrously?

We do not know what frost it was that killed this blossoming ecstasy. Nannerl has long since ceased to be his confidante. Once again it is his muse alone that tells us anything of him.

He was seized by a sudden aversion to "gallant" music and he turned from it. The four last months of this year were not very productive, and his compositions were mostly confined to church music. Was he going through a religious crisis or had another illness laid him low? The Bolognese portrait painted at this period, the original of which has been lost, suggests the latter. For all the inadequacy of its execution, this copy is undoubtedly more revealing than any other of his portraits. The eyelids are heavy, the gaze is that of a convalescent. The lovely lips are closed. In it are expressed the bitterness and sweetness of suffering withstood, but not entirely overcome. The bearing is manly and austere. The breast is decorated with the Order of the Golden Spur. His father had it painted, no doubt in view of the impending parting. This was still far off, but Leopold was already anxiously making all necessary preparations for a journey on the part of his son. Conditions in Salzburg, it would seem, were no longer endurable. Leopold Mozart busied himself writing letters, accumulating letters of recommendation—all in the greatest secrecy lest the Archbishop might hear of it. A sum of money, too, was borrowed—and here the Abbé Bullinger once more showed himself to be the indefatigable friend he was—for Wolfgang must go out into the world equipped as befitted the Chevalier de Mozart.

An interesting document has been preserved in the shape of a letter addressed by Wolfgang to Padre Martini on September 9th. In it he enclosed the motet composed the year before for the Elector of Bavaria, and urgently requested his erstwhile teacher for his opinion of it. It is a grave and despondent letter; there are passages in it which betray great spiritual loneliness and in which we hear the voice of that Mozart who so seldom reveals himself.

> "Dearest and Most Esteemed Father and Maestro,
> . . . we live in this world so as continually to improve ourselves, to enlighten each other and to assist each other's development both in the sciences and the arts by means of an exchange of views . . . Ah, how often have I wished that I might be nearer to you and be able to converse with you and open my heart to you. I live in a country where music is in a somewhat languishing state . . . Oh, esteemed Father, how glad would I be could I tell you more of all these matters . . ." And he concludes: "It is a perpetual grief to me to be so far from the being whom I most love, esteem and reverence in the world."

He mentions only church compositions in the letter, as though these alone occupied his thoughts, and, as a matter of fact, except for three Masses, we know of no other compositions dating from this period.

It was not until January that he wrote, for the famous French pianist, Mademoiselle Jeunehomme, who made a brief and, for Mozart, stimulating, visit to Salzburg, the Piano Concerto in E flat major (K.271), perhaps his most beautiful concerto; which, with its great melancholy andante, is as expansive and as mysterious as a clouded and restless sea. Mozart was still turning his back on the "gallant" style. Free and in full consciousness of his powers, he now stood on the threshold of his twenty-first year—in the sphere of music already a master, in the things of life untaught and unteachable. His father knew this, knew the unpractical side of his son so thoroughly; he planned, wove schemes, commended him to God and the world, and renewed their connections with Munich, Augsburg and

Mannheim. With the help of a textbook, Wolfgang once more took up the study of French. For if they were not to succeed in finding him a post as *Kapellmeister* at one of the South German courts, then Paris was this time to be the objective and there, of course, their great hope was once more friend Grimm, who would pave the way as he had done before. Leopold Mozart bought a coach, moreover, and raised a comparatively large sum of money; his son should make his fortune abroad and his relatives would join him there and the family would be re-united. For Leopold had to resign himself to staying behind; leave of absence for them both was out of the question. And so he prepared to make that most difficult of all sacrifices: to let Wolfgang out of his sight, to see him slip from his watchful care; and for his sake, too, he resolved to part from his wife and to let her go as well. Her authority, it is true, was as good as non-existent, but Wolfgang was so feckless in practical matters and so credulous a dreamer in dealings with people who flattered him that it would have been too great a risk to allow him to set off alone.

By the end of March all their preparations were so far advanced that Wolfgang's request for leave of absence was submitted to the Archbishop. It was formulated so naïvely that Colloredo gave both of them their *congé*. He subsequently changed his mind and retained the father in his service, which only shows how difficult it would have been to replace him.

The chief delight of the summer of 1777 was provided by the young and beautiful Frau Josepha Duschek, a singer from Prague. Mozart went into raptures over her and in her honour he composed the superb dramatic scena, *Ah! lo previdi* (K.272). In Frau Duschek he had gained a faithful friend and patroness for life.

And now autumn was upon the land. Mozart, it is true, had come to detest his native town, and he hoped and believed that he was turning his back on it for ever. But now, when this countryside, the stirring contours of these mountains, are seen in the light of farewell, so many an hour radiant with bliss and emotion finds an echo in his incalculable heart that there pours forth from it that wonderful and solemn farewell greeting, the *Sancta Maria* (K.273), which is to be ranked amongst his greatest masterpieces, and which was completed a few days before his departure on September 9th.

❧

Munich

SEPTEMBER 23RD IS SHROUDED IN THE GREY OF early twilight. Morning is still far off. But outside the open door of the Mozarts' house a carriage is waiting. Dimly discernible, old Leopold stands there busied with the final arrangements for the travellers, who have already taken their seats. The luggage is piled on the carriage. His wife, over whose knees he now spreads the rug, he is never to see again. How quickly is the parting, the climax of such long preparations, over! The horses are on the move in a trice. But all too soon do the travellers vanish from the view of the bowed father and the weeping daughter, for the town gates are still closed. A quarter of an hour goes by before the carriage is able to pass through. Day has dawned. The citadel floats in the mist like a ship. Wolfgang gazes up at it, his heart swelling with wild jubilation. He is free. Free of all the oppression and restraint! The world lies open before him, waiting to be conquered. The letter which, as a dutiful son, he sends home that evening, is full of exuberance. He plays the role of the head of the family towards his mother. Incidentally he has left his diplomas and testimonials at home. A symptomatic act of forgetfulness.

"Wasserburg, September 23rd.

"*Viviamo come i Principi.*[1] We lack nothing but Papa. Ah well, it's the will of God; no doubt all will be well. I hope that Papa is as well and as happy as I am. I am managing capitally. I am quite a second Papa, I see to everything. I arranged from the outset to pay the postilions, for I can talk to the fellows better than Mamma. Here at the 'Stern', in Wasserburg, the service is excellent. I am treated like a prince . . ."

Leopold Mozart is overjoyed to get news so soon. And now comes, thanks to the lively exchange of letters, a period of Mozart's life of which we learn a great deal.

"Salzburg, September 25th, 1777.

"I was overjoyed to receive dear Wolfgang's letter this morning. The Abbé Bullinger, too, has just read it . . . and laughed heartily. Am delighted that you are both so well: I am now, thank God, a great deal better. After you had driven off; I went wearily up the stairs and threw myself on to a chair. I took all possible pains to keep out of the way at your departure so as not to make our parting the more painful, and in all the bustle and confusion I forgot to give my son my paternal blessing. I ran to the window and sent a blessing after you both. I did not, however, see you driving out by the gate, and we could only suppose that you had driven through some time past, since I had been sitting for a long time without thinking of anything. Nannerl wept quite astonishingly . . ."

[1] We live like princes.

He was to return to the subject of this fateful morning in another letter, in which he enclosed the "certificates", entreating Wolfgang not to lose them.

> "I was unable to discuss certain important matters with you on your departure, because I was ill, confused, upset, downhearted and very sad, because, moreover, talking almost choked me, and I had a great deal to think about and arrange in regard to the baggage."

In the gloom of these days Leopold found himself admirably supported by Nannerl, who, herself sick with misery, had by the same evening sufficiently pulled herself together to play piquet with him. But he might have been a Chinese father, so little had his daughter meant to him from the very first, compared with Wolfgang. Whenever the children recovered from severe illnesses three thanksgiving masses were always said for Wolfgang and only one for Nannerl. And yet it was she who was to be the prop, the solace, the inadequate consolation, of his embittered old age. Such is, only too often, the fate of parents.

"I am ever in the best of moods, my heart has been as light as a feather ever since I left all that chicanery behind," writes Wolfgang from Munich on September 26th.

Munich's delight at his powers was as extreme as Salzburg's regret at his departure, and his father had plenty to write with regard to the deep interest of Countess Lodron and her predictions with regard to Wolfgang's future, and of the dismay of Count Firmian, who had just bought four riding horses and had been looking forward to placing them at Wolfgang's disposal; nevertheless his grand connections did not carry him one step further in

Munich than they had done in Salzburg. By the 29th we find him writing: "I don't believe we shall achieve much here." Prince Zeyll, it is true, had intervened on his behalf with the Elector of Bavaria, but the latter had "only shrugged his shoulders". At an audience which he managed to snatch at an odd moment the following characteristic conversation took place between him and the Elector: "You've left Salzburg for good? Why? Did you have a row?" And when Mozart expressed his desire to enter his service and pressed his claims: "Yes, my dear boy, but there is no vacancy . . . if only there were a vacancy . . ." Mozart was undeterred. "I assure your Highness I should do credit to Munich." "Yes, but it's no use," returned the Elector, already turning to go, "there is no vacancy," therewith uttering the watchword that was to play a decisive role in the whole course of Mozart's career.

Count Salern, the Director of the Opera, was of the opinion that if Mozart stayed things would work out satisfactorily for him. Count Seau, the Intendant, raised no objection, but all the same Mozart seemed to him too young as yet, not enough of a celebrity and too un-Italian. A certain Herr Albert proposed to produce ten friends each of whom would contribute one ducat a month. "If in addition I were to get even 200 florins a year from Count Seau, that would make 800 florins in all. How does Papa like this idea? Is it not a kindly thought? Ought the proposal not to be accepted if it is made in earnest?—I am extremely delighted with it." Leopold had his doubts about these ten contributors of a ducat. Wolfgang, however, wanted to remain in Munich and had made many friends there. " Were I alone, it would not be impossible for me to contrive to live here, for I should get at least 300 florins from Count Seau. I should have no need to worry about my board, as I am frequently invited out, and if not, Albert"—this was his landlord— "is always delighted to have me to dinner. I eat but little, drink water, and finish with some fruit and a small glass of wine. I would make the following contract with Count Seau: I should undertake to produce four German operas a year, some *buffe* and some *serie*. I should then get a benefit night for myself on each opera, that being the custom here, and that alone would bring me in at least 500 florins, which, with my salary, would make 800 florins, if not more. For Reiner, the actor and singer, took 200 florins on his night, and I am a great favourite here. And how much more of a favourite would I become were I to contribute towards raising the reputation of the German national theatre in the world of music! And that I should certainly do, for on hearing the German music-drama I was seized with a longing to write. . . . The piece was called *Das Fischermädchen*, a very good adaptation with music by Piccini. They have no original pieces as yet." The exchange of letters between father and son is particularly lively at this period. But Leopold cannot make up his mind to leave Wolfgang alone; the continued absence from home of the mother, however, is likely to prove too great a financial burden, and he therefore urges them to move on, so that no more money shall be spent to no purpose. Disappointed, Wolfgang bows to his wishes.

On October 11th they set off for Augsburg. It was the second stage of their journey, and it brought them just as little success as the first.

❧

Augsburg

THE SUDDEN CHANGES IN THE YOUNG MOZART ARE AN indication of his vitality, which we have already said bid fair to last up to the age of seventy or even longer. On his father's side he came of a long-lived family, and he pictured himself, "as sure as fate", as a rich old gentleman, living in a splendid mansion, like Gluck. And, indeed, why not?

His self-assurance was superlative. It was fully borne out by his real worth, but not as yet in the very least by his reputation. An "extremely good composer"—even his most enthusiastic admirers called him no more than that, and the Italian laurels had withered away. Even Padre Martini's glowing testimonials had been unable to keep them alive. Hence the bitter agony of spirit, which was at once to fortify and consume him.

We are now dealing with a Mozart whose impetuosity and caustic tongue are as yet alike unfamiliar to us. In his letters home the Augsburg infant prodigy, Nanette, the eight-year-old daughter of the pianoforte-maker Johann Andreas Stein, is aptly held up to ridicule. He gives a young Herr von Langenmantel, who is pleased to make fun of his papal cross, a thorough snubbing, and he finds neither Augsburg nor its niggardly, close-fisted city fathers to his liking. The only things from which he derives any gratification there are playing the organ in the Church of the Barefooted Friars and at St. Ulrich's, and an ardent friendship struck up with a girl cousin two years his junior, whom he refers to as "the *Bäsle*".

> "I shall be truly glad to be once more in a place where there is a court," he writes to his father. "I must say that if it were not for the presence of my good cousins,"—that is, his uncle and aunt—"and if my dear *Bäsle* were not here, my regrets would be as innumerable as the hairs on my head at having ever come to Augsburg. I must give you some account of my dear *Bäsle*. But I shall postpone this until to-morrow, for one must be in a gay mood to praise her as she deserves . . . I now write to tell you emphatically that our *Bäsle* is pretty, intelligent, sweet, clever and gay; and this is probably because she has been a good deal in society. She was also some time in Munich. We really suit each other splendidly, for she too is inclined to naughtiness, and we enjoy quizzing people together, and have great fun."

In relation to her, however, it must be admitted he revealed a degree of ruthlessness that would be hard to match. Was this a reaction to the long period of restraint, the day-dreams of the past which had led to nothing, or was that element of chaos rising up within him out of which an artist such as he fashions a world for himself in all its harmonies and discords? What is Leporello if not an undertone? This much is certain: Mozart had now cast off the aura of the Salzburg Palace; the Lodron ladies would not have recognised him, and we are still far from Tamino.

But was she really so common, the poor *Bäsle*, that she should release such gross tones in Mozart? Or did she tolerate his familiarities in the hope of being able to hold him, being herself far too crude to gain a glimpse into his complex soul and perceive that through her very complaisance she must forfeit all serious interest in her on his part?

Leopold would in course of time have looked not unfavourably upon a match, but when he hinted at this Wolfgang replied that he would have to marry far too many women if he had to propose to every woman with whom he had had a little innocent fun. The *Bäsle* showed soon enough that despite all her disappointment she was quite capable of a disinterested and unselfish friendship, and that she possessed none of the latent meanness of Constanze, whom Mozart, seeing that he chose her as his wife, took so much more seriously than the *Bäsle*, who, alone and unprotected, was to sink lower and lower in the social scale and end her days in far humbler circumstances than Mozart's widow, who lived to an honoured old age as Frau von Nissen, the wife of Herr von Nissen, Aulic Counsellor to the King of Denmark.

Mozart's success in Augsburg was meagre. On October 25th, the day before his departure, he gave a concert, which brought in 70 florins before expenses had been deducted.

> "You do not know yourself how well you play the violin," writes his father. "If only you will do yourself justice and play with *style, vigour and spirit,* indeed, as though you were the *leading violinist in Europe!* Oh, how often you will hear a highly esteemed violinist for whom you will feel nothing but pity."

In his letters both to Munich and to Augsburg he writes of the Countess Lodron's keen interest in Mozart's career. "Mozart is sure to go to Mannheim, and, come what may, I cannot dismiss it from my thoughts. The Elector is sure to keep him there," was a remark of hers that was passed on to Leopold. She sent for him, and invited Nannerl to her house, ostensibly to play a rondo on the clavier, but really to get first-hand news of Wolfgang.

From Salzburg Leopold pulled strings to get the Augsburg concert written up. A report of it appeared in the "Machenbaurische Zeitung" and was couched in such highly complimentary terms that the people of Salzburg opened their eyes wide. "They could say no more," he writes delightedly. But he is seriously vexed by another piece of news. "Did you know that on the day of your concert our good friend M. Grimm arrived at the 'Drei Mohren', hard by the concert hall? I saw this announcement in the 'Augsburger Intelligenzblatt': 'On the 22nd Herr v. Grimm, Palatine Ambassador, arrived by post-chaise from Saxony, and is staying at the "Drei Mohren" . . .' presumably he arrived very late, and departed early the next morning, or he would have read the notice of your concert or have heard you spoken of . . . What pleasure it would have given him," the father continues naïvely, "and you both, had he arrived in time and attended the concert."

Grimm, however, *had* arrived in time and *had* been present at the concert. The fact that he did not make himself known to Wolfgang, did not exchange greetings with him after all this long time, was an ominous sign. We know how Mozart varied in appearance and what differing impressions he made on people; had he, perhaps, considered his second best coat good enough for the people of Augsburg, for whom he had no great liking, and had he seemed to Grimm, measured by the standard of the Paris salons, quite impossible? One may assume that purely external motives determined his attitude of reserve towards the former "prodigy", for the discovery of whom twelve years before he had taken so much credit. He may well have asked himself whether the child prodigy had after all become anything more than a provincial musician. Was it to be supposed for a moment that the Marquise de Pas-du-tout, or the Duchesse de Merci-bien would deign to notice the little man? The recently ennobled Baron Grimm was a snob; he possessed intellect, no doubt, but no character, and by his failure to recognise Mozart's status and importance he has betrayed the superficiality of his judgment.

All in all Augsburg was even less profitable than Munich as a stopping place. On October 26th, our travellers set off for a brief visit to Prince Ernst von Öttingen-Wallerstein, a great music-lover, who held court at the Castle of Hohenaltheim. There they made the acquaintance of the pianist and composer, Ignaz von Beecké. By October 30th they were in Mannheim.

Mannheim 1777

MANNHEIM AT THIS TIME HAD A POPULATION OF 25,000. The Elector Carl Theodor, who was, a year later, to become Elector of Bavaria, was a lover of pomp, a ruler who was given to playing the Roi Soleil and who took Louis XIV for model in his private life, but who also expended large sums on the arts and sciences, founded a German theatre, in which Schiller won his first laurels, and above all made his capital the most famous musical centre of Germany. Just as he imitated Louis XIV, so the inhabitants of Mannheim imitated their ruler in their mode of life, devoting themselves with zest to both intellectual and artistic pursuits. Mannheim rejoiced in the possession of the best possible orchestra, the most perfect instrumentalists. It was a town after Mozart's heart and he proposed to enjoy his freedom to the full.

Konzertmeister Cannabich, a man of considerable talent and musical knowledge, who had known Mozart as a child, and whom he visited on October 31st, the day after his arrival, gave him the warmest of welcomes and took him off to the final rehearsal of Händel's *Messiah*, which was taking place on that day. Incidentally, it failed to find favour in Mannheim, nor, indeed, did it make any particular impression on Mozart. Church music by the Abbé Vogler concluded the programme.

This Abbé Vogler was the most influential musical personality at the Mannheim court. Like Mozart a "Knight of the Golden Spur", he was on good terms with old Hasse in Venice, and, himself a famous teacher, he opposed the methods of Padre Martini. Carl Maria Weber, who became his pupil, retained throughout his life reverent, indeed, grateful memories of him. "I hope," writes Leopold, admonishingly, "that Wolfgang will be at pains to make a friend of everyone by his complaisance and courtesy, and His Reverence *Vice-Kapellmeister* Vogler must be a clever man, for he stands in high esteem with the Elector." But Wolfgang was at no pains to do the Abbé Vogler justice. Influenced by Cannabich and the Viennese composer Holzbauer, he immediately took sides against him, seeing in him only "a dreary musical jester, who has a very great conceit of himself and small capacity. The whole orchestra from top to bottom dislikes him and he has been a source of much annoyance to Holzbauer." This was quite enough for him, for Holzbauer was one of the pioneers of German opera, which for a time held its own against the "Italianomania", as Leopold called it, in Mannheim. "The music of Holzbauer (to his opera *Günther von Schwarzburg*) is very beautiful," he assured his father, . . . "What surprises me most of all is that so old a man as Holzbauer should still have so much spirit; for one can scarcely credit what fire there is in his music." It was not

Holzbauer, however, but the Abbé Vogler, the very man whose favour he so frivolously forfeited, who could have helped him to obtain an appointment. This might have meant his staying in Mannheim, and German opera might, as a result of his and Holzbauer's influence, have gained a firm footing even at that early period and permanently established itself. But alas! how incapable he was to prove, both now and henceforth, of studying his own interests, what fantastic, hare-brained schemes he was to evolve! A plan had only to be tempting, and he believed it possible to carry it into execution there and then. During his stay in Mannheim, he showed not the slightest trace of what the French call "*esprit de conduite*". He ought also, urged his father, to seek to ingratiate himself with the Intendant, Count Savioli. "That is both a duty and politic. All this is neither intrigue nor deception . . . for your years and your person would lead no one to suspect the magnitude of the divine favour with which you have been endowed through your talents; many are the places you have left where they have not perceived the half of your talent."

If, however, "a slight melancholy" attacked the father whenever he went home because he fancied he could hear Wolfgang playing the violin, the son for his part had no wish to be reminded of Salzburg. "I hope, too, that you now have less vexation than when I was in Salzburg," replied the son. "For I must admit that I was the sole cause. I was treated ill; I did not deserve it. You, as was natural, felt for me—but too much so. That, you see, was my principal and most urgent reason for leaving Salzburg in such haste." "You are certainly right," was the father's answer. "I did feel the greatest vexation at the scurvy treatment you were obliged to endure; it was that which tore at my heart, robbed me of sleep, filled my every thought and was bound in the end to consume me."

There is still evidence on Leopold's side of generous and sympathetic understanding of his son, on Wolfgang's of an emotional attachment to his father.

A letter written on the occasion of his father's birthday begins as follows: "I cannot write poetically, for I am no poet. I cannot arrange my phrases so skilfully as to give light and shade, for I am no painter. Neither can I express my feelings and thoughts by gesture and pantomime, for I am no dancer. I can, however, do so in music, for I am a musician." Why, he is an artist through and through! Even in words he sometimes plays about with a rhythm as though with notes.

Meanwhile he was making no progress professionally. Count Savioli's reception of him on November 4th proved to be very condescending. "I hear that you play the clavier quite passably," was the remark the Count deigned to make to Mozart. But the Elector was charmed when he played two days later at a court concert. He called his playing not merely passable, but incomparable, and granted him an audience for the very next morning. Wolfgang offered to write an opera for Mannheim, and the Elector replied: "We may very well arrange that." After this he played frequently at court, but the desired appointment was still not forthcoming. "Count Savioli," he wrote to his father, "has already spoken three times to the Elector, and the answer has been on each occasion, with a shrug of the shoulders: 'I shall give my answer in good time, but I have not yet made up my mind.'"

Instead of the ducats which he so sorely needed he received in payment, to his great annoyance, a gold watch; he already possessed five. His father still went on hoping, it is true, although he had never approved the journey to

Mannheim or the costly detour via the Castle of Wallerstein, and he mistrusted Savioli. "For Heaven's sake," he wrote, "you must set your minds on making money." How much of the money borrowed had already been spent? The Abbé Bullinger's 300 florins, over 90 here and 40 there. "You must see to it that you not only let the Elector of Mainz hear you play, but so arrange matters that you obtain a present in money, and an opportunity to give a concert in the town whenever possible, which a great number of the nobility will attend." There too, went on Leopold, he would find *Konzertmeister* Kreiser and the singer Franziska Ursprung, who would assist him. For Leopold assumed that the travellers were already in Mainz, would have preferred them to be in Munich, urged them to go on to Paris, worked out in detail the various routes, was at a loss to know what was for the best, wrote letters the length of pamphlets, whole pages of them in cipher, and complained, not without reason, that he was not being kept *au courant* with their news. "We have received no letter from you today, perhaps one will come to-morrow by Friday's post. Of the German opera, who composed it, who sang, and how, not a word do you write! And as for the concert, who played, who sang, who blew and who whistled . . . you are strange folk." A letter of Wolfgang's of November 20th was, as it happened, on the way, but in it he did not go into any details. "To-day I must write quite briefly, for I have no more paper at home," he wrote, and indulged in witticisms at the expense of a "brand new" composition of the Abbé Vogler's. When writing nonsense to his "dearly beloved *Bäsle*" in Augsburg, he allowed himself more time.

Yet on "the evening of November 22nd, or rather punctually and precisely on the stroke of 10 of the clock," he once more addressed a lighthearted letter to his father.

It also contained a few repentant lines for the Abbé Bullinger, who wrote him a postscript in nearly every one of his father's letters. "When I reflect that I have never yet written to him, who is my best and truest friend !" And he signed himself "Wolfgang Amadé Mozart, Knight of the Golden Spur, and as soon as I marry, of the Pair of Horns, member of the great Academy of Verona, of Bologna, *oui, mon ami!*"

From Mannheim, come what might, he refused to budge. He had made friends with the violinist Franz Anton Wendling, and his brother, Johann Baptist Wendling, the flautist, whose beautiful daughter Auguste was the mistress of the Elector: "It positively cuts one to the heart," was Wilhelm Heinse's comment, and he called her a "hundred-petalled rose in full bloom". Mozart gave her clavier lessons for love, and wrote songs for her, which she "sings incomparably", among them the recitative *Basta vincesti*, and the aria *Non lasciarmi*, with which she, and the whole Wendling family, fell "madly in love".

He was held even more in thrall by Rose Cannabich, for whom he composed the Sonata K. 309, and of whom he was to write to his father: " . . . his daughter, who is fifteen and the eldest child, is a very pretty and pleasing girl. For her age she has great good sense, and a demure demeanour; she is grave, talks but little, but when she does, is always gracious and friendly. Yesterday she again afforded me inexpressible delight by playing my sonata most admirably. The andante (which must not go fast) she plays with the greatest possible feeling. She likes playing it, too, very much. You know I finished the first allegro when I had been here only two days, and had therefore only seen Mlle. Cannabich once. Young Danner asked me how I proposed to compose the andante. 'Entirely in accordance with Mlle.

Rose's character . . . what the andante is, so is she.' " And to her too, filled with joyous self-assurance, he gave clavier lessons for love. But what did all these songs and arias, the compliments and assurances of his friends, bring in for the young spendthrift? "I have already mentioned to you in my letters, I hope, that Holzbauer's great opera is German?" Yet what consolation was this to Leopold in the midst of all his cares?

"I received your letter of the 20th, written on a scrap of paper, because you had no more paper at home, on Thursday the 25th . . . Here am I wearing my brains out, and writing myself nearly blind, concerned to provide for all eventualities, while you and your mother regard everything as a trifle, are wholly indifferent, bind my hands so that I am unable to advise and help you, by not letting me have a word as to where you propose to go." And just as he had previously urged them to leave Munich, he now urged them to leave Mannheim.

Meanwhile Wolfgang had already replied to his father's reproaches on November 29th, in a strangely sobered tone, "I received your letter of the 24th this morning, and from it perceive that you are incapable of reconciling yourself to changes of fortune, good or ill, whichever should overtake us. Hitherto we four, such as we are, have been neither fortunate nor unfortunate, and for that I thank God. You heap reproaches upon us that we are far from deserving." The rest of his letter makes it abundantly clear that he had been kept dangling by half promises and that his patience had been sorely tried, but also that it would have been most inadvisable to throw up the game at this particular moment and leave Mannheim. For Nannerl he enclosed the allegro and andante of the sonata composed for Rose Cannabich, and since he was so delighted with it, he devoted a postscript to it. "Doubtless you will have heard some bits of this sonata, for at Cannabich's it is either sung, played on the clavier or violin, or whistled at least three times a day, but *sotto voce* of course."

His father, however, called the sonata "peculiar" and considered that it had something of the "mannered Mannheim gout" about it.

We cannot agree with him. It is the sheerest baroque, the curves, the relief of which are brought to life for us in sound, and if Rose Cannabich was like this andante, we can only profoundly regret that it was not she to whom he remained attached. It moves forward with stilted grace, in certain passages clearly breathed upon by an echo of the *Nachtmusik*; it is as though the colour-tones of the sunlit and shadowy green mountain-slopes of his native Salzburg had been infused into the flat Mannheim countryside.

Salzburg was forgotten, but for Frau Mozart Mannheim was but a poor exchange. We learn from her somewhat wheezy pen how wretched were their quarters, from which she in particular was the sufferer.

"To-day, the 7th, Wolfgang dines with Herr Wendling, so I am alone at home as is commonly the case, and suffer grievously from the cold, for when a little fire has been made it burns away so soon that the room is cold again, and it is never laid again afterwards. A tiny fire costs 12 kreutzer, so I have only a little one lit early in the morning, when I get up, and in the evening. During the day I am obliged to suffer great cold. As I now write I can scarce hold the pen for shivering . . ." She too has not yet given up all hope of an appointment for Wolfgang. "We have not yet been to a single ball, only to one *galla comedi*, for the tickets are very dear, the stalls 45 kreutzer per person and in the poorer boxes, 1 florin. No one is allowed in free, everyone must pay, the director of the theatre gets 3,000 florins yearly and the poorest singer 600, the musicians, too, are paid well, herr Canewich as director of the orchestra now

> has 1,800. . . herr capellmeister holzbaur about 3,000 and when they compose something new they receive presents how very different from omezbhrg,[1] it makes one's mouth water, so that we pray God to grant, if it is His divine will, the Churifrot[2] will keep us here, things move slowly here, we must wait in patience, it is something at least that he has not refused."[3]

She did not like being so much alone, poor woman, and, after all, how much pleasanter it would have been for her to be within the cosy four walls of her own home or at archery practice with the Robinigs and Adlgassers, Barisanis and Hagenauers, gossiping about this and that, rather than to be sitting, alone and silent, in the icy-cold, gloomy inn-room, which she was afraid to have heated, waiting for Wolfgang, who would not come back until late in the evening.

By December 10th, Wolfgang found it impossible to wait any longer in uncertainty. He accosted Savioli, who was trying to avoid him, and learned that the Elector "had made up his mind", but in a negative sense. Once more, then, he was a hope the poorer. What now? And what availed it that the whole Cannabich family wept? Nevertheless he has at last one piece of good news to give his father: A Dutchman, he reports Wendling as saying, will give him 200 florins "if you write three little and easy short concertos and a couple of quartets for the flute." "Now at last, God be praised, we have left the inn," writes Frau Mozart on December 14th, "and have a clean room, with two nice beds and an alcove, in the house of a hofkammer Rath . . . he has a good wife, a mamselle of 15, who has played the clavier now for eight years, Wolfgang has to give her lessons, and in return we pay nothing for our lodgings

[1] Salzburg.

[2] Cipher for Kürfurst, Elector.

[3] Postscript to Wolfgang's letter of December 6th.

or for wood and light. Wolfgang eats at Monsieur Wendling's and I take my food with young Herr Danner, and in return he takes lessons in composition from my son, and that is how we have arranged things . . . you cannot credit how highly Wolfgang is esteemed here, both among musicians and others, they all say he has not his like, they completely worship his compositions. Often I do not see him the whole day long. Most of the time I am alone at home, for owing to the cold and bad weather I cannot go out much, for I have no umberel when it snows or rains."

The news that his son "has an astonishing amount to do" and can provide for his mother's keep, reassured the father. The plan now was for Wolfgang to go to Paris with Wendling "who is a very dear friend of our dear friend Grimm," but for the mother to return to Salzburg. This also, and the fact that his dear wife was returning home to them, delighted both husband and daughter. The skies had once more cleared. And what had not been achieved in Mannheim might yet be accomplished in Munich. "I shall write next post day to Prince Zeyll, to bring matters forward in Munich," we read in Wolfgang's next letter. "If you also would write to him, I should be very glad. But briefly and to the point. No fawning, for that I cannot endure," a remark that enraged Leopold afresh. Wolfgang, for his part, was irritated at his father's wanting to know whether he had been to confession. "What you write with regard to confession has already been seen to on the Feast of the Immaculate Conception," the mother writes reassuringly. ". . . that all goes very well with us, God be praised and thanked, I have already told you, I have to be the whole afternoon with the frau hofkammer Räthin's, and eat with them every evening, Wolfgang is everywhere highly esteemed . . ." And she, like Wolfgang, wishes them "a happy New Year, let us hope it may be better than the last . . . and that I may have the joy of seeing you both again in the New Year."

Before the old year was out Wolfgang's first meeting with the fateful Weber family took place. It was as though a flowery ravine had opened out before the guileless young man, which was to draw him into its depths. The way in which he had suddenly contemplated the journey to Paris as though it were a mere pleasure trip, should long since have made his father restive. He intended, he wrote, to burden himself with as little luggage as possible; his "puce-coloured Spanish coat and the two waistcoats" seemed to him ample. The rest was to be left behind in Mannheim. The Wendlings, too, proposed to travel lightly.

Whereupon his father replied fussily: "You must not and cannot model yourself on your foolish travelling companion. Your circumstances are very different . . ." The gaining of fame, honour and a great name and hence money were not a matter of a few months, let alone a few weeks. But Wolfgang had by now dismissed all thought of Paris from his mind.

Since their letters frequently crossed, the matters to which they referred were often out-of-date. A decided chilliness had crept mto their relations. But when Leopold, grieved at the way in which his wife was passing her time in Mannheim, wrote: "You should not and must not leave your Mamma to eat her heart out alone," and "see to it that you keep her company and take care that she wants for nothing, even as she takes thought for you," the son was able to reply that now it had been decided that the journey was out of the question, things had arranged themselves in the best possible way. "That my Mamma and I have capital lodgings, you know already . . . nor was it ever my intention that she should live elsewhere than with me."

In the meantime the Mozarts' interest was once more concentrated entirely on Munich, where, on December 30th, the Elector had died of the smallpox, and on the same day Carl Theodor had been proclaimed his successor. The new Elector left immediately for Munich, and within a short time also transferred the Court to his new capital. This put Mannheim at a serious disadvantage.

Every possible topic is now mentioned in the letters—the possibility of war against "our Elector, whose right of succession is contested," valises, and the "chaise" which must be sold, clothes which must be taken to Paris, others that are to be left behind—everything except the one thing that was fettering Mozart to Mannheim more than ever. Amongst other things he writes of his meeting with Wieland, who had arrived on December 21st. "I must tell you that I have made the acquaintance of Herr Wieland. But he does not as yet know me as well as I know him, for he has heard nothing of me. I should never have imagined him to be what I find him. His manner of speech appears to me to be somewhat affected. A somewhat childish voice; a glassy stare, a certain studied insolence and yet at times an idiotic condescension. It does not surprise me, however, that he should choose to behave thus here (if not at Weimar or elsewhere) for people here look upon him as one who has fallen from the skies. People are uncommonly constrained in his presence; no one speaks, everyone is silent; they hang on every word he utters; the pity is that they have often to be kept so long in suspense, for he has an impediment in his speech, which obliges him to speak very slowly and he cannot utter six words without pausing. For the rest he is, as we all know, a man of excellent parts."

Wieland showed Mozart every mark of friendship.

"Herr Wieland, after having heard me twice, was quite enchanted. The last time he said to me, after loading me with all manner of praise: 'It is indeed a piece of good fortune to have met you here,' and pressed my hand."

In reply to an anxious enquiry on the part of his father with regard to the Dutchman's 200 florins, Wolfgang wrote that he need have no misgivings, everything was perfectly all right.

❧

Mannheim 1778

"On Wednesday next" Mozart writes to his father on January 17th, "I go to spend some days with the Princess of Orange at Kirchheim-Poland . . . A Dutch officer, who is a good friend of mine, was given a terrible scolding by her for not having taken me with him when he went to pay her his New Year compliments . . . I shall get at least eight louis d'or; for since the Princess is passionately fond of singing, I have had four arias copied for her, and I shall also present her with a symphony, for she has a quite delightful little orchestra and gives a concert every day. The copying of the arias, moreover, will cost but little, for a certain Herr Weber, who is to accompany me thither, has copied them for me. This Herr Weber has a daughter, who sings admirably and has a lovely pure voice, and is only just 15 . . . My De Amicis aria with the dreadfully difficult passages she sings most admirably; she is to sing it too at Kirchheim-Poland."

He had heard such good reports of the Princess of Orange, he said, that he had at last resolved to pay her a visit. In other words, he had made his going there dependent on whether Aloysia Weber could accompany him.

How easily the young Mozart let himself be won over and ensnared by flattery, we have already seen. How little he studied his own interests, is clear from the rash way in which he drew upon himself the enmity of the Abbé Vogler. He had been prodigal of his talents and knowledge in his eagerness to win the favours of Auguste Wendling, even more so to win those of Rose Cannabich. Was not the devotion lavished on the thirteen-year-old Rose Cannabich, also the due of the fifteen-year-old Aloysia Weber? argued the Webers. And was this treasure of a Mozart, who gave lessons for love, to be allowed to slip through their fingers? His prestige as a musician of exceptional talent was enormous amongst the initiates. With or without an appointment, he did not lack recognition in Mannheim. To be taught by him, to have ones name coupled with his, could not but be advantageous. Now self-seekers are wont to extol an unselfish person for his very unselfishness, and, moreover, to warn him of other self-seekers, so that they may all vie with one another in exploiting him. Poor Wolfgang, who would so gladly have played the *homme d'affaires* in the eyes of his father, could not even assert that a certain Herr Weber was copying for nothing the four arias which he had composed for his daughter, but only that "the copying will cost but little". But his father had already calculated that this new family connection would cost his son quite half the fee he would receive from the Princess of Orange? But what was to be done about it? The Webers were already sure of their prey, for Wolfgang was mortally in love with Aloysia. Forgotten was the poor *Bäsle,* no more arias for the hundred-petalled Gustl Wendling, faded from the memory, too, was Rose Cannabich, together with the sonata which so resembled her.

"Wolfgang is not yet back from Kirchheim," his mother writes home on February 1st, "herr weber has written to his wife that the Princess will not permit them to leave till the end of the week, so I too must be content with that. As to his journey to Paris, however, you cannot have more fears than I, if only Monsieur Grim were in Paris, I should have no misgivings, he might perhaps let him lodge with him or do him some other service, for he is certainly a true friend to us, on whom we can depend. I have just now received a letter from wolfgang, he is at worms and is coming back tomorrow, how glad I shall be to see him again."

But Wolfgang could think of nothing else now than of roaming the world with the Webers. He returned to Mannheim in a state of intoxication. There can be no other explanation for the truly grotesque letter which, on the very next day, as though burning to let the cat out of the bag, this usually reticent young man wrote to his father; and the postscript which his mother added without his knowledge was one day to cut him to the heart.

"Monsieur mon très cher père,

"I could not possibly wait till the usual Saturday, for it is too long since I had the pleasure of conversing with you by letter. The first thing I must tell you is how I and my good friends fared at Kirchheim-Poland. It was simply an excursion. We left here on Friday morning at eight in the morning, after I had breakfasted with Herr Weber; we had a capital chaise to seat four. We arrived in Kirchheim-Poland by four. We had to go straight to the castle . . . Mlle. Weber sang three arias. I shall pass over her singing—in a word superb . . . Mlle. Weber sang in all thirteen times and played the clavier twice. . . On my honour I would rather hear my sonatas played by her than by Vogler. I played in all twelve times, and once by request on the organ in the Lutheran church, and presented the Princess with four symphonies, but received no more than seven louis d'or, *notabene* in silver, and my poor dear Mlle. Weber five.

This I should never have expected . . . we have, however, lost nothing thereby; I still have a profit of 42 florins, and the indescribable pleasure of having become acquainted with thoroughly honourable, good Catholic and Christian people. I only regret not having got to know them long since. Now comes something important concerning which I beg you to give me an immediate answer.

"Mamma and I have discussed the matter, and we are agreed that we do not at all care for the Wendling's mode of life."

With startling suddenness the lack of piety of the Wendlings and the questionable virtue of the daughter are put before his father with pious horror.

"Wendling is a thoroughly honourable and very good man, but unfortunately he is without religion, and so is his whole family. I need say no more than that his daughter was the Elector's mistress. Ramm is a fine fellow, but a libertine . . . friends who are without religion one never keeps. I have already given them a hint. I said that three letters had arrived during my absence of which I could tell them nothing further than that it was hardly likely I should accompany them to Paris. Perhaps I might follow them, but I might go somewhere else; they were not to depend on me. This is my plan:

"I shall finish the music for de Jean here entirely at my leisure. For that I shall receive my 200 florins. I can stay here as long as I wish, for neither food nor lodging cost me anything. In the meantime Herr Weber will endeavour to obtain various concert engagements for himself and me. We shall travel together. If I travel with him it will be just as if I were to travel with you. The reason why I am so fond of him is that, except in appearance, he resembles you in every way and has just your character and way of thinking. My mother, if she were not, as you know, too comfortable and lazy to write would tell you the very same thing. I must admit that I very much enjoyed my excursion with them. We were merry and gay. I heard a man converse as you do. I had no need to worry about anything. Anything that was torn I found mended. In a word I was waited upon like a prince."

One can imagine how little his father was moved by his supposed resemblance to Herr Weber. But better and better is to come.

"I am so attached to this unfortunate family that I could wish for nothing more than to be able to make them happy. And perhaps I may be able to do so. My advice is that they should go to Italy. Hence I should like to ask you to write, the sooner the better, to our good friend Lugiati, and ask him how much, and what is the most, a *prima donna* receives—the more the better, for it is always possible to accept less—perhaps it would be possible to get the Ascenza in Venice. I will stake my life on it that her singing will do me credit. She has already profited so much in this short time from my teaching, and how much more will she have profited by then? I have no fears, either, with regard to her acting. If all should turn out well, we, that is, Herr Weber, his two daughters and I, will have the honour of staying for a fortnight with my dear Papa and my dear sister. My sister will find a friend and companion in Mademoiselle Weber, for she has as high a reputation here, as a result of her careful upbringing, as has my sister in Salzburg, her father is as respected as is my father, and the whole family as the family of Mozart."

And further on:

"I can tell you I shall be delighted to bring them to Salzburg. If only that you may hear her. My De Amicis arias, and the bravura aria, *Parto, m'affretto*, and *Dalla sponda tenebrosa*, she sings superbly. I entreat you to do your utmost to enable us to go to Italy. You know my dearest wish—to write operas.

"I think we shall go to Switzerland, perhaps also to Holland. Pray write to me soon on the matter. If we stay long anywhere *en route* the other daughter, who is the eldest, will be of the greatest use to us, for, since she can cook, we can keep house for ourselves. *A propos*, you must not be too astonished that of the 77 florins I have no more than 42 left. I was reckless for sheer joy that honourable and like-minded people had come together again . . ."

In other words, he had to a considerable extent made himself financially responsible for the Webers' trip . . . And having rashly, and, as will later transpire, in fulfilment of a promise—it is easy to guess who was pulling strings—unburdened himself of this letter, he rushes out of the house. His mother, however, secretly appalled, takes advantage of his absence to add a postscript.

"My dear husband, from this letter you will no doubt have perceived that when Wolfgang makes new friends, he would give his all for them.

"It is true she sings incomparably; but one should never lose sight of ones own interests; I never cared for his friendship with Wendling and Ramm, but I did not venture to object to it, and he has never listened to me.

"But no sooner did he become acquainted with these Webers, than he instantly changed his mind. In a word, he would rather be with other people than with me, I complain from time to time of things that do not please me, and that he does not like. You will, then, consider what is to be done; I do not look upon the journey to Paris with the Wendlings as at all advisable, I would rather accompany him myself later on; it would not cost so much by diligence; perhaps you will yet receive an answer from Herr Grimm; meanwhile we are losing nothing here, I am writing this in the greatest secrecy, for he is at dinner and I do not wish to be taken by surprise. Addio, I remain your true wife

"MARIANNE MOZART"

Scarcely was this letter, dated February 4th, despatched than Wolfgang repented of it. A certain apprehension can clearly be read between the lines of the letter addressed to his father a day or two later. The kindhearted Frau Mozart was also worried about her postscript. This son of hers, at this time so impulsive and wayward, was for her a more powerful magnet than home and hearth, than the familiar, snug Salzburg surroundings by the side of husband and daughter. She was entirely on his side again and had made up her mind, since he did not want to travel with the Wendlings, to set out with him for the dreaded Paris, to face complete insecurity, perhaps serious want. And while he was seeking for a living for them both, she was to have to cope afresh with totally strange lodgings, with anxiety, bitter privation, and, did she but know it, to face death, on which her thoughts must have dwelt from time to time. Truly, a heroic woman, this mother of Mozart's!

Leopold's letters of this period contain notes of genuine feeling. Fame, prestige and money, however, were for him inseparable conceptions, and the word money in particular he was specially fond of underlining. This point was increasingly to become a bone of contention. Let us assume that Andreas Schachtner, an old friend of the family who had known Mozart from the age of three, was fully justified in saying of him: "I fancy that in the absence of so advantageous an education as he had he might have become the most ruthless scoundrel," so susceptible was Mozart to every passing attraction, the good or ill effects of which he had not had time to test; nevertheless, whatever the course of his life, he must inevitably have developed into a visionary and dreamer in practical matters. But we must remember that he was a musical genius whose sublime aims were bound constantly to interfere with all thoughts of material gain; producing in him, rather, impatience, a sense of impotence, and that dullness of gaze which so struck a contemporary. It was only dimly and imperfectly that he appreciated such hard facts as the difference between 96 and 200 florins, which were so obvious to his father. Leopold's trust in him suffered its first severe blow when he read that fateful letter of Wolfgang's, which he called "a raving letter, which was nearly the death of me"; and when Wolfgang read the reply to it, he cursed himself over and over again for having let himself go. He admits, in his next letter, that he had not written it on his own initiative, agrees with his father on all essential points, abandons all his plans for wandering, making his mother the excuse, and vents his spleen, not, of course, on Aloysia, who was responsible for the whole thing, but on the completely innocent Nannerl. "I embrace my sister with all my heart; tell her she is not to weep about every piddling trifle, or I shall never return as long as I live."

We must dwell a little longer on the ups and downs of these letters. They shed a brighter light on Mozart's development than all the accounts of his contemporaries. And we shall not be able much longer to consult the correspondence in its entirety. Within a short time the artless letters of Frau Mozart come to a sudden stop. Leopold's letters to Wolfgang have been kept from posterity. A mean and criminal act has robbed us of these important documents. They would have told us too much with regard to his wife, and she therefore destroyed them. In her base thirst for revenge she was one day to try to have her father-in-law thrown out of his very grave; as though it were not enough that she had shown that of her own husband so fateful a lack of respect.

The evil presentiment that assailed Leopold when, for the first time, he heard of the Webers, was only too well founded. They had already set their seal on Wolfgang's fate and were never again to let him go. They formed a sombre background to his life, and already Constance was concealed in the wings.

The family storm seems to have subsided, and Frau Mozart tried to soothe her husband with soft words, but the waves rose high again when he heard the hapless story of the 96 gulden:

> "So once again I have guessed aright? . . . After all this time it turns out that you could have had pupils, but simply because once or twice you did not find them at home, you stayed away altogether. You would rather give lessons for love, forsooth, would rather leave your old father in want . . . it is more fitting that your fifty-eight-year-old father should run hither and thither to earn a pittance . . . and *instead of paying his debts*, support you with the little that is left him, because you in the meantime amuse yourself by giving lessons to a young girl for nothing. Reflect, my son, summon your common sense to your aid! Reflect whether you are not treating me more cruelly than our Prince, for from him I had nothing to look for . . . but you are my son . . . My dear Wolfgang, all your letters convince me that you will always be turned aside by the first heated fancy that comes or is put into your head without duly reflecting on the matter or giving it careful consideration. You write, for example: I am a composer, I must not bury my talent for composing. Who has ever said that you should? By roaming the world like a gypsy you really would be doing so . . . Why should it not be possible for you to learn to know people? To divine their intention? To hide your feelings from the world? . . . My dear Son, God has blessed you with an admirable intelligence. There are, so far as I can see, only two reasons which sometimes prevent your applying it properly . . . a thought too much arrogance and self-love; and then the fact that you immediately get on too familiar terms with people, and open your heart to anyone and everyone; in short, that, desiring to be natural and unconstrained, you fall into the error of being too open-hearted . . . even people who do not know you should be able to read on your brow the stamp

of genius. To flatterers on the other hand . . . you can open your heart with the greatest of ease . . . all that I say to you is only intended to make of you an upright and honourable man. There are millions of people who have not been so favoured by God as you. What a responsibility! Would it not be a pity if so great a genius took the wrong path! And that can happen in the twinkling of an eye . . . Mamma goes to Paris with you, you must repose all confidence in her verbally and in me by letter."

This piece of advice, "to hide his feelings," Wolfgang was now to follow in his correspondence with his father.

"Shall give all needful information in my next letter, together with all addresses and letters, to Diderot, d'Alembert, etc. . . ." adds Leopold.

Pages and pages are devoted to this, accompanied by instructions, good or otherwise, for his behaviour. Leopold Mozart, who has a claim on the gratitude of posterity for all that he did for his son, was a little man, Wolfgang in comparison an immeasurably great figure; but we live in a queer world, which loves to turn things upside down, delights in mazes and jigsaw puzzles, prefers snapshots to all other forms of portraits, and maintains things not only in a smooth flow, but in a whirl, leaving it an open question what is to live, what to perish. It was Leopold Mozart who at this period gave of his best in his role of father, and to a great extent, also, of mentor, and it was Wolfgang to whose head the freedom at last won mounted like wine. Which does not exclude the probability of its always having been for a temperament such as his a sorer trial than any other to be unable to give of his full measure, only to attain the level of his less inspired work and—if only like a masterpiece painted over—not to be the immortal Mozart that he yet was. Compared with the Salzburg months of the year 1776 the time spent in Mannheim was not very productive. With the exception of the lovely aria, *Non so d'onde viene*, the passion for Aloysia Weber at first gave rise to no fresh works. But in almost every letter Mozart urges his father—no doubt at her instigation—to send him songs from his Salzburg collection. Again Leopold has an inkling of the true state of affairs, but he complies with his son's requests, in order not to antagonise the Webers, though in every line he betrays his exasperation.

"So I am to have the honour to despatch five arias and to pay for the copying of three more and their transport to Augsburg, when I myself, God knows, have no money; I look like poor Lazarus, my dressing-gown is so full of holes that if anyone rings the doorbell in the morning I am obliged to run away," etc. A side-light is thrown on Nannerl, too, in this letter (of February 25th) and the echo of the affair of the 200 florins was bitter enough. "She was not weeping over a piddling trifle when she wept over your letter, and yet when you wrote that you had not received the 200 florins she said: 'God be praised that it is no worse.' For we cannot deny that she has your affairs at heart, and she knows that her own note of hand must now be pledged to enable you both to leave Mannheim, for how could I, without blushing with shame, approach Hagenauer again without giving him something as security? This your sister has done cheerfully and without giving it another thought, although she knows that if I die to-day, she will be left a pauper."

Meanwhile it was not the father but the son who this time had taken refuge in illness; in "catarrh, headache, sore throat, pains in my eyes, and ear-ache". He takes "anti-spasmodics", black powders and "elder-flower tea" to made him sweat. And although he makes excuses for not being in the mood to write, he once more comes out with Aloysia's requests. How she must have dinned them into him!

Warm, but thoroughly shame-faced, thanks to Nannerl follow, "for the 50 florins which she so kindly borrowed for me, but which I so needed".

Poor Wolfgang was never to succeed in playing the spendthrift with impunity. For every frivolous action on his part circumstances were to put him in the wrong; life was not to permit him to let pupils slip because on one or two occasions he had not found them at home and to give talented young women lessons for love instead. It was to apply to him the standard, not of a genius, but of an ordinary Philistine, and since he was found wanting as such—and of that there can be no doubt—it was to abandon him to misery. At the very height of his powers as a master he was to be reduced to composing tunes for musical boxes for a mere pittance.

As yet he realised nothing of the precariousness of existence. To him all avenues lay open, the prospect was lovely and enticing. The fact that his father had to go about ill-clad brought tears to his eyes, but he was confident that, given his head, he would be a rich man. "All my hopes are now set on Paris," he writes home, "for the German princes are all niggards." Frau Mozart backs him up in everything. It had been right from every point of view, she insists, for Mozart not to have travelled with the Wendlings. Wendling was the best man in the world "but the whole family knows nothing of religion, and sets no store by it, the mother and daughter do not go to church the year round, never go to confession, and hear no masses, but they frequently go to the theatre. They say the church is not healthy. We have only learned all this bit by bit, partly from their own friends, and some things Wolfgang has heard and seen for himself. I have prayed daily that God might prevent this journey, and God be thanked, so it has turned out. Most of the people here have no religion . . ."

Leopold continues to tender advice, sends them countless addresses, and busies himself in a thousand and one ways on their behalf. "The contract with the carriage-jobber has just been concluded," writes Wolfgang on March 11th. "For 11 louis d'or he is to drive us to Paris in our own chaise, which he has bought from us for 40 florins. To-morrow I shall set it down in writing that I am to pay him only 7 louis d'or and 4 florins in Paris, since I have not yet been paid for the chaise."

On the 11th he set out with his mother. On the 23rd they were both in Paris.

❧

Paris I

THIS IS NOT THE SAME MOZART WHO, SIX MONTHS AGO, as he drove out through the gates of Salzburg, felt his heart leap for joy because he believed that he had cast off all his chains and that the world lay before him. The intimacy between him and the mother who was so boundlessly devoted to him has deepened, his sense of responsibility towards her has grown; no longer does he play the role of head of the family merely in jest. The experience gained on their travels, all the mistakes he has made, his own often immature behaviour, have themselves matured him, his passion for the fascinating Aloysia and the parting from her have sobered him. And so the two of them go driving along in their little travelling-carriage, each silently musing upon their respective hopes and fears.

Meanwhile the father has been worrying about them and has once more raised four or five louis d'or, so that they shall not arrive in Paris penniless, "since, as you wrote to me on February 19th, you have no more than 140 florins, it is clear to me that Wolfgang has not earned anything from pupils, and that once again it was all idle talk."

He issues innumerable warnings and instructions for their conduct, again and again referring them to Grimm. "I pray God that He will send Wolfgang better fortune in Paris . . . It is fortunate for him that Herr Baron von Grimm is in Paris; he must have complete confidence in him and do everything that he tells him, and as he tells him . . ." But Grimm has already conveyed a hint to him not to stake everything on one card; why else should he have written of a possible journey to Russia? ". . . then you would again be at a dead end. For if things were to continue like this, all our possessions would be mortgaged and we should find ourselves suddenly reduced to poverty, and in the end none of us could help the other," writes Leopold in a fever of anxiety. But he continues to place all his hopes on Grimm. "Who knows that you may not be able to live somewhere near him?" Nor does he fail to reproach them for not reading his letters with sufficient care. "H. Baron v. Grimm will not be able to lodge you in his house. That is not to be expected; you had best, therefore, make enquiries at M. Mayr's." And, in conclusion, "by way of precaution write down H. Baron v. Grimm's address in several places. Rue de la Chaussée d'Antin près le Boulevard." Grimm, Grimm, Grimm all the time.

On March 23rd at four o'clock in the afternoon our interesting travellers have arrived safely in Paris, and dutifully write off at once to Salzburg. "We are lodging at Herr Mayr's in the house where herr von Waldburg lodged and do not yet know what we shall have to pay . . . for eight days of our journey we had the best possible weather, astonishingly cold in the mornings and warm in the afternoons, but the two last days the wind almost choked us and the rain drenched us so that the two of us in the carriage were soaked to the skin and could scarce gasp . . . to-day we called on herr baron von grim," Frau Mozart continues, "he was not at home, but we left a card to let him know of our arrival . . ."

Their journey had taken nine days. Wolfgang had "never endured such tedium", and at St. Joseph's in Clermont they had drunk the health of the Abbé Bullinger. This is all they have to tell of the impressions gathered on the journey and of the various stopping places.

Of "Herr Baron von Grimm", to whom he found himself referred as the *arbiter mundi*, Wolfgang, who knew himself to be a master of his craft, was sick of hearing. His irritation is clearly discernible in the letter which, with his mother, he writes to Leopold on March 24th, the day after their arrival . . . "Today we are to take a *fiacre* and go in search of Grimm and Wendling. To-morrow morning, however, I am to call on the Palatine Ambassador, Herr von Sückingen, a great connoisseur and devoted lover of music, to whom I have two letters from Herr von Gemmingen and M. Cannabich. Before leaving Mannheim I had the quartet which I wrote in the evenings at the inn in Lodi, the quintet, and the Fischer variations copied for Herr von Gemmingen. And he wrote me a most civil note, expressing his pleasure at the memento I had left for him, and sending me a letter to his good friend Herr von Sückingen, adding: 'I am persuaded that you will be a far greater recommendation to the letter than it can possibly be to you.'" Wolfgang, who was extraordinarily susceptible to praise, was easily won over by such felicities. "And to meet the expenses of the copying," he continues, "he sent me three Louis d'or, assuring me of his friendship and begging for mine in return. I must say that all those gentlemen who knew me, privy counsellors, court officials, other persons of repute, and all the Court musicians were very reluctant and grieved to see me go. Of that there can be no question."

Was he now to put himself in Grimm's hands like a mere greenhorn?

Cannabich had held a concert in his honour, he writes, at which Aloysia had sung the *Aer tranquillo* from the *Re Pastore* and his latest aria *Non so d'onde viene* with signal success. "The members of the orchestra never ceased praising the aria and talking about it. I have very many good friends at Mannheim (people of wealth and position), who very much wished to keep me there. Well, well, I am quite ready to go where they pay well"—he puts this in to please his father— "who knows but it may yet still come about—I wish it may, for I am like that, always full of hope." But Leopold no longer even allowed himself to hope. In this he was to show that he still saw eye to eye with Grimm, who knew as good as nothing of Wolfgang's compositions apart from the early works to which he himself had stood sponsor; in his eyes the only important question was whether Mozart would be able to get a footing in the musical world, and of this he was highly sceptical from the start. Wolfgang was unknown; a fact that he himself did not quite realise, since wherever he went he received the homage of the *cognoscenti*. But a genius who did not make his way in the world cut no ice with Leopold. And so there was more and more friction between the two of them. Wolfgang could not refrain in his first letter from Paris from harping on the Webers and writing sentimentally: "Mlle. Weber was so kind as to knit two pair of mittens for me and present them to me as a keepsake and a small token of gratitude. Herr Weber did all the copying I required *gratis*, provided me with music paper, and made me a present of Molière's comedies (knowing that I had never read them) . . . and when he was alone with Mamma he said: 'Our best friend, our benefactor, is about to leave us. There can be no doubt that your son has done much for my daughter, has taken a great interest in her welfare, and she cannot be too grateful to him, and so forth.'" What could Leopold suppose but that Wolfgang had not shaken off the Webers? The mistake he made, however, was not to give him a free rein while he was in Paris, not to give him time—in his own fashion Wolfgang was able to make a way for himself and the sympathetic interest he aroused on all sides was quite extraordinary. At the very moment when his prospects were most rosy, Grimm and his father were to compel him to cut short his stay in Paris and to leave it for ever, empty-handed. Great cities, it is true, are cruel; they hang round the neck of a conqueror who knows how to capture them; the less fortunate they leave lying by the wayside; and there was nothing of your Rastignac about Wolfgang. From the first glance Grimm never saw beyond that side of him which made him seem seriously ill-equipped for the struggle for existence. He was ready, however, to stretch a point—by recommending him to the Duchesse de Chabot. Let us hear Wolfgang's account of this affair in his letter of May 1st:

"M. Grimm gave me a letter of introduction to her, and so I went there. The letter was mainly to recommend me to the Duchesse de Bourbon (who when I was last here was in a convent), and to introduce me afresh to her and recall me to her. A week went by and I heard nothing, but since she had already asked me to call at the end of a week I kept the engagement and went. I was made to wait for half an hour in a vast icy, unheated room without a fireplace. At length the Duchess came in, and was extremely civil, begging me to make allowances for her clavier, as none of her instruments were in good order; perhaps I would try it. I said that I would very gladly play, but that it was impossible at the moment, for my fingers were numb with cold; and I asked her at least to have me taken to a room with a fire. *'O, oui, Monsieur, vous avez raison,'* was all the answer she vouchsafed me, whereupon she seated herself among a group of gentlemen who were all sitting in a circle round a big table, and began to draw. I had the honour to wait for a whole hour. The windows and the doors were open, so that not only my hands but my whole body and my feet were frozen; and my head, too, began to ache. And so there was *altum silentium*, and I scarcely knew what to do for cold, headache and tedium. I kept thinking that but for M. Grimm I would take my leave there and then. At length, to cut a long story short, I played on the wretched, miserable pianoforte. The most vexatious thing of all was that the Duchess and all the gentlemen went on drawing without a pause, and were completely absorbed, so that I was obliged to play to the chairs, tables and the walls. In such unpropitious circumstances I lost patience, and after playing through half of the Fischer variations I rose. I was at once overwhelmed with compliments. But I said the only thing there was to say, namely, that I could not do myself justice on such an instrument, but should be very glad to choose another day on which a better one might be provided. But the Duchess would not hear of my leaving, saying that I must wait another half hour until her husband came. He, however, sat down beside me and listened with rapt attention, and I—forgot cold and headache completely, and despite the wretched clavier, played as I can when I am in the mood. Give me the best clavier in Europe and an audience which understands or wishes to understand nothing and is insensible to what I am playing, and I lose all pleasure in it. I subsequently related all this very fully to M. Grimm. You urge me to pay a great number of visits, in order to make fresh acquaintances and to renew old ones. This is, however, impossible. The distances are too great and the roads too miry to go on foot, the filthy state of Paris being indescribable. And

> if one takes a coach, one may very soon drive away four or five livres, and all for nothing, for the people merely pay one compliments, and there it ends. They ask me to come on such or such a day—I play, and they exclaim: '*0, c'est un prodige, c'est inconcevable,*' and then '*adieu*'. I spent money enough at first in driving hither and thither, and often to no purpose, for I frequently found the people not at home. No one who is not here can conceive how disagreeable it all is. Altogether Paris is much changed, the French are by no means as polite as they were fifteen years ago; their manners now border on rudeness and they are abominably supercilious."

The society which was one day to find such a relentless observer in Marcel Proust was even at that period equally open to criticism on the score of its shallowness, and had already thrown up the type of the *grande dame mal elevée.* It is not without good reason—and let this be taken as a word in favour of kings and castes—that castes forfeit their status and kings their countries.

Fortune did not smile on Wolfgang even in Parisian musical circles. He wrote four alternative numbers for a *Miserere* by Holzbauer, but to no purpose. The performance was not a success and the best of the choruses were omitted. Legros neglected to send his *Symphonie Concertante* to the copyist. He found it extremely hard to get a hearing, his impatience, a heritage from his father, was great at all times, hence he was in a tearing rage with Paris and the state of music there. "Well, here I am, and I must bear up for your sake, but I shall thank God Almighty if I come off with my natural taste unimpaired. I pray God daily to grant me grace to bear up steadfastly here, that I may do honour to myself and the whole German nation, to His greater honour and glory." He urges his father to help him to go to Italy once again. "—so that I may be restored to life again . . . I shall hew my way through here as best I can, and only hope that I shall escape safe and sound. Adieu!" There is no doubt that he was leading an unusually serious life in Paris, and it is not because he neglected her, but because he was looking for work, that Frau Mozart was again left alone so much. By May 14th he is able to write to his father almost triumphantly:

"I have so much to do already that I am wondering how things will be when the winter comes." The Duc de Guines, who "plays the flute incomparably", has a daughter, he writes, who plays the harp "*magnifique*", and he is giving her lessons in composition. He is also expecting shortly to receive the libretto for an opera and has been asked to compose the music for a ballet. Further, he has been offered the post of organist at Versailles. Nothing was to come of these offers, but it put him in an advantageous light to be able to write of them to Salzburg. And how his mother boasts of him from the very first! "Wolfgang has a great deal to do," she informs her husband as early as April 5th, "for Easter week he is to compose a miserere for the *Consert Spirituell* with three choruses and a fugue and a duet and I know not what," and she retails a list of all the people who have invited him out to dine and of his pupils. True, she adds the bitter reflection:

"We shall not receive a Kreutzer before Easter. But," she assures him, "it is impossible to describe how famous and what a favourite Wolfgang is here again, herr wendlig spoke so well in his favour before his arrival . . . he is a truly kind-hearted man," she adds repentantly of the man they have so often maligned, "and Monsieur Von grim, too, promised wendling, since he has a greater reputation than he as a musician, to do all he can to see that he shall soon become known." What actually was the position with regard to his reputation? We may take her at her word when she continues: "As far as my way of life is concerned it is not at all agreeable, I sit alone the whole day like a prisoner in my room, which, moreover, is so dark and looks upon a little courtyard so that all day long one cannot see the sun and does not even know what the weather is like . . . the entrance and the stairs are so narrow that it would be impossible to get a clavier up here, and so Wolfgang must go to Monsieur le gro to compose because there is a clavier there, so I do not see him all day and am completely forgetting how to talk. The food I get from the theatre too is superb, for 15 sol at mid-day I get three dishes, first a soup made with butter which I do not relish, secondly, a morsel of bad meat and thirdly something made of calves' feet . . ." Far away are the good Salzburg puddings and dumplings and pancakes! Mme d'Epinay looks out for better and cheaper lodgings for them, invites Wolfgang to the house and shows herself to be more kind-hearted than "friend Grimm," who is glad to leave the worry over Wolfgang to her. "Yesterday herr Baron von grim came here to pay me a visit; he asks me to tell you not to fret, everything will yet turn out well, we must be patient for a little while longer, he will answer your letter presently, he is very occupied at the moment."

And what do the two of them, so far away from home, talk of when Wolfgang comes home in the evenings and they go out together for a meal? About Salzburg and their Salzburg friends. Frau Mozart, for all her simplicity emotionally far freer than Leopold and in consequence the nobler nature of the two, does not trouble her head about the nobility, whether of the first, second or third rank, but she keeps a sharp look-out for the changing fashions, so that Nannerl in Salzburg shall always be able to go one better than her neighbours. "Tell her she should get a good walking stick, for here it is the latest fashion for all women (with the exception of maidservants) to use a stick when they venture abroad, to go to church, to pay visits, to take the air, or wherever they go, in the streets, not in their carriages, of course, no one goes on foot without a stick, because it is so slippery walking here, especially when it has been raining, that some time past a woman broke her foot, and a doctor said it would be better if females were to make use of sticks, and so it forthwith became the mode." Full details as to the latest hair-dressing fashions are appended.

Ever since the death of the old Elector there had been a dispute over the succession, and the war situation came in for a good deal of discussion. Salzburg was in a very exposed position and Wolfgang advised his father to come with Nannerl to Paris. This provided his father with welcome opportunity to speak of his debts and to use them as a peg on which to hang the usual moralisings and advice. And so the two people of whom he thought incessantly, no longer sent him much news of themselves, pleading as an excuse the high postage fees, whereas poor Leopold's letters to them were twice as frequent and three times as long. They, for their part, were on their guard with him, concealing some things and glossing over others. He stood high in the esteem of both wife and son, but there was no real contact between him and them, and thus little ease in their relationship. And whereas Leopold harps again and again on "Herr Baron von Grimm," Wolfgang now only writes of the Palatine Ambassador, Count Sückingen, who is "a charming man, an enthusiastic lover and true connoisseur of music". He is no doubt tilting at Grimm when, in his short letter of May 29th, he writes: ". . . often I can see neither rhyme nor reason anywhere. I am neither hot nor cold, and take little pleasure in anything. What, however, cheers and fortifies me most is the thought . . . that I am an honest German, and that, though I cannot always say, I can at least think, what I please." "I have dined at least six times with Count Sückingen, the Palatine Ambassador," he writes on June 12th, "and always stay from 1 till 10. Time, however, passes so swiftly there that one is not aware of it. He likes me very much and I for my part enjoy being with him, for he is a most friendly and sensible person, with sound judgment and a true understanding of music. I was there again to-day with Raaff. Since he has for a long time now begged me to do so, I have taken him several of my compositions. To-day I took with me my new symphony, which I have just completed, and with which the *Concert Spirituel* on Corpus Christi day is to open . . . "This is a piece of good news to give his father. In Paris he had struck up an intimate friendship with Raaff the singer, whom he had kept at a distance in Mannheim, and also with Wendling. Frau Mozart is for ever blowing Wolfgang's trumpet. She loves him beyond measure and understands him better than anyone. The time when he is at home compensates her for all the discomfort and boredom of the long days alone. On the whole, she had not fared badly in Paris. "I am right sorry to leave this house, the people are excellent folk with whom I can talk German." And even the new lodgings were excellent. "You will wish to know where we lodge. Look first for the Rue Monmartter, and then the Rue Clery, in this Rue Clery it is the first street on the left hand, when one goes in from the Rue Monmartter, it is a handsome street, and mostly gentlefolk lodge there, very clean, not too far from the pulvar,[1] and a

[1] Boulevard.

healthy air, the people in the house kind and honest not self-seeking which is rare in Paris." She too writes of Count Sückingen and the weekly invitations to his house. "Herr Raaff comes to visit us nearly every day, he calls me mother and is very fond of us, he often stays with us two or three hours or more, he came once specially to sing to me . . ."

But they certainly know what it is to feel homesick in a foreign country. "Oh, how often when we sit down together to our evening meal do we speak of our friends in Salzburg. Adio keep well both of you I send you many 1,000 kisses and remain your faithful wife Marianna Mozart." And in her last letter, written on June 12th, she says: "We are having a most beautiful summer, truly pleasant, god be praised, we have so far had no storms. Wolfgang and I (when he eats at home) get a midday meal for 15 sols, but our evening meal for only 4 sols . . . we talk almost every day of our Salzburg friends and wish them with us."

Wendling and Raaff, who had proved such excellent friends in Paris, had ended their concert tour and were going back to Mannheim. During the difficult period that now set in for him, Mozart was alone.

It meant considerable success for a twenty-two-year-old musician, who was as good as unknown in the wider musical circles of Paris, to have his symphony (D major, K.297) performed at the *Concert Spirituel* and greeted with applause. In every town he visited his fate was to be the same. Only sporadically did he attract the attention of a wider public; among the cognoscenti, who recognised in him a genius, he invariably gained enthusiastic friends and admirers.

Meanwhile he was making but little contact with musical circles. "I spoke with Piccini at the *Concert Spirituel*," he writes. "He is very civil to me, and I to him, if we meet thus by chance, as it were. Beyond that I make no acquaintance, either with him or with other composers. I know my business, and they theirs, and that is enough." It was by no means enough, but his father would have it thus; so short-sighted was he that he isolated Mozart, cut him off from many a stimulating influence, many an interesting exchange of views, and taught him to see in every other musician a competitor. And so he remained aloof from the dispute between the pro-Gluck and the pro-Piccini parties, and failed to perceive its implications. His father warned him expressly against Gluck, towards whom he felt attracted. Queen Marie Antoinette, who so ardently espoused the cause of Gluck, understood far more about music than Grimm, who took up the cudgels for Piccini—for Italian music stood much higher in general esteem. When he realised later on that he had backed the wrong horse, Grimm's remarks on the subject were hopelessly vague and non-committal. "I do not know," he declared after the first performance of *Iphigenia in Tauris*, which established the triumph of Gluck, and thus proclaimed his adherence to the victorious party, "whether it is singing or far more than that. In listening to *Iphigenia* I forget that I am at the opera, and imagine that I am listening to a Greek tragedy." Of the real roots of the dispute, he had no idea. Richard Wagner was one day to give the clearest exposition of its underlying causes, its fundamental significance. Mozart secretly sided with Gluck and chafed under Grimm's tutelage. "I only regret that I cannot remain here, if only to show Grimm that I have no need of him, and that I can do as well as his precious Piccini, although I am only a German," he writes in September, 1778. We know, however, that he was fighting a losing battle and that Grimm was literally to drive him out of Paris. He had not wanted Mozart to come there; ever since seeing him at Augsburg he had regarded him with distaste. What concern of his was this pale-faced musician with the enormous head, the quondam handsome prodigy to whom all the ladies of the court had lost their hearts and who had given promise of developing so very differently; who had never learned to be modest in his demands, but, on the contrary, had the temerity, penniless and unprepossessing as he was, to behave in the most cavalier fashion to persons of rank who treated him *de haut en bas?* All this was beyond dispute, and here we have a key to the nature of a man who, though sociable and fond of the pleasures of life, yet came into such tragic conflict with the world. Even at the height of his fame life was to bring him sternly to heel; again and again to pull this genius, so devoured with ambition, down from his pedestal, bid him fall in line with, nay, even march behind, mere celebrities of a day; him, who *a priori*, so to speak, was so acutely conscious of his own uniqueness and rank as an artist, but who was, alas, too naïve to grasp that his world must also be convinced of it, and that, moreover, it inevitably took a connoisseur, a man not only of sensibility and taste, but a true music-lover, a rare spirit, to discern true worth with any assurance. Grimm at any rate did not combine these attributes. He had himself, as we say, "in hand". He schooled himself to be cold, aloof, in feeling. This is the only explanation for his mistaking Mozart's proud bearing for arrogance and, for assessing him, like any Philistine, at his face value. Had young Mozart secured for himself the patronage of a single *grande dame?* And how was it that the Duchesse de Chabot had not even paid him the compliment of placing one of her choicer instruments at his disposal, and had not scrupled to continue her sketching party while he, his fingers numbed with cold, had played on her very worst piano? Simply because he did not know how to impress people. It lay in Grimm's power to have warmly espoused the cause of his young countryman, even though it was not such child's play as it had been fifteen years ago. But he would have had to be a man of an entirely different stamp; he was too small-minded to be affected in the slightest by Mozart's simplicity, by his poverty, the very things which seem to us today such touching things about him. "He is too simple-minded," is the verdict he pronounces on Mozart in a letter written on August 13th, *"peu actif, trop aisè à attraper, trop occupè des moyens qui peuvent conduire à la fortune. Ici pour percer il faut être retors, entreprenant, audacieux."* From his point of view he was certainly right, but what a point of view! Particularly when he goes on: *"Je lui voudrais pour sa fortune la moitié moins de talent . . ."*

Posterity, forsooth, does not share his wish! Actually Grimm found Leopold the more congenial of the two, for he, after all, knew how to adopt that submissive tone which was so alien to Wolfgang's character. Grimm, however, had too much intelligence, knew too well what he was doing, to be able to square his behaviour with his conscience. Hence his fury when another German—and a colleague at that—Count Sückingen, declared his willingness to take over his role, to keep Wolfgang in his stead, to take him into his house and under his protection. And thus it came about that Mozart left Paris for ever, empty-handed, just when he was on the point of making a way for himself; for he was to become a German composer, German influences were to bring to maturity the glorious tree which has to-day become the property of the whole world, bestowing its fruits on all who know how to savour them.

All the arrangements for the performance of his new symphony went off this time without a hitch. It was included in the programme of the *Concert Spirituel* on June 18th and was a success. Yet the account that Wolfgang sends to his father sounds strangely detached; it is as though he were looking back on something that lay in the shadows of a distant past.

"Raaff stood next me," he writes, "and in the very middle of the first allegro came a passage that I knew would be bound to please. The entire audience was transported, and there was a torrent of applause, but since I knew when I wrote it what an effect it would have, I had brought it in once more in the last allegro—it came in there *da capo* . . . so out of sheer delight I went straight off after the symphony to the Palais Royale and ate a delicious ice . . ." and so on.

Frau Mozart was not present at the concert. His letter is dated July 3rd, 1778, the day of her death. Wolfgang prepared his father for the news without actually telling him of it.

❧

Paris II

WE KNOW THAT WOLFGANG DEVOTED HIMSELF TO his mother during the two weeks of her illness with the greatest selflessness. We know, too, that he was so worn out with anxiety and anguish that by the time the slender thread of his mother's life had snapped his own capacity for suffering gave out. A few hours afterwards he wrote to the Abbé Bullinger, requesting him to convey the sad news to his father. This letter, with its exquisite characters, which seem as though drowned in grief, can be seen in a glass case at the Mozarteum in Salzburg. Very different is the one written on the same day to his father, in which he prepares him for the worst. The words: "And now for another subject; let us leave these melancholy thoughts," are like a cry, almost, of an animal at bay. It was in the late afternoon that Frau Mozart died, and he wrote these lines at two o'clock in the morning. Presumably with the corpse in the room. And what is a corpse? "*Sterbliche Überreste*," the Germans call it, the English "mortal remains" . Yet it is less than that: no longer a thing, but a mere affair that has no significance and no relevance. *La dépouille mortelle* is the more precise definition which the French language has invented for it. However unforgettably its features may have been smoothed out in death, beautified, transfigured, it is offensive, nauseating—away with it! But lo! once hidden away in its coffin, vanished from our gaze, it puts off the finite, becomes a beacon that sends out beams far and wide; whether, an insentient burden on the shoulders of the bearers, it makes its entry through wide-open doors into the church as though into its domain and there sets up its throne, guarded by a ring of flickering candle-flames; whether, in stately flower-decked funeral carriage, it proclaims its *ritardando* in broad daylight in the crowded street; or whether it is dragged on a wretched cart, without a following, along a rough field track, a sustained note in the midst of nature.

"Let us pass to other matters, for there is a time for everything," Mozart writes again a day or two later, and it is only with the greatest reluctance that he is able to bring himself to return to the details of the mournful event.

There is a time for everything?

Yes, but who can say what surprises the soul of a Mozart has in store, what seeds it causes to spring forth from its soil as the result of a particular happening? Mozart's sense of the immanence of death, which dates from this period, sets him apart from all other musicians. No one before him has ever set to music the unbridgeable remoteness of the realm of shadows, its insubstantiality, in accents of such intense perception. Gluck conveys to us its grandeur, but not its horror, the grave Bach is a lyricist in comparison, of this world Wagner and Beethoven, and

Schubert, who was so profoundly attracted by the eerie splendour of the supernatural, romanticise it. The light-hearted, pleasure-loving, sportive Mozart, he alone is a realist, an initiate, in this sphere. None but he gauged with such acute awareness that gaping, all-devouring abyss into which he beheld the kindly Frau Mozart dragged, far from the land, which was so much a part of her, where she felt so much at home, the banks of the stream on which Salzburg stood beneath the vault of the sky; where the conversation all turned on the little happenings of the day, one's love for one's own kith and kin, on archery, on this and that, and one laughed with one's friends, and discussed the price of butter.

"I am consoled not only now, but have been so this long time past! . . ." we read in a letter written by the twenty-two-year old Mozart to the Abbé Bullinger. ". . . In her extremity I prayed God for but two things, first a happy death for my mother, and for myself strength and courage—and the good Lord heard me, and bestowed those two blessings on me in full and overflowing measure."

Mozart had had to provide both for his own and his mother's keep in Paris. It may easily be imagined to what a penniless state he was reduced by the additional expenses of his mother's illness and death. On July 9th he wrote to his father: "I write this in the house of Madame d'Epinay and Herr Grimm, where I am now living; I have a pretty little room with a very agreeable view, and in so far as my circumstances permit, I am happy here . . ." But he did not attain spiritual equilibrium as rapidly as all that, and if he remained devoted to Madame d'Epinay, there was soon to be friction again between him and Grimm. In the latter's view Mozart was a hopeless case; no longer a star turn, not even a turn; talented, yes, that he could not deny. But there were talented young men enough and to spare all over the world; despite their talent, or perhaps even because of it, unless they had the capacity to make their way in the world, they were crushed beneath the wheels and had to be content to be "little people". This young man, who ought to go back home and the sooner the better, was feeding on delusions.

Mozart, who harboured such a different opinion of himself and his future, and was already conscious of having composed many an immortal work, sensed with rising irritation what Grimm thought of him and how offensive he found his poverty. From the point of view of a Philistine he was perfectly justified. But how came it that a man who set himself up to be a judge and critic of ideal values, yet failed to recognise that this pauper was a rich man in disguise, one who had a perfect right to his demands for the choicest instruments and to his passion for noble rooms, suits of fine cloth and elegant buttons; and that here was a man who loved riches in the manner of a poet, because for him *"la richesse est le mépris de la banalité et de la laideur"*, as Giraudoux so aptly puts it in his *Lafontaine*. Grimm's pedagogic attitude towards the most priceless artistic treasure that came his way in the whole course of his life, and above all the crude way in which he drove Mozart out of his house, out of Paris and out of the country, holds him up to censure for all time. His sin, the most heinous that a man such as he could commit, was a sin against the spirit. And thus in the procession of those who crossed Mozart's path his place is far behind the janitor, Deiner, who, confronted by the poverty and want that did indeed close in upon Mozart at the end of his life, never failed to accord him the respect due to a supreme darling of the gods.

In the letter to his father of July 3rd, in which he does not yet disclose the news of his mother's death, Mozart slips in, in the fulness of his grief, a revealing sentence: "You will have realised for some time past that I am not happy here—I have so much cause . . ."

It would have been difficult, indeed, for Mozart to have loved Paris. No one likes a town in which he has been dogged by misfortune; he makes the town itself—at least if he is young—responsible for the melancholy experiences that he has endured. And what, with the exception of the loyalty of his Mannheim friends and the hours spent at the house of Count Sückingen, had Mozart to place on record in Paris's favour? Had advances been made to him from any other quarter, he would not have failed to bring them to his father's notice. But instead of such advances he had been treated to a display of ill manners on the part of the Duchesse de Chabot and the Duc de Guines. Never before had he been shown so little consideration, never before had he experienced what it was to trudge the pavements from pupil to pupil as an unknown musician, forced into the odious task of giving lessons. Hitherto he had found himself everywhere acclaimed by the *cognoscenti*. But in Paris no curtain was drawn aside to enable him to elude the general indifference to his talents. The foolish counsels of Leopold, who warned him like a petty shopkeeper to shun other composers as competitors, were bringing their reward. And so Mozart came scarcely at all into contact with other artists. His Mannheim friends had introduced him to Le Gros, the Director of the *Concerts Spirituels.* These concerts were reputed to be the oldest musical institution of their kind and were held on Saints' days and Sundays, when the opera was closed, in the Swiss Hall of the Tuileries. Mozart had been asked to write choruses for

Holzbauer's *Miserere*, but the whole thing had proved a failure, and everything, indeed, went wrong. A *Symphonie Concertante* that he had submitted interested Le Gros so little that he forgot, or else neglected, to have the parts copied. Noverre, the Viennese ballet master, whom the King had summoned to Paris, made frequent approaches to him, it is true, and it was agreed between them that Mozart should write an opera–*Alexandre et Roxane.* Highly elated, Mozart announces the news in his letter home. By the beginning of April the first act of the libretto was completed. But Noverre could give him no assurance that it would be performed. And thus Mozart had no incentive to apply himself to the work. Noverre, he believed, had only kept him dangling so that he should write the music to his ballet–*Les petits riens.* This was given on June 11th; it bore Noverre's name alone, however, and was soon forgotten. The score, fortunately, was discovered in the library of the Paris Opera in the year 1872.

Mozart had broken with Le Gros after the experience with his *Symphonie Concertante*, but he met him one day when calling on Raaff, the singer, who lived in the same house, and Le Gros, with profuse apologies, commissioned him to write a symphony for Corpus Christi Day. This was the D major symphony, already mentioned, which was performed on June 18th with conspicuous success. Now as ever he had little or no contact with other musicians. "I know my business and they theirs. That is enough," he had written to reassure his father.

Perhaps it was enough. But his isolation was now unbounded. The last of his Mannheim friends, Raaff, had left Paris. Grimm no longer brought him into touch with anyone, and his only wish was to be rid of him. Unfortunately we are not in possession of Grimm's letters to

Leopold. It would be interesting to see how he managed to bring his influence to bear on him and how very easily he impressed his counsels on the obsequious little man, just as though they had been words of the greatest wisdom. The two now worked hand in glove with one another. In Leopold's case at least, there were nobler motives at work; his solicitude for Wolfgang, his longing to see him again. But now not only was the son playing at hide-and-seek with the father but the father with the son. Leopold was doing his utmost to secure for Wolfgang a post that had fallen vacant at the court of the hated Archbishop; but he deluded Wolfgang into believing that there had been a change of heart on the part of Colloredo, who, he seemed to suggest, was burning to take him back into his service at a higher salary and was prepared at the same time to allow him all sorts of facilities for travel. Salzburg was all of a sudden pictured as a town, fortunately situated between Italy and Munich, where they would all live in comfort, and settle without any difficulty the debts incurred on Wolfgang's journey—a constantly recurring theme. Count Florian's riding horses were already waiting for Wolfgang's return.

Mozart's Paris host, meanwhile, was making his sentiments abundantly clear.

> "M. Grimm recently said to me," Mozart writes in his letter of July 31st to his father, " 'What am I to write to your father? What are your plans? Do you intend to remain here, or are you going to Mannheim?' I really could not help laughing. 'What should I do now in Mannheim? Perhaps if I had never come to Paris—but as it is, I am here, and must do my utmost to find my feet.' 'Well,' he said, 'I hardly think that you will manage to make your way here.' 'Why? I see here a crowd of wretched bunglers who managed to succeed, and am I then

with my talent not to do so? I assure you that I like Mannheim, and would greatly like to secure an appointment there—but only if it were to bring me honour and repute. I must be sure of my position before I take a single step.' 'I fear,' he said, 'that you are not active enough here, do not go about enough.' 'Well,' I said, 'that is what I find most difficult; besides, I have of late been unable to go anywhere on account of my mother's long illness; two of my pupils are in the country, and the third (the Duc de Guines' daughter) is about to be married . . .' The very next day after this talk with Grimm I went to call on Count Sückingen. He was entirely of my opinion, that is, that I should have patience and wait until Raaff arrives, who will do everything in his power for me, and if this comes to nothing, Count Sückingen has offered to secure an appointment for me at Mainz. Meanwhile my plans are to do my utmost to make a living here by taking pupils, and to earn as much money as possible; I am now doing so in the fond hope that there will soon be a change in my fortunes, for I cannot deny, indeed, am bound to admit, that I shall be glad to be free of Paris, for giving lessons here is no joke, but a most wearying task, and unless one takes a great many, one does not earn much. You must not imagine that it is laziness—oh no !—but simply that it is entirely contrary to my genius, my way of life. You know that I am completely absorbed in music, so to speak, that it occupies my thoughts the whole day long, that I like speculating, studying, reflecting. Well, my present mode of life prevents this. I shall have, of course, a few free hours, but I shall need those few hours for recuperation rather than work."

Poor Mozart! His one burning desire now is to write an opera. He is not daunted at the prospect of difficulties. "*Au contraire*, when I fancy to myself, as I often do, that I am really to write an opera, I feel my whole body aflame, and I tremble from head to foot in my eagerness to teach the French to know, esteem and fear the Germans more and more." Unfortunately he cannot refrain from drawing his father's attention to the Webers and their affairs. The

Mannheim court, he writes, is to be transferred to Munich, and Aloysia is to be engaged at the theatre there. Owing to the complications of the war, all these arrangements have come to a standstill. "If I could only help them! Dearest father, I commend them to you from my heart. If only they had the enjoyment of 1,000 florins for a year or so!" And this to Leopold, who never ceased to remind him of his own debts, and whom it strengthened in the conviction that Wolfgang could not be left to himself. Particularly since to him the Webers were like a red rag to a bull. He looked upon them as the real cause of his wife's death. Had there been no Aloysia and had Wolfgang gone to Paris with the Wendlings, she would have been safe and sound with him in Salzburg. He was never to relinquish his grudge against these people.

Four months is no time in which to conquer a city like Paris—and Mozart was there no longer than that. Things, it is true, could never move fast enough for him. His father often rebuked him for his impatience, but that impatience was inherited from him, and at this period it was not the son who showed himself to be rash and in too much of a hurry. Since he was there, he decided to bear up. "I place my hopes on the winter when everyone returns to Paris from the country." From this time disagreements and conflicts between father and son were to come thick and fast. With what unwillingness was Mozart to leave the Paris of which he had so lately longed to be "free"? According to Grimm's, and therefore according to Leopold's, judgment, however, he was wasting his time there and Paris was not the place for him. They were both mistaken, for he would without doubt have made his way. In August the clouds were lifting for him in all directions. Le Gros, very much impressed by him after the success of his symphony, arranged a further performance of it for Ascension Day, this time with a new andante, and commissioned him to write an oratorio for the *Concerts Spirituels* of the following winter. Moreover, there was a reunion with Johann Christian Bach, the friend of the London days, and this was a source of real delight to Wolfgang. His next letter to his father is written from St. Germain. Bach had induced his host, the Maréchal de Noailles, a well-known amateur of music, to extend an invitation to Mozart. What a relief it must have been to him to escape for a while from Grimm's patronising presence!

"St. Germain, ce 27 aoust 1778.

"*Mon très cher père,*

I write in the greatest haste. You will see that I am not in Paris. Mr. Bach of London has been here for the last fortnight; he intends to write a French opera. He is only here to hear the singers, after which he returns to London, where he will write it, then come back here to put it on the stage. You can well imagine his delight and mine at seeing each other again. Perhaps his delight is not so genuine"—again a characteristic remark to please his father, for no sooner does he make it than he gives it the lie—"yet one must allow that he is an honourable man and gives people their due; I love him (as you doubtless know) with all my heart, and hold him in great esteem . . . This is the residence, as you perhaps know, for I am told that I was here fifteen years ago, but I remember nothing of it, of the Maréchal de Noailles, and it is because he is very fond of me that he has tried to bring about this meeting. I shall not earn anything here—maybe a small present—but I shall lose nothing, since it costs me nothing, and even if I get nothing out of it, I shall at least have made a very useful acquaintance. I must make haste, for I have to write a *scena* for Tenducci for next Sunday—for pianoforte, oboe, horn and bassoon, the performers being the Maréchal's own musicians, all Germans, who play extremely well. I should have liked to write to you long since . . . but then I drove out to St. Germain, intending to return the same day, but I have now been here a week . . . have patience; everything proceeds very slowly, France is just like Germany, they put one off with compliments, but there is yet hope that one may thereby make one's fortune." One can tell that he is once more in his element.

On September 8th a second symphony by him was performed at the *Concerts Spirituels*. His sonatas were already at the copyist's. These included the lovely Sonata in A minor (K.310) which we remember for the agonising luminosity of the *allegro maestoso*, the singing and, as it were, veiled melancholy of the *andante cantabile* and its dramatic middle section, and the scurrying presto. He wrote the Sonata in E flat minor for violin and pianoforte (K.304) and the Sonata in A major (K.331). Latterly he had been occupying himself once more with the works of Schobert. But he was not to stay much longer in Paris now, and he had no time even to settle up his affairs. The symphony was to be lost. The connection with the Maréchal de Noailles remained unexploited. The publication of the sonatas would have brought his name into the limelight. But there was no help for it. Leopold was insisting—obviously under pressure from Grimm—that he leave Paris. And he found himself hustled out of Paris even sooner than his father could have wished. This precipitate departure was utterly distasteful to him.

" . . . Besides, I tell you frankly, my affairs are beginning to prosper," he writes on September 11th. "It is no use trying to hurry matters; *chi va piano, va sano*; my complaisance has secured me both friends and influence . . . I shall prove to you clearly that M. Grimm may be capable of helping children, but not grown people, and—but no, I will say nothing—yes, but I must; do not imagine that he is the man he was; were it not for Madame d'Epinay I should not be in this house; and he need not plume himself on the fact that I am, for there are four houses where I might have lodged." Yet Grimm would not allow him to move. My only regret is that I cannot stay here, if only to show Grimm that I have no need of him and can do as well as his precious Piccini . . . Madame d'Epinay, however, has a kinder heart; the room in which I am belongs to her, not to him; it is the sick-room, that is to say, if anyone in the house is ill, he is put here; there is nothing agreeable about it but the view; it consists of bare walls; no chest or anything else in it. Now judge for yourself if it would have been possible for me to endure it any longer; I would have told you all this long since, but I feared you might not believe me. But now I can keep silence no longer . . ."

Many biographers of Mozart have endeavoured to exonerate Grimm. St. Beuve writes of him: "*bel esprit, fin, piquant, agréable, mais coeur égoiste et sec*." Later, however, he felt constrained to formulate a milder judgment on the friend of Diderot. But if we allow the facts to speak for themselves, we must admit that he was too mild. At the worst possible moment, emptyhanded, robbed of whatever advantage he had gained, Mozart was forced to depart. Grimm would not in any circumstances permit another man, and a German and a colleague into the bargain, Count Sückingen, to take Mozart into his house. The father's eyes were at last opened. ". . . what you say in your letter of a certain person does not occasion me great surprise, for his letters have always aroused my suspicions."

Too late. And Leopold's good wishes for the journey did not reach his son in Paris, for he had long since set out. He found himself obliged to depart, not at the beginning of October, but as early as September 26th.

"At the last moment I had a mind to have my baggage taken to Count Sückingen instead of the offices of the diligence, and to stay for a few days longer in Paris, and, on my honour, I should have done it had I not thought of you, for I did not wish to vex you . . . Just imagine, M. Grimm deceived me into thinking that I should go by diligence and reach Strasbourg in five days; and I did not discover until the last moment that it was quite another vehicle, that travels at a snail's pace, without changing horses, and takes ten days. You can picture my indignation . . . On getting into the coach I received the agreeable news that we should be twelve days on the journey . . . there is the great good sense of Baron v. Grimm for you . . . I endured a week in this conveyance; I could not have borne it any longer . . . you know I am never able to sleep in a coach, and therefore I could not go on without risk of falling ill . . ."

Among his fellow travellers, he writes, is a German merchant who lives in Paris, and who has attached himself to him. The two of them break away from the rest and travel from Nancy to Strasbourg by another conveyance. Leopold is beside himself. "I cannot conceive what purpose Grimm had in hurrying you off so disgracefully, and it would have been well for you if Count Sückingen had detained you for a few days longer in Paris, and you had waited for my last letter, that is, if you had been *assured* of earning more money. I am incensed at him on another count . . . it is always thus when people do not write with complete frankness. You ought long since to have informed me of his double dealing . . . Basta! it is all over now, it was a lesson to you and will have convinced you of what I have told you a hundred times: that a disinterested friend, a true friend, a friend who will stand by one in good or ill is the rarest thing in this world." The self-righteous man is forgetting that he did not give his son even the remotest hint of his changed opinion of Grimm, and had therefore in no way encouraged him to express himself freely on the subject of his strange patron. Wolfgang stood in awe of his father. Frankness towards him had for a long time been out of the question. But he was exasperated now and in no hurry to leave Strasbourg. Two concerts, given by him to empty houses, brought him in next to nothing. He let himself be persuaded, however, into giving a third, and with the same result. But he welcomed any excuse to postpone the date of his return to Salzburg. For the nearer it approached, the more was he seized with horror and dread, whereas his father was burning not only with the desire to see him again, but also to have him under his watchful eye once more. Their views no longer coincided on any point.". . . had I not been subjected to so much vexation in the house where I was lived," Wolfgang writes on October 15th, "and if the whole thing had not come on me like a thunder-clap, and I had had time to think things out in cold blood, I should certainly have begged you to have patience for a little longer and let me stay a while in Paris; I assure you I should have gained honour, fame and money, and have certainly freed you of all debt. Well, what is, must be; do not think that I regret it." Yet how greatly he did regret it! "For you alone, my dearest father, you alone can sweeten for me the bitterness of Salzburg, and you will, I am convinced, do so too. Yet I must freely admit that I would come to Salzburg with a lighter heart did I not know my self to be in service there; that thought alone is intolerable to me . . ."

What he himself had striven for in vain, the Webers had secured with the utmost ease: Aloysia's engagement at the Munich Opera. They were to receive 1,600 florins, the daughter alone 1,000, the father 600. Wolfgang was overjoyed. "Yet what I desire so much, I may, alas, no longer hope for," he confesses to his father, "that is, to secure an appointment for her in Salzburg, for the Archbishop would never give her what she now gets . . . the poor creatures were all in the greatest distress on my account; having received no letter from me for a whole month, they thought I had died in Paris . . . and they were confirmed in this belief because people were saying in Mannheim that my poor mother had died of a contagious disease; they had already all prayed for my soul; the poor girl went every day to the Capuchin church. You may laugh, but I did not; I cannot but be touched by it . . ." Who, we wonder, had been pulling his leg? Or had the story been passed on to him in good faith? "He is too simple-minded," Grimm had said of him with justification. We cannot see Aloysia going daily to the Capuchin church to weep for him. She was greatly obliged to him for the lessons he had given her and all he had taught her, but she now had other things to think about.

October went by. Mozart was still in Strasbourg; far too long a time for his impatient father, who feared that if Wolfgang stayed away too long, the Archbishop would change his mind, and then how were the debts so incessantly referred to in his letters to be met?

But Mozart in Strasbourg has not yet recovered from his final impressions of Paris, and the manner in which he had been bundled off. In his letter of October 26th we find a last mention of Grimm:

> " . . . I hope you have received my last letter from Strasbourg, of October 15th I believe. I will rail no more against M. Grimm, yet I cannot refrain from saying that it is entirely owing to his stupidity in hurrying on my departure that my sonatas are not yet engraved or rather have not yet come to light, or at least that I have not yet received them. When I do, I am like to find them full of errors. If only I had stayed three days longer in Paris, I could have corrected them myself, and brought them away with me. The copyist was in despair when I told him that I should be unable to revise them, but would have to entrust the task to someone else. And why? Simply because M. Grimm, when I told him that, since I could not

stay three days longer in his house, I proposed to go and lodge at Count Sückingen's in order to attend to the sonatas, replied, his eyes blazing with fury: 'Listen to me. If you leave my house without leaving Paris, I shall never set eyes on you as long as I live; in that case do not ever presume to come into my sight again, for I shall be your bitterest enemy.' Restraint was indeed necessary . . ."

It was only natural that he should have been so reluctant to leave Paris, after having at length settled down there, for it provided him with endless stimulus. Between March 23rd and September 26th *Armide*, *Alceste*, *Iphigènie en Aulide* and *Orphée* had been included in the repertory of the Opera. We can feel a breath of them in the wonderful choruses of *Idomeneo*. In addition, a vast number of comic operas had been performed during this year, among them Rousseau's *Le devin du village*. Grétry, Monsigny and Philidor took the lead in this field; Pergolese, Cambini and others at the *Concerts Spirituels*. French influences began to be clearly discernible in Mozart's work. Without becoming involved in the dispute between Gluck and Piccini, he had sided, not with the latter, but with his great countryman, whom, however, he had had no chance of meeting, for when Gluck returned to Paris Mozart was no longer there.

❧

Homecoming

MOZART WAS NOW EXPECTED TO RETURN TO SALZBURG with all speed by the most direct route. But in defiance of his father's express injunctions, he went on to Mannheim, where he stayed with Frau Cannabich, whose husband had by this time taken up his post with the court orchestra, now transferred to Munich. Happy to be once more among his friends, he indulged in all kinds of day-dreams; he fondly imagined, for example, that the Elector, out of disgust with the Bavarians, would transfer his Court back to Mannheim. In any case he hoped to obtain an appointment from him, and, by some miracle, to shake off the Salzburg yoke. "I may perhaps make as much as 40 louis d'or here. True, I should have to stay here six weeks, or even two months," he writes home on November 12th. "Seiler's company, which must be known to you by repute, is here. Herr v. Dalberg, who is the director of it, will not let me go until I have composed a duodrama, and, indeed,

I did not take long to think it over, for I have always wished to write that kind of drama . . . Just imagine my delight at having to do the very thing I have always wanted to do! . . ." He even assumes that his father will share his delight, and begs him to take a strong line with the Archbishop and demand a higher salary. "There is no knowing," he continues, "whether I shall not cock a snook at the Archbishop." His father's patience was sorely tried, but how one understands the son when he writes: "I am filled with joy at the thought of paying you a visit, but nothing but irritation and dread when I picture myself back in that beggarly court." And, indeed, how much better off than he were his protégés, the Webers! "What pleases me most in the whole Mannheim and Munich affair is the fact that Weber has done so well for his family. They now get 1,600 florins, for the daughter alone receives 1,000 and her father 400 and then a further 200 as prompter . . ."

Mozart was profoundly attached to Frau Cannabich. Of Rose there was no more talk, but he must have poured out his heart about Aloysia. He could no longer suppose that she went to the Capuchin church to weep for him. But he was not averse to letting her worry a little over him, for he was so sure of her. And, after all, she knew that he was coming, that he had no picture in his heart but hers. But there was no hurry, for Munich was so near Salzburg, and he gave his father an address where letters to Mannheim could always reach him. He would have preferred to abandon all thought of returning. Whereat Leopold, who saw all his plans going agley, flew into a furious passion; not the passion of an angry father so much as that of an irate landlord who sees himself bilked of his bill. On November 19th he presented his account in no uncertain terms. He now repented even of the small credit he had opened for his son for the journey.

"So it was only in order to idle away your time in Mannheim that you had the forethought to make 8 louis d'or in Strasbourg? You hope to obtain an appointment in Mannheim? An appointment? What do you mean by that? You have no business to obtain an appointment at present either in Mannheim or in any other place in the world—I refuse to hear that word appointment again . . . I refuse to hear anything more of the 40 louis d'or which you may possibly earn. Your intention is evidently to bring me to ruin merely in order to carry out your airy schemes. You had over 15 louis d'or in hand on your departure from Paris, that is to say, 165 florins. In short, I refuse absolutely to be brought to shame and plunged into debt for your sake, still less to bequeath your poor sister nothing but poverty and misery. You know as little as I how long God will grant you to live. If I write to Madame Cannabich that to finance your journey

I borrowed	300 florins
that I raised for you in Mannheim	200
that I paid in Paris out of money received from Geschwendtner	110
that I have to pay Baron Grimm 15 louis d'or	165
that you received from me in Strasbourg 8 louis d'or	88
that in the course of 14 months, you have thus put me into debt to the tune of	863 florins

if I tell her to convey this information to all those who advise you to remain in Mannheim and inform them that I desire you to take up service in Salzburg for a few years because thereby I foresee some prospect of paying these debts, none of them will utter a single word to hold you back but will pull quite different faces . . . I hope that on receipt of this letter you will immediately expedite your journey and so order your affairs that I may receive you with joy and not meet you with reproaches . . ."

Leopold's indignation at Wolfgang's proneness to make grandiose plans, which were never to be based on anything more solid than his own desires, and, likewise, his insistent reference to his outstanding debts, are comprehensible from his standpoint; for he was utterly unable to instil any conception of the hard facts of debit and credit into his son's unpractical mind. But there follows the sinister and unpardonable sentence: "I hope that, remembering that your mother met an untimely death in Paris, you will not burden your conscience with the hastening of your father's death also . . ."

Gone is the noble composure with which he had accepted the grievous blow of his wife's death, pondered on its inevitability. "Her rosy complexion, far too lovely for an old woman," he had then written, "and a certain cough were sure signs that an internal inflammation was at any moment to be feared . . ." The journey had been a risk for her; nevertheless he had made the sacrifice of surrendering her to Wolfgang. But the seeds of disease had already been at work in her before her departure from Salzburg; had she remained snugly at home by the side of husband and daughter, she would, despite all the distractions and the feeling of security to be found in her own circle, despite all the simple pleasures and amusements, have felt constant anxiety for the son who was so far away; and it is questionable whether the disease would not have made more headway in Salzburg than abroad, where, in spite of the discomfort of wretched lodgings, uncongenial and strange company or even none at all, and unpalatable fare, she was at least with him. As we have already said, when he returned to her in the evenings she was fully recompensed for the loneliness and tedium of the day. One can imagine how much the physical presence of this son of hers meant to her, on what terms of unconstrained intimacy with him she found herself during these moments when they were alone and undisturbed. *She* believed in him—for that we have his father's testimony—and *she* refused to be disconcerted by his incompetence, or shaken in her belief because he was no longer a favourite of fortune. To be with him was a perpetual feast, he moved in a cloud of glory, peerless for the sweetness of his temperament, his wit, his inexhaustible flood of ideas, the fulness of his being . . . The worthy Leopold, of course, could not compete with such brilliance. As head of the household he was decidedly overbearing, and had long since exhausted his wife's patience. For even loyalty (oh, did married men but know it!), nay, loyalty above all, has its caprices. Moreover, poor weary woman that she was, in Paris she was absolved from having to act as intermediary between them. Cruel though may have been the circumstances of her death, yet a happier death than in the presence, in the arms, of this son, could not have been vouchsafed her . . . "Your good mother," so ran a letter of the father's written at the time of her death, "the apple of whose eye you were, and who loved you beyond measure, who was so proud of you and who (as I know better than you) lived wholly for you . . ." Yes, they knew it, all three of them.

How did Mozart react to the grievance of his father, which were now almost past remedy? He gave up all his plans and prepared for his departure, but for weeks on end preserved complete silence. ". . . my not having answered you for so long," he writes at length, "is the fault of no one but yourself and your first letter to me in Mannheim. I really never would have believed it possible that—but enough, I will say no more, for it is all over now . . ." What dignity there is in those few words! ". . . next Wednesday, the 9th, I leave here—sooner I cannot, for, believing I should be here a few months longer, I accepted some pupils, and I wish of course to complete the course of twelve lessons. I assure you you can have no idea what kind and true friends I have here."

It was all to no purpose. Leopold, it is true, feeling that he had gone too far, had in the meantime moderated his tone, but he still persisted in his demands.

> "I could wish that this letter might no longer reach you in Mannheim . . . I am weary of your schemes . . . for you cannot, or will not, consider anything in cold blood—often, it is true, because you are carried away by the impetuosity of your youth and by the flattering proposals which first one and then another makes to you, and look upon everything as gold, though it turns out in the end to be nothing but tinsel . . . two things fill your head and keep you from all sensible reflection. The first and principal thing is your love for Mlle. Weber. To which I am not entirely and absolutely opposed; I was not so when her father was poor, why should I be so now that she can make your fortune and not you hers . . ." But he is seized with an evil presentiment . . . "My dear son. You know too little of the world. But when you are at home again you will remember my letters and all my forebodings and predictions of human ingratitude. Herr Fiala waited yesterday on the Archbishop, who inquired how matters stood in Mannheim. Herr Fiala told him that the best music they had in Mannheim was by Mozart; that . . . Mlle. Weber had sung an aria by Mozart the like of which he had never heard in all his life. Whereupon the Archbishop questioned him closely, asking him in particular about everyone who had performed your work, and when told, displaying very great pleasure . . . My dear Wolfgang, I keep thinking that Herr Weber is a man like most of his kind, they parade their poverty and then when things go well with them refuse to know one. It flattered you to think that he had need of you; perhaps he will refuse even to admit that you helped her or taught her anything . . . I hope, therefore," he concludes, "that you will leave without delay, or I shall write to

Madame Cannabich. I hope, God willing, to live a few years longer, to pay my debts, and then, if it pleases you, you may run your head against a wall. But no! You have too good a heart. There is no evil in you. It is merely that you are heedless. Time will set that right."

"I received your letter of the 23rd safely," Wolfgang writes, after his long silence, in the letter already quoted, and he repeats: "I leave on Wednesday next, and do you know with whom I am to travel? With His Reverence, the Imperial Bishop of Kaisersheim. He at once knew my name when a good friend of mine spoke of me to him, and expressed great pleasure at having me as a travelling companion. He is (in spite of being a priest and prelate) a really amiable man. I shall therefore go via Kaisersheim and not by Stuttgart, but that is no matter, for it is a good thing to be able to spare one's purse, slender as it is in any case, a little on the journey . . ."

To this plan his father was to raise no objection, but another ten days went by, and Wolfgang was not to conceal from him his vexation at having to leave Mannheim.

"Kaisersheim, December 18th, 1778.

". . . my journey from Mannheim to this place would have been one of the most agreeable to a man leaving a city with a light heart . . . but for me, who have never before left a place with so heavy a heart, the journey was only in part agreeable. It would not have been agreeable at all, would have been, rather, positively tedious, had I not from youth up been so accustomed to leaving people, countries and towns, and did I not cherish very great hopes of seeing the good friends I have left behind again, and that very soon." There follows a eulogy of Frau Cannabich.

Troops had just been quartered in Kaisersheim, and a great deal of drilling was going on.

"What strikes me as most absurd is the horrible military. I should like to know what use they are. At night I hear perpetual shouts of ' Who goes there?' I invariably make a point of replying—'Use your nose'."

With what delicious lack of prejudice does Mozart express himself as to the importance of soldiering at a time when such a thing as pacifism did not even exist in name, and only the sister of Frederick the Great, Wilhelmine, the wife of the Margrave of Bayreuth, had avowed her pacifist principles in her correspondence with Voltaire.

He still had not received his sonatas.

"I shall really be ashamed to arrive in Munich without my sonatas. I cannot understand the delay. It was a stupid trick of Grimm's. I have written to tell him so, too, and he will now see that he was in rather too much of a hurry. Nothing ever vexed me so. Just think of it; I know that my sonatas were published at the beginning of February, and I, the author, have not yet received them, and cannot therefore present them to the Electress, to whom they are dedicated . . ." He takes appropriate measures to get them, and then turns his attention to the *Bäsle*.

He made a further stay of ten days in Kaisers heim, and Leopold, despite his impatience, by now almost pathological, was obliged to approve Wolfgang's travelling on with the Prelate and accompanying him also on the journey to Munich. "That his Reverence the Prelate is a truly amiable man, you know; but that I may count myself among his favourites, you do not. This, I imagine, will be neither to my advantage nor my disadvantage, although it is always a good thing to have one more friend in the world . . ." The thing that was most evident to the father was that the journey would thus cost nothing; to the son that it would be delayed, for every mile was now bringing him nearer to Salzburg. Since their route did not lie via Augsburg, he wrote to the *Bäsle*: "If it will give you as much pleasure to see me as it will give me to see you, come to the worthy town of Munich. Be sure that you are there before the New Year . . . one thing I regret—that I cannot give you a lodging, for I am not staying at an inn, but with—well, whom do you think? I should like to know myself. But, joking apart, that is just why it is so important for me that you should come. You may have a great role to play. So be sure to come . . ." There follow obscenities. "Well adieu, my angel, my darling, I await you with impatience. *Votre sincère cousin,* W.A.

"P.S. Pray, write to me at once, to Munich, Poste Restante, a brief note of 24 pages, but do not say where you are to stay so that I may not find you nor you me."

Knowing perfectly well that he was going to stay with the Webers, for Herr Weber had been unable to avoid giving him an invitation, he undoubtedly meant her to be a witness of his happiness, his hoped-for bethrothal, and not for a moment did he pause to reflect that the role he had allotted her might cause her disappointment. But for all his levity, he appraised her correctly in relying on her understanding, her friendship and good-nature. Her behaviour proved, at least, that he had been wrong to indulge his wanton humours on this young girl, his junior by two and a half years. For she must at that time have been still a girl of unblemished virtue, otherwise the strict and particular Leopold would never have desired her as a daughter-in-law. Mozart placed the talented Aloysia on a pedestal, and when one compares the exaggerated reverence and awe he displayed towards her with the tone he adopted towards the *Bäsle*, one cannot help feeling that he wronged his cousin. Somewhat bedraggled, she was from now on to go her unprotected way, and it was not she but the worthless Constanze who was to find in Mozart the most chivalrous of husbands, to cherish, watch over and spoil her. From his letters to her, which were passionate to the very end, it is clear how severe and devoid of all illusions, nevertheless, was his judgment of her. But here we encounter for the first time the uncannily vast span of his spiritual keyboard, those sharp contrasts in his character, which permitted of no compromise, only of plunges into the abyss, flight. From the highest regions in which his spirit dwelt, from the utterly dematerialised exaltation of his vespers, he was impelled towards the depths. As one who had learned how to fear–for he was no "heroic" character–he clung to all that was generally accepted as normal, to the limited, the circumscribed, to that which, of the day, lived only for the day. He sought his satisfaction in it, identified himself with it, was infatuated with it, lost himself in it. He was caught in the toils of Susanna, the mercurial queen of this realm. Unalloyed earthiness he transformed into birdlike lightness, for such metamorphoses sprang from the profound inner workings of his genius. Compare, for example, Marcellina in *Fidelio*, or Annchen in the *Freischütz*, with Mozart's soubrettes. Mozart's gaiety was an unconscious drive; as witness Blondchen, Despina, Barbarina searching for the lost needle, Zerlina who could so lightly forget a Don Giovanni in the arms of a Masetto, the bird-spirits, Papageno and Papagena, the primitive Leporello and the sub-human creature Monostatos. What *brio* is let loose in these characters. An unconscious drive, too, in Mozart, was his fooling, his drollery, his love of jollity and laughter. For him the ephemeral was no mere symbol, but flight, the intoxication of oblivion.

On December 25th Mozart arrived in Munich in the company of the Prelate, and whether it was still day or the winter night had already settled upon the city, for him all the streets were veiled in golden clouds, and the lamps were like golden trees in the reflection of his joy at seeing Aloysia again. He proposed to obtain an appointment in Munich, in order at long last to be able to snap his fingers at the Archbishop. Did not Cannabich already hold a post there? Had not the Mannheim Orchestra, his Mannheim friends, the Wendlings and Raaff, always so loyally concerned for his welfare, followed the Elector to his new capital? Would he not too meet with success in this town where Aloysia now lived and moved and had her being? This made the prospect even more tempting.

But fresh letters were on their way from the indefatigable Leopold, who was well able to imagine what his son was up to.

". . . do not imagine that you are going to make a prolonged stay in Munich," he lets him know on December 28th. ". . . I insist that if you find no favourable opportunity of setting out earlier, you will travel here by the first diligence that leaves in the first week of January. Should you have it in mind to persuade Herr Cannabich to write to me with regard to a longer stay, it will be to no purpose for I should write to him at length and give him such a convincing and detailed account of the whole matter that he would forthwith appreciate my reasons and be very surprised at some of the things I should tell him . . ." And once more the debts, which he expects his son to help him to pay off in Salzburg, are set out . . . "you left Paris on September 26th; had you travelled direct to Salzburg, I should already have paid off 100 florins of our debts, *have been able to pay*, I should say . . . or am I to get into the postchaise myself and fetch you. Surely my son will not allow things to go as far as that! . . ."

Alas! it was not on florins or debts that poor Mozart's mind was set. Aloysia had dashed his hopes. She had made a career for herself, he had not. A penniless lover like Mozart could not possibly appeal to her. She gave him to understand without much ceremony that she no longer needed him and hence no longer loved him. Did he imagine he was still a good match for her? And she even permitted herself to jeer at the red coat he happened to be wearing—the Archbishop's livery, which he was expected to don once more, was of the same colour. It is only possible to write laconically of this incident in his life.

Wolfgang was profoundly shaken, but, his biographers say, he preserved his composure. Sitting down at the piano, he hummed the famous song of Götz von Berlichingen, *"Ich lass das Mädel gern, das mich nicht will."* With regard to his emotional state of mind we have another piece of evidence, the famous aria, *Io no chiedi, eterni . . .* , with the recitative, *Popoli di Tessaglia* (K.316), which he completed on January 8th, 1779. In its main outlines it had already taken shape in Paris as an expression of his "yearning for the far-off beloved".

> *"Mon très cher père!*
>
> "I am writing this at the house of Herr Beecké. I arrived here safely, God be praised, on the 25th, but have found it impossible to write to you until now. I shall keep everything until I once more have the happiness and pleasure of speaking to you in person, for to-day I can do nothing but weep; I have far too sensitive a heart. In the meantime I must tell you that I received my sonatas safely the day before I left Kaisersheim, and that I shall therefore present them myself to the Electress. I shall only wait until the opera is staged, and then leave forthwith, unless it turns out to be expedient and profitable for me to stay here a while longer, in which case I am convinced, indeed assured, that you would not only approve, but yourself

> advise it . . ." What was he still hoping for? "I am naturally a bad writer, as you know, for I never learned to write; but in all my life I have never written worse than to-day, for I am quite unfit for it—my heart is too full of tears. I hope you will write to me soon and console me. I think it will be best if you write Poste Restante, then I can fetch the letter myself. I am staying with the Webers. But stay, I think it would be better, yes, far better, if you addressed your letters to our dear friend Beecké. I intend (strictly between ourselves) to write a Mass while I am here. All my friends advise me to do so. I cannot tell you what good friends Cannabich and Raaff are to me . . ."

> "I was very perturbed to read your letter and that of Herr Beecké," Leopold replies on December 31st. "Should your tears, your sadness, have no other ground but your doubts as to my love and affection for you, you may sleep in peace . . . It seems from our friend's letter as though this were the chief cause of your sadness. Oh, I hope that there is no other. For you have no cause to fear either a cold reception or an unhappy life with me and your sister . . ."

On the father's part the same fear as ever lest Mozart may in the end stay away altogether, on the son's an inexpressible reluctance to return home. But the efforts of his Mannheim friends, almost every one of whom had moved to Munich with the Court, met with no success; now as ever there was no post as *Kapellmeister* vacant for him, he could see no other path but the one that led to Salzburg. It was fortunate, at least, that the *Bäsle* had overcome all the obstacles in the way of her joining the cousin who had summoned her to his side. She climbed into the stage-coach in Augsburg in high spirits. It was not until she reached Munich that her eyes were opened. Although Wolfgang refused to go home without her, she was only the crutch on which a sick man leans. She did not, however, let him sense her disappointment; the very fact of being in his company, and, too, no doubt, a gleam of hope, buoyed her up, and without further ado she declared her willingness to accompany him to Salzburg, although no invitation from Leopold had yet arrived; the moment was not a convenient one for him, and he would have preferred her to come in the spring. But in this matter Wolfgang had his way. He no longer had any valid excuse for postponing his return home.

> " . . . You cannot imagine," he writes in his last letter of January 8th, 1779, "what I suffered from Madame Robinig's visit, for it is long since I have spoken with such a fool . . . yesterday I waited on the Electress with my dear friend Cannabich, and presented my sonatas. Her apartments are exactly what I should like mine to be one day, exactly like those of a private individual, really charming and delightful . . . "Well, in short, I burn with eagerness, believe me, to embrace you and my dear sister once again. If only it were not to be in Salzburg . . . My *Bäsle* is here. Why? To please her cousin? That is indeed, the ostensible cause, but well, we shall speak of that in Salzburg, and that is why I very much wished her to come with me to Salzburg . . . she will be glad to come; so, if it would give you any pleasure to see her, be so kind as to write immediately to her brother so as to settle the matter. When you see her, she is certain to please you, for everyone likes her. . . ."

And so about the middle of January they both set out. We may presume that the journey was a merry one. The jokes and pleasantries in which he indulged with her were like a warm coverlet spread over him, and her gay company deadened to some extent the agony of his spirit. One can imagine how wretched he would have been had he travelled all alone on this January day, into the January gloom, to face a father who was estranged from him, and to return to a yoke that he utterly abhorred; abandoned entirely to the chill horrors of loneliness, the icy pangs of grief for the cruel Aloysia whose image was ever in his heart, an image which the ingratitude she had shown and the mortification she had caused him had been unable to shatter. This last affliction he was spared on this journey, otherwise so full of frustration, and we are glad to know that the pretty young cousin sat by his side in the coach. For pretty she was.

Her comeliness had not escaped his notice when he had first met her in Salzburg. But in Mannheim he had soon forgotten her; Rose Cannabich had first put her in the shade, then Aloysia. Oh, had he but caught the brief, revealing glimpse of the latter that we get in a picture painted of her in old age! The muses and the graces have dismissed her without a word of farewell, and the first Donna Anna has survived with the face of a housekeeper. The massive brooch, the long earrings, the very stuff of her dress, point to great parsimony. Every feature is ignoble; the full nose, the pursed lips, the line of the neck, of the shoulders, the breast. But to-day at seventeen she is a talented and interesting young woman and it will be long yet before Mozart will have overcome his infatuation for her. The break with her came, so to speak, as the last straw in a series of disappointments. What a journey! When Mozart so cheerfully and confidently left Salzburg behind him, as he thought for ever, on that September morning, he could not have glimpsed the unlucky star which was to dog him from place to place so that his bright prospects always faded, and he nowhere achieved what he had hoped for. In those places where he would most gladly have lingered, he was not permitted to stay; in those where he found everything against him, he was compelled to hold out; and if ever he settled down, if ever his affairs took a turn for the better, he was bustled on; and inexorably he found himself at last sent back to the place whence he had set out.

It may be that all this was to his profit and advantage, had happened so that, steeled in the running fire, he might attain perfection on the peaks of his mystic devotion! For there was to be no lingering by the wayside for him; never was he to have "exactly" the same kind of apartments as the Electress of Bavaria, those of "a private individual"; in other words, never was he to live comfortably and free of cares. How far Brother Frivolity, the sensuous, nay perhaps dissolute, sybarite, the wild young rake, the dashing cavalier found real expression in his manifold nature, is a riddle that will never be answered. The shadows, it is true, that gathered round him, the dread accents, the cries of agony that ring out so terrifyingly and painfully in his work, however desolate may have been their depths, they too were consumed in the light. Many of his biographers are of the opinion that Mozart had no feeling for the beauties of nature. What an error! Bright skies, gardens tastefully laid out, trees festooned with fragrance, the first red of morn, the sun-lit morning and the summer are unmistakable features of his spiritual landscape. Never do we feel the close air of over-heated rooms, even in his chamber music. Flickering candles, for the windows are open, the night air streams in and a bright sickle moon hovers above the tree-tops.

The rest of his life is nevertheless a kind of brilliant mourning. Some outlive their time; Mozart anticipated the span of a man's life at a gallop. By thirty-one he was to learn, as he himself admitted, to recognise in death "his truest and best friend."

LEOPOLD MOZART WITH HIS CHILDREN
Copper engraving by Jean-Baptiste Delafosse (1721-1775) based on a water painting by Louis Carrogis de Carmontelle (1716-1806)
"Nannerl", aged 11, is singing; Wolfgang Amadeus, aged 7, is at the harpsichord.

Mozart wearing a diamond ring
Anonymous painting, about 1775

The Palais Lodron in Salzburg
Oil by J.M. Sattler about 1828

CONSTANZE MOZART

W.A. MOZART
Engraving by Johann August Eduard Mandel (1810-1882) after the drawing by Dorothea Stock (1789), Berlin 1858

MOZART WITH HIS PARENTS
Oil painting by Johann Nepomuk della Croce, 1780/1

Archbishop Hieronymus von Colloredo
Anonymous painting, 18th century

WOLFGANG AMADEUS MOZART AT THE PIANO.
Unfinished portrait painted by Joseph Lange, 1789

❧

Salzburg

On January 17th 1779, the day after Mozart's return, his appointment as Court organist was confirmed. He was from now on to be paid a higher salary; and he had stipulated that he should no longer be obliged to play the violin. On Saints' Days he presided at the organ, and in addition to accompanying the choir, it was his duty to play the voluntaries, which offered him a welcome opportunity of giving free rein to his musical inspiration. But this, no doubt, was the sum total of the pleasure he derived from being in the service of the Archbishop, who had not the slightest intention of allowing him to be any less conscious of his dependence.

Of a change of heart such as Leopold had deluded Wolfgang into expecting, there could, of course, be no question, and the thing that more and more estranged father and son was the innate submissiveness of the one and the innate pride of the other. Mozart was absolutely determined to take himself off at the very first opportunity. This, however, did not occur so soon, and he was obliged to possess himself in patience; for almost two years he had to hold out, to help his father to pay off his debts—always the chief item on the programme. For the rest the curtain has remained lowered over this last Salzburg period. Two affectionate but distraught letters to the *Bäsle*, written in the usual style, are the only records that we possess. His cousin had stayed on as a guest in the Mozart household for a few weeks and then gone home. Mozart was now reduced exclusively to the company of his former acquaintances, and he found them even less bearable than before, for by now he had seen a little of the world, and his innate critical faculties had become keener than ever. He felt out of place in Salzburg. At the same time these joyless months were uncommonly productive, for the impressions gained in Paris and Mannheim were working themselves out. So none of his experiences ran to waste. The works 327 to 360 of the new French classification belong to this period. And if in his Church music he had to bear in mind the Archbishop's taste, he nevertheless composed, in addition to the Coronation Mass, the two vespers, already mentioned, from the apparent brightness of which a breath of infinite loneliness is wafted to us. He wrote Symphonies 33 and 34, the *Symphonie Concertante* for violin and viola, and the Concerto in E flat major for two pianos. In the year 1780 Emanuel Schikaneder introduced a little excitement into the life of Salzburg with his company of strolling players. An air which he agreed to compose for Schikaneder, Mozart completed in Munich.

For the long-hoped-for commission from Munich had at last arrived. His Mannheim friends there had not been idle; the Elector, too, had remembered him, and he was asked to write the *opera seria* for the Carnival of 1781. An old French libretto was chosen as a model, and the task of adapting it entrusted to the, unfortunately, exceedingly untalented Abbate Giambattista Varesco, Court Chaplain in Salzburg. This was *Idomenée*, first produced in Paris in the year 1712 and repeated in 1731. So it was that Mozart's *Idomeneo* came to birth.

On November 5th Mozart set out for Munich. A clear sky once more opened out before him. Letters once more flew to and fro between father and son—so united in their common joy. The bond between them, so close despite all disagreements, once more found the very happiest expression. Being unable, out of respect for the Munich Court, to do otherwise, the Archbishop had granted Mozart six weeks leave of absence. When in December, this time was up, it was Leopold who wrote reassuringly, saying that he would intervene to obtain a prolongation of Wolfgang's leave; he no longer, moreover, opposed Wolfgang's hopes of obtaining an appointment in Munich. "You know, my dearest father, that it is only for your sake I am in Salzburg, . . . on my honour I find, not Salzburg, but the Prince, the proud nobility, more and more unendurable every day . . . Adieu! Come to Munich soon and hear my opera, and tell me then whether I am wrong to be sad when I think of Salzburg . . ."

Leopold went into the details of the libretto with the greatest interest; and Wolfgang was very ready to pay heed to his suggestions as to theatrical effects. It was only in the matter of the music that he refused to accept advice, either from his father, who urged him to compose in a more "popular" style, or from the singers. With his friend Raaff, who sang the part of Idomeneo, and who had grown no younger since the Mannheim days, he had a good deal of trouble. "He is too fond of chopped noodles, and pays too little regard to expression." The *castrato,* Dal Prato, who sang the part of Idamante, had to be coached by Mozart from start to finish. "He has not a ha-porth of method . . . the lad is no good at all," he grumbled to his father. There were plenty of intrigues, too, to report to Leopold. The two women singers, Lisl and Dorothea Wendling, friends from the Mannheim days, were highly delighted with their lovely arias. There is no mention in his letters of Aloysia Weber. One of her patrons, a certain Count Hardeck, had secured for her an engagement as principal singer in Vienna, and she had departed thither with the whole Weber tribe. Mozart lived only for, thought only of, his *Idomeneo.* Both Court and musicians were favourably disposed towards him. Cannabich introduced him to the Countess Baumgarten, the most recent favourite of the Elector, in whose presence the rehearsals went off brilliantly. "I was quite astonished," the Elector declared later on. "No music has ever so impressed me; it is *magnifique.*" (Cannot one imagine one is listening to His Serene Highness in Pocci's Marionette Theatre?)

With the completion of each act Mozart's joy in creation grew. He caught a severe cold, but had neither time nor patience to look after himself properly. The news of the beauty of the opera reached Salzburg, and Fialla, a member of the orchestra, and the ladies Barisani, prepared to set out for Munich. Frau von Robinig, too, could not possibly miss the premiere. Fortunately it was postponed several times, and Leopold and Nannerl, therefore, who did not set out until January 25th, arrived in time for the dress rehearsal. The Archbishop having gone to Vienna for a lengthy stay, there was no need to ask him for the permission which he would certainly have refused. This visit of father and daughter has unfortunately deprived us of any account of the first performance of *Idomeneo*, which took place on January 29th, with, as far as one can tell, great success. Mozart was now anxious to bring his Church music to the notice of the Court. He sent home for two of his Masses, and composed the great Kyrie in D minor (K.341). He was popular, he was acclaimed, and he could now join in the festivities of the Munich Carnival. We may presume with fitting abandon. "In Munich, it is true," he was himself to admit to his father later on, "I placed myself, against my will, in a false light in your eyes. I amused myself too much. But I swear to you on my honour that, before the opera was put on, I did not go to a single theatre, and never visited anywhere but at the Cannabichs. It was out of youthful folly that I later on made too merry. Where is there for you to go? I thought to myself. To Salzburg. In the meantime you may as well enjoy yourself . . . "

He had now been in Munich four months instead of six weeks, and a peremptory order came from the Archbishop that he was to proceed without delay to Vienna, where Colloredo still lingered with his retinue and his best musicians. Ever since the end of the period of public mourning for the Empress Maria Theresa—she had died on November 29th, 1780—the musical life of the city had been in full swing again. Mozart, who wished for nothing more ardently than to make a name for himself in Vienna, as well as elsewhere, left Munich with a far lighter heart than if the password had been Salzburg. We do not know whether he passed through Salzburg on his way to Vienna, to see his father, sister and friends; it was only, after all, because of the Archbishop that he hated the place.

And *Idomeneo?* Lightly come, lightly go. It had been

but a short-lived triumph. Even before the first performance Mozart had been aware of the shortcomings of the libretto, and he made a good many changes in it when the opera was repeated in 1786 in the Palais Auersperg in Vienna. The critics seem to have ignored it completely. This is what Mozart read when he turned to "Die Münchner Staats—, gelehrten und vermischten Nachrichten"—of February 1st, 1781: "On the 29th of last month the opera *Idomeneo* was performed for the first time in our new Opera House. The authorship, both music and translation, are products of Salzburg. The designs and Settings, amongst which the view of the harbour and Neptune's temple create a superb effect, were masterpieces by the famous stage designer, *Herr Hofkammerrath* Lorenz Quaglio, of this city, and called forth general admiration." The Quaglios, employed, father and son, at the Munich Court and National Theatre till well on into the nineteenth century, were local celebrities, who were always highly esteemed in the town. Herr Lorenz Quaglio was obviously already a celebrity, and the critic considered it expedient to neglect to mention the name of the young composer side by side with that of Herr Quaglio, so as to be sure of not committing a faux-pas—deaf to the masterly appeal of this work, to the splendid choruses, worthy of a Gluck, completely deaf to Ilia's graceful melodies, to an aria such as *Se il padre perdei*, to Idamante's moving, Electra's passionate, accents, to the tragic momentum, the animation of the overture. This does not surprise us. We are writing in the year 1936, and are people of experience. The Germany of Mozart's day, dismembered into little principalities, ruled over by petty princes, entirely decentralised, but forming important centres of art, culture and thought, was at this time living through its great period. Although that Germany did not count for much even in the world of music. And this at a time when Johann Sebastian Bach had been dead for only thirty years, Händel only twenty, when Haydn was alive, Beethoven had already been born, Mozart was a much-travelled young man and knew that the home of music was no longer Italy. It was Germany, *la belle inconnue*, that, in so interesting and promising a fashion, was nearing her prime. Existing only as a hypothetical factor of power and not at all as a coherent whole, this Germany called into being a splendid array of poets and produced a miracle such as Goethe. Its mind not really set on the merciless game of politics, not very concerned for its external unity, it was still unaware of its state of spiritual disruption, but was hearkening to the workings of its own soul. Its true home could not be measured by its acreage but by the extent of its horizon, the very vastness of which characterised it, was the symbol of its place in the van of the nations. The founders of its especial fame were representative, it is true, neither of the majority nor of that norm of which the critic of "Die Münchener gelehrten und vermischten Nachrichten" was the personification, and could thus never hope to gain a large following. They would, had they appealed to the public, have received only a pathetically small number of votes: a half or at the very best one per cent. Were they wasted, then? It may be. For we live in a perilous, a menaced, sometimes one is tempted to say, a lost world.

❧

Vienna II

MOZART ARRIVED IN VIENNA ON MARCH 16TH *"mutter seeliger allein"*[1] in a postchaise, as he wrote to his father on the 17th. How many hopes and plans must have thronged his mind on the journey, for planning and hoping was second nature to him. In Munich, he had been fêted, had lived, free as a bird, the unfettered life of a gentleman; now he was resolved to make his way in Vienna, too, to refuse henceforth either to be kept under or paraded by the Archbishop. Thus the arena had already been cleared for the fray. For the Archbishop had quite other views; incensed in any case at Mozart's overstaying his leave, he was contemplating a tightening of the reins, and "treated him thenceforth as a lackey".[2] So as to keep a more watchful eye on him he installed him in his own palace, in a "charming room" of the kind to which Mozart was so

[1] "All by myself."
[2] *Abert*, Vol. I, p.779.

exceptionally susceptible, but—he was to eat with the servants, and the two valets, moreover, were to take precedence of him. Beside himself at such humiliation, he gave full vent to his indignation in a letter home. We seem to see him more vividly before us in this letter than in any of his portraits; we can almost see the quick shrug of the shoulders, catch the expression on his face of wounded indignation, glimpse the flashing eye, the white, strained look. "... I have at least the honour of sitting above the cooks. Well, I can almost imagine myself back in Salzburg. At table stupid, coarse jokes are made. No one jokes with me, for I never say a word unless I am obliged and then always speak with the utmost gravity, and as soon as I have dined I go my way ..."

Leopold in Salzburg is once more seized with panic, and endeavours to calm his son. We only gather this, however, from the son's replies. For we shall read no more of Leopold's letters to Wolfgang. The last is dated January 22nd, 1781, and is addressed to Munich. Constanze was one day to destroy all the letters that came to her husband in Vienna; and because of her hatred of her father-in-law, to rob us of these important documents.

> "What you write," Mozart replies on March 24th, "of the Archbishop's vanity being tickled at having me in his service has some truth in it—but of what use is that to me? One cannot live by it. Believe me, he serves here only as a screen to keep me in the shade. What distinction does he accord me? Herren v. Kleinmayer and Benecke,[1] and the illustrious Count Arco have a special table to themselves; it would be some distinction if I were at their table, but not to sit with the valets, who. . . light the candles, open the doors and wait in the anterooms, and with the cooks. And then, when we are summoned

[1] The Archbishop's valets.

to a concert anywhere, Herr Angelbauer has to keep watch for the arrival of the Salzburg gentlemen and then send word to them by a lackey that they may enter, as Brunetti himself told me. I thought to myself: just wait till my turn comes. So the other day, when we were summoned to Prince Galitzin's, Brunetti said to me in his usual polite manner:

"Tu, bisogna che sei qui sta sera alle sette, per andare insieme dal Prencipe gallizin. L'Angelbauer ci condurrà. Ho riposto: va bene—ma—se in caso mai no fossi qui alle sette in pun to: ci andate pure, non serve aspettarmi."[1] I contrived to go alone, for I am ashamed to be seen about with them, and when I reached the top of the stairs, there stood M. Angelbauer ready to tell the lackeys to conduct me in. I took no notice, however, either of the valet or the footman, but went straight through the apartments into the music room, all the doors being open, and so straight up to the Prince, paid my respects to him and stood there conversing with him. I had quite forgotten my friends Cecarelli and Brunetti, for they were nowhere in sight; I found them leaning against the wall right at the back of the orchestra and not daring to advance a step . . . I have dined twice with the Countess Thun, and go there almost every day. She is one of the most charming, most delightful women I have ever met in my life, and I stand high in her esteem too . . ."

"But what makes me nearly desperate," he writes on April 11th, "is that on the very evening that we had this filthy music at home I was invited to Countess Thun's, and of course could not go. And who do you think was there? The Emperor. Adamberger and Mlle. Weigl were there, and each received 50 ducats. What an opportunity!"

The Archbishop had forbidden him to perform on his own, but he paid no heed to the prohibition. One of his symphonies was conducted with great success by the old *Kapellmeister* Bonno. A concert, permission for which was

[1] You must be here at seven this evening, so that we may go together to Prince Galitzin's; Angelbauer will take us there. Very well, I answered, but if I am not here on the stroke of seven, pray proceed there yourself, and don't wait for me.

wrung from the Archbishop and which was given on April 2nd, in aid of the widows and orphans of Viennese musicians, went off with even greater éclat.

But now he was told to pack up his things and return with the rest of the Archbishop's suite to Salzburg, again empty-handed, and without having gained the ear of the Emperor. With every day his resentment grew, and everything was working up towards the final break. It came on May 7th, and was to entail separation from Salzburg, a breach with his father, and, alas! his walking straight into the Webers' trap.

"I am still in a fever of indignation! And I am sure that you, my best and kindest of fathers, will be so too. My patience has so long been tried that it has at last given out. I no longer have the misfortune to be in the service of the Archbishop of Salzburg, and to-day is a happy day for me. Twice has the—I know not what to call him—said the most insulting and impertinent things to my face, which I have not repeated to you out of a desire to spare your feelings, and have only refrained from taking instant revenge because I always have you, my dear father, before my eyes. He called me a knave and a profligate, and bade me get out of his sight and I bore it all, although I felt that not only my honour but yours was being impugned, but as you would have it so, I kept silence."

Mozart well knew the submissive side of his father's nature. "Now hear what happened," he nevertheless went on, in an endeavour to convince him. "A week ago the courier came up to me quite unexpectedly and told me that I must leave at once. Notice had been given to the others, but not to me. I hastily packed up my things, and old Madame Weber was so kind as to take me into her house, where I have a charming room, and am with obliging people who are ready to see to all those things that one often needs in a hurry (but cannot get done when one is alone) . . . ”

By the Archbishop, from whom he was to fetch a package to take to Salzburg, he was addressed in the following manner: “ ‘When are you going, young fellow?’ I: ‘I intend to go tonight, but all the places are engaged.’ Then he burst out and said that I was the most dissolute fellow he knew, no one served him so badly as I did, and he advised me to leave that very day, or he would write home and stop my salary. It was impossible to get a word in, for he blazed away. I listened calmly to it all. He lied to my face and said that I received a salary of 500 florins, called me a ne’er-do-well, a scamp, a scurvy rogue and—oh, I should not care to tell you what else. At last my blood was up, and I said: ‘May I take it that your Grace is not satisfied with me?’ ‘What, you would threaten me, you rogue? There is the door; I will have nothing more to do with such a low rascal.’ At last I said, ‘Nor I with you.’ ‘Go!’ he ordered. I, on taking my departure: ‘The matter is settled then; to-morrow you shall have it in writing.’ Tell me, my dear father, if I did not say this rather too late than too soon? I assure you that I prize my honour above all else, and I know that you do too.”

But no, he knew otherwise, knew that he was bombarding his father in vain, knew that their conceptions of honour were poles apart. “So long as the Archbishop is here I will give no concert,” he continues. “If you think that I have put myself in bad odour with the nobility or with the Emperor himself, you are entirely mistaken, for the Archbishop is hated here, and most of all by the Emperor. He is in a rage because the Emperor has not invited him to Luxemburg. I shall send you a little money by the next post, to show you that I am not starving here. I entreat you, moreover, to be of good heart, for good fortune is now coming my way, and I hope it will be your good fortune, too. Write to me privately that you are content, and indeed you may well be so Publicly, however, abuse me roundly, so that you may in no way be blamed. Should the Archbishop, however, be guilty of the slightest impertinence towards you, come immediately with my sister to Vienna; I assure you on my honour that we can all three contrive to live here. Nevertheless, I should be glad"—he bethinks himself in time—"if you could bear up for another year."

He will not hear another word about Salzburg and he hates the Archbishop "to the point of frenzy". This letter was written from the house *"Zum Auge Gottes"* in the Petersplatz, where the Webers lived.

The abyss between father and son has now opened out and nothing can bridge the disparity between their two natures. The father is not a day, not an hour, ahead of his age. And therefore the waters of the ephemeral, which he never overtops by a hair's breadth, will one day break over him and bury him. Mozart is even in his father's eyes not "in a position to demand satisfaction", and he must swallow slights, in so far as they come from "persons of rank". Any other course of behaviour would be "unwise". He is therefore hardly likely to be moved at his son's writing three days later to say that he had been obliged to leave the opera in the middle of the third act to go home and lie down, "for I was feverish, trembled in every limb and staggered in the street like a drunken man . . . "

At length Wolfgang is stung into writing the lovely and disconsolate letter of the 19th May, from which we gather that Leopold "can never approve" of his having left the Archbishop's service in Vienna. "I really do not know where to begin, my dearest father, for I have not yet recovered from my astonishment, nor shall I if you persist in thinking and writing as you do. I must confess that I do not recognise my father in one single feature of your letter! A father, yes, but not the kindest, most affectionate of fathers, a father concerned for his honour and that of his children. . . "

But all this meant nothing to Leopold. Honour was a luxury for fine gentlemen, and one which he did not permit either himself or his children. The fact that, as Mozart insisted, the Viennese were on his side and that the Archbishop was highly unpopular both with the Emperor and the court did not impress Leopold in the least. It was in vain that his son tried his best to get round him. He assured him that he was a changed character and regarded nothing, next to his health, as of such importance as money! Wolfgang, who had as little conception of money as had his father of the honour of a gentleman! He enclosed 20 ducats as a proof of his ability to make a way for himself. The debts were presumably not yet settled.

On June 13th occurred that disgraceful interview in the course of which Count Arco, who was expected to play the role of mediator, for nothing can have been less to the Archbishop's liking than to be deprived of the services of a genius like Mozart, so far forgot himself as to kick Mozart out of the room. Even after this incident, Leopold continued apparently to be of the opinion that it was possible for Wolfgang to remain in the Archbishop's service; at this point the thought of living with his father must have become as intolerable to him as the yoke of servitude to the Archbishop, and he freed himself once and for all from both.

Vienna was to be the final destination of the twenty-five-year-old Mozart, and in that moment when the blissful hour of freedom struck, the hour in which he was to assume responsibility for his own life also struck. Life itself, the dangers and dangerousness of which he was incapable of perceiving, was to be his new taskmaster. However wretched had been his position hitherto—instead of the agreed annual sum of 500 florins he had received only 400 in Salzburg—he had yet had security, had had a genuinely devoted and affectionate, if censorious and didactic, father on whom to fall back in case of need. But now he stood on his own feet, and his end we know. Yet he was to be vouchsafed the bliss of self-fulfilment, and his one passionate, supreme desire—to write operas—was to be granted; he was to write six in the ten years that lay ahead of him. This fact weighed heavy in the scale of his earthly happiness, and the penury and want of his external circumstances, which far exceeded Leopold's worst fears, never succeeded in counterbalancing it.

Until September, 1781, he lived with the Webers. Old Weber had died two years previously, Aloysia had married the actor Joseph Lange, and the mother had taken to letting rooms. There were three unmarried daughters still at home. Mozart undoubtedly felt at home in this environment. Arthur Schurig supplies us in a few lines with an admirable pen-picture of him at this period. "When he had but lately been lingering on the most distant heights of the visionary world, he loved to sit in Madame Weber's kitchen and get her to retail to him the most trivial domestic gossip, or he would jest and romp with her three daughters. Without being conscious of it, he felt the need for the contrast between the heights of sublimity and the depths of banality." Never a good word in the letters now of Aloysia; Mozart, always so easily influenced, joined her family, who were at daggers drawn with her, in inveighing against her. He admits in a letter to his father, it is true, that he cannot yet think of her without a pang, and he is glad that her husband guards her so jealously. Taking it all in all, it was a halcyon period, with no lack of friends and patrons, and not without its compensations. The Archbishop had picked upon a well-known pianist at the Viennese court, by the name of Kozeluch, as his successor, and had offered him a yearly salary of 1,000 florins, but had met with a rebuff. If he could treat a man like Mozart as he had, said Kozeluch, how was he going to treat, and declined the post, for he was better off in Vienna.[1] Even Leopold, distressed as he was at his son's independent behaviour and at the separation from him, took his part before strangers. "Since His Grace treated my son so exceptionally ill in Vienna," he wrote to Breitkopf, "and the entire nobility, on the other hand, showed him signal honour, they were easily able to persuade him to resign a humiliating post with a wretched stipend and remain in Vienna. . ."

The aforesaid nobility, it is true, now withdrew to their estates, and Mozart was left with only a single pupil. Despite the patronage of the Countess Thun, he only found seventeen people to take up subscriptions for six violin sonatas he decided to publish. Nevertheless, Vienna was "the most marvellous place in the world" for his profession, as he wrote in a letter home. The Emperor

[1] Leopold Kozeluch (1752-1818), a bungler, but an experienced and assiduous intriguer. At first he tried to set Mozart against Haydn. "I should not have written it in that way," he declared to Mozart of a bold passage in a new quartet by Haydn. "Nor I either," said Mozart, "but do you know why? Because neither you nor I would have hit on the idea." Kozeluch then vented his spleen on Mozart. He declared that the overture to *Don Giovanni* was full of faults, and that of the *Zauberflöte* pretentious. During the première of *La Clemenza di Tito,* in Prague, he protested loudly, to his own detriment. Later he even ventured to approach Beethoven, who conferred on him the title—"miserabilis."

Joseph's musical talent was distinctly mediocre, but he cultivated both the opera and the drama, and was a true lover of the arts. The antithesis in every respect of the Archbishop of Salzburg, by raising the prestige of the theatre, he also raised the prestige and the social status of the writers, actors and musicians. He knew, too, how to raise the level of taste in the public, which was now drawn from all the educated classes. An increasingly marked contrast between North and South Germany was becoming discernible. "Lutheran composers", "Lutheran singing" grew to be familiar terms even on Mozart's lips. Under this tolerant and intellectually alert ruler, Vienna became one of the most artistically alive of all the European capitals. Although he himself may have had a weakness for Salieri, it was owing to his influence that Gluck was the dominant figure in the musical world, and Vienna at that time lived as much under the aegis of Gluck as of the Emperor. Indeed, a city after Mozart's heart! The popular notion that he cared for music to the exclusion of everything else will be best dispelled by the following passage from a letter written to his sister on July 4th, 1781: "My only relaxation is the theatre; I wish that you could see one of the tragedies put on here! I know of no other theatre where every kind of play is produced *so excellently*. Here every role, even the smallest and most trivial, is well played and is understudied . . ." He enquires in this letter also about the ribbons which he has sent her as a present, and apologises to his father because, owing to its being the dead season, he is only sending 30 ducats.

He was still living with the Webers, and this, of course, gave rise to a certain amount of gossip. Of Reifenberg, a place near Vienna, he writes, stirred by the beauty of nature, to his father: "The house is nothing much, but the countryside—the forest!" and goes on to say that he has long intended to seek fresh lodgings. He denies that he has any intention whatever of marrying. "If there has ever been a time in my life when I did not contemplate marriage, it is the present . . . God did not give me my talents to throw away on a woman and waste my life in idleness. I am only just beginning to live, and am I then to spoil my own life? I have certainly nothing against matrimony, but it would be a misfortune for me at present . . . if I were obliged to marry every woman with whom I have jested, I should be saddled with at least 200 wives . . ." All this sounds very proud and confident, and it is quite true that at this time he was far more occupied with other things than with his flirtation—for there was no question of love such as he had felt for Aloysia—with Constanze, which was encouraged by Madame Weber. All the same, the affair had already begun, and it was autumn before he yielded to his father's exhortations and at last moved out; in the meantime the net in which he was finally to be caught was being drawn round him more tightly, for his prospects had improved, and for the completely penniless young girl he was a tolerably good match. On August 1st he was able to write jubilantly to his father: "Young Stephani[1] has given me a libretto to set to music. I must confess that badly as (for all I care) he behaves towards other people, of that I know nothing, he is a very good friend to me. The libretto is very good. The subject is Turkish and the title is *Belmont and Gonstanze*, or *Die Verführung aus dem Seraglio*. I shall write the music of the symphony, the chorus in the first act and the final chorus in the Turkish manner . . . I am so delighted to be writing the opera that I have already completed Cavalieri's first aria, and that for Adamberger, and the trio

[1] Inspector of the Viennese Opera.

which concludes the first act. The time is short, it is true; for it is to be performed in the middle of February; but the circumstances connected with the time when it is to be given, and indeed everything else to do with it, fill me with such delight that I hurry off to my writing-table with the greatest eagerness and sit there working in the most blissful of moods. The Grand Duke of Russia is coming here, and so Stephani begged me, if possible, to finish the opera in this short time . . ." By August 8th he is able to announce that Adamberger, Mlle. Cavalieri and Fischer "are uncommonly pleased with their arias". Yet things were not to proceed so rapidly as had at first appeared; the Grand Duke and the Grand Duchess postponed their visit, and it was not the *Entführung*, but Gluck's *Iphigènie en Tauride*, in German, and his *Alceste* in Italian, that were put on in honour of the distinguished guests.

The Emperor had a particularly high regard for Mozart as a pianist, and on December 24th he invited him to play at the Burg in competition with the famous Clementi.

> "I had been in Vienna but a few days," wrote Clementi to one of his pupils, "when I received an invitation from the Emperor to play to him on the fortepiano. On entering the music room, I found someone already there whom I took, on account of his elegant appearance, for a gentleman-in-waiting; but we had scarcely entered into conversation when he embarked on the subject of music, and we soon recognised and greeted each other very warmly as fellow artists—Mozart and Clementi."

The Emperor had made a bet with the Archduchess, which he won, that Mozart would emerge the victor. He then sent him a present of 50 ducats. If Clementi was charmed by Mozart's playing, Mozart expressed himself positively acidly on the subject of the "worthy harpsichordist" Clementi, who had not a ha'porth of feeling or taste, in his opinion, and was a mere automaton.

With the beginning of the winter season the number of his pupils increased. The best of these, the one to whom he felt most drawn, was Frau Therese von Trattner. To her he dedicated the great Fantasia and Sonata in C minor (K.457). He now had an enormous amount of work on hand. On May 3rd he gave a concert at the instigation of the Countess Thun, the programme consisting of some of the best portions of *Idomeneo*. He apologises in a letter to his sister for not writing to her more frequently.

Nevertheless, he sent presents home to Salzburg: to his father a snuff-box and two watch-ribbons which he had been given by Count Szapary, and to Nannerl two caps worked by Constanze.

For meanwhile Frau Weber had caught him. In her eagerness to get one of her unmarried daughters off her hands, she had conspired with their guardian, a former valet of the name of Thorwart, to trap Mozart into giving a written undertaking, which bound him to Constanze for life and represented her, justifiably or not, as having been compromised. The fact that Constanze, in a burst of feeling and as a sign of her confidence in him, tore up the document, in no way altered the fact that Mozart regarded himself as bound. Very different from the letter to his father of July of the same year is that of December.

"An unmarried man," is now his cry, "is, in my view, only half a man. That is my view, and I cannot help it. I have reflected and pondered on the matter enough, I shall always feel the same. Well, now, who is the object of my love? Do not be alarmed, I beseech you. Surely not one of those Webers? Yes, one of the Webers; not Josepha, not Sophie—but Constanze, the middle one. I have never met with such diversity of disposition in any family." A fine family this, into which he marries! The eldest he describes as coarse, idle and deceitful, Aloysia as deceitful, evil-minded and a coquette, the youngest as frivolous—but Constanze as a martyr . . . Among other things he insists that she knows all about house-keeping, dresses her own hair, and "has the kindest heart in the world . . . I love her, and she loves me, dearly. Tell me if I could wish for a better wife".

Leopold had learned from another source the story, which had been withheld from him, of the blackmailing tactics employed by Frau Weber and Constanze' s guardian in the matter of the marriage contract, which bound Mozart either to marry Constanze or to pay her an annual sum of 300 florins. We can gain some idea of his only too comprehensible indignation and disappointment from the following passage from his son's letter in reply to one of his: Wolfgang admits that the guardian behaved far from well, "but not so ill that he and Madame Weber deserve to be put in irons like criminals, made to sweep the streets and wear a placard round their necks bearing the words 'seducers of youth'. That would really be too much". But only too much. What good reason he had for being ashamed of his mother-in-law is apparent from the fact that he has to admit "that she is fonder of drinking, perhaps, than a woman should be. Still, I have never yet seen her drunk, I should be lying were I to say that I had".

Drunk or not drunk, this Frau Weber, who was notoriously avaricious, a busybody, common, and above all a slattern, exerted in a world such as ours a power and a force before which a shrewd but honest man like Mozart's father had perforce to capitulate. He and Nannerl, in their grief and disappointment, had nothing to distract them in the little town of Salzburg, and the streets must have seemed more than ever to close in on them, the mountains to bear down on them more heavily, the daily round to drag more dismally, the rushing stream to echo their loneliness more loudly. For Wolfgang, who was surely drifting farther and farther away from them, would be all the more perceptibly lost to them if he entered into this dubious marriage.

He, meanwhile, was now able to turn his attention once more to his work on the *Entführung*. Joseph II preferred "courtly, salon" music like Salieri's, and both Haydn and Mozart were much too modern for him. And yet this Emperor, as cultured as he was just and tolerant, desired Mozart, whom he so highly esteemed as a pianist, to try his hand at composing an opera. The intrigues that were afoot he countered with the command that the *première* was to take place on July 16th, 1781.

❧

Die Entführung Aus Dem Serail and Marriage

WHAT A CONTRAST BETWEEN THE TURMOIL, THE whirlwind character of this first year in Vienna and the dullness of musical life at the Archbishop's Court! Was Mozart able any longer to distinguish the world of his imagination from the world of reality? Caught up in the spell of his new work, he invested his two Constanzes with the same halo, bestowed on the young Constanze Weber the nobility of Belmont's Constanze and paid homage to the one in the person of the other. During this undoubtedly happy period his passion for Constanze became at once more confused and more profound. He had reached the stage of seeing a Helen in every female, with the exception of the ugly and fat Fräulein von Auernhammer, his best pupil, whom he described in such drastic terms in his letter to his father of August 22nd, 1781. The not exactly pretty, but well-built Constanze Weber was sure of her game from the start. It is the bliss of springtime that the brilliance, the radiant ideas of *Die Entführung* convey to our senses. Imperishable is the impression made upon us by the andante which, in C minor, forms the middle section of the Overture, and then in such happy sequence unveils itself, as it were, in C major as Belmonte's aria.

Mozart was obliged to make a good many concessions to please the cast. Constanze's first air: *"Ack, ich liebte, war so glücklich"*, opens in sweetly penetrating strains; but in deference to the *prima donna*, Catarina Cavalieri, it had to be continued as a *bravura* air. And the Pasha Selim, lord of all destinies, declaims, as he moves across the stage, in a speaking voice—a risky thing, but one which Mozart may not have found altogether inconvenient, for the inevitable pathos of an unhappy lover would have introduced an element altogether too heavy for *opera buffa*. Schurig calls the opera a mixture of German, French and Italian stylistic elements, German only in the sphere of feeling. That it is essentially German in its vigour and its lyricism there can be no doubt, and its shortcomings cannot detract from its charm. One cannot agree with him, however, when he goes on to declare that Mozart was an innocent child not only in *life* but in the very best of his creative work, and that his intelligence, which never fully developed and remained to the end childish, played an extremely small part in his music in comparison with his indefatigable, powerful and spontaneous imagination. Is one not conscious, on the contrary, of intensive reflection in his work and of a careful marshalling of his material? His imagination, it is true, bore him, like a hurricane, wherever he wished. But we find him childish only in relation to life. In this sphere alone, indeed, his genius was deficient. He was possessed, it is true, of a sharp tongue, but he was no judge of people. Fully occupied as he was with his own inner problems, he lacked the necessary concentration for a study of human nature, just as he lacked a head for business matters, lacked all sense of the meaning and value of money. How could it have been otherwise?

Mozart's account of the première, which took place by the Emperor's command on July 16th, has been lost, and we have only the account which he gave his father four days later: "I hope you have safely received my last letter in which I told you how well my opera was received. It was given yesterday for the second time. You will scarcely credit it; there was an even stronger cabal against it than on the first evening. The whole of the first act was hissed, but this did not drown the loud bravos that greeted the arias. . . In the second act both the duets and Belmonte's rondo, *Wenn der Freude Thränen fliessen*, were encored as on the first night. The theatre was almost more crowded than at the première. The day before there were no reserved seats to be had, either in the stalls or in the third gallery, nor a box of any kind. The two performances have brought in 1,200 florins. . . Count Zichy has this moment sent word to me," Mozart adds, knowing how glad his father will be to read these words, "asking me to drive out with him to Laxemburg, so that he may present me to Prince Kaunitz. I must therefore conclude, in order to dress, for when I do not expect to go out, I always remain *en négligé*." The postscript can have aroused less pleasure: "My dear Constanze presents her compliments to you both."

The die, then, had been cast. True, there had been a lovers' quarrel, but it had no consequences and was as characteristic of Mozart as of the lady of his choice . . . "I beg you once again," he writes to Constanze on April 29th, 1782, "to consider and reflect upon the cause of all this unpleasantness, which arose from my displeasure at your being so shameless and thoughtless as to tell your sisters, in my presence, be it noted, that you had allowed your calves to be measured by a fop. No woman who set store by her honour would do such a thing . . . even if; as you say, the Baroness[1] permitted the same liberty; that is quite another matter, for she is a woman who is no longer as young as she was and cannot possibly attract any longer; in any case she is a friend of etceteras . . ."

Madame Weber must have taken good care to see that this disagreement was smoothed over, for a breach with this future son-in-law, who might now be said to be a rising star, would have meant the end of everything. We also find the Baroness Waldstätten playing for a time an important role in this troubled period of Mozart's life. *Die Entführung aus dem Serail* had been an undoubted success. Behind the scenes, it is true, there was a clique of musicians bent on discrediting it. According to them it was not to be taken seriously. Joseph II gave this clique his encouragement by declaring after the performance: "It was nothing out of the way." An anecdote that went the rounds at the time is characteristic of Mozart, who is never known to have expressed himself obsequiously. "Too fine for our ears, and a prodigious number of notes, my dear Mozart," the Emperor is said to have declared to Wolfgang, who thereupon retorted: "Just as many notes, Your Majesty, as are necessary." The opera was performed fourteen times more that year. Prince Kaunitz was enchanted with it, and Gluck, to Mozart's delight and astonishment, arranged for a special performance on August 6th, congratulated him after it, and invited him to dine on the following day. "My opera was given again yesterday (at the special request of Gluck). Gluck complimented me very highly on it. I am to

[1] The Baroness Wadstätten.

dine with him to-morrow," he unfortunately announces to his father in his delight, for his father was, of course, once more to warn him against Gluck.

Die Entführung, which was in general highly praised by the critics, was included in the repertory of several German theatres as early as the following year. It was accorded its most enthusiastic reception in Prague, from now on the true "Mozartian" town. Except in Vienna, where Mozart made 50 ducats, the proceeds were hardly worth mentioning. By neglecting to arrange for the publication of the piano score at the right moment, he let slip all the profits he might have made from it, a fact which exasperated Leopold far more than himself. Elated by his success, Mozart plunged into work as never before. Ever since his escape from the archiepiscopal yoke, his old affection for Salzburg and his Salzburg friends had revived. During July, when he was already overwhelmed with work, he received an urgent commission to write a fresh Serenade for the Haffner family, and in order not to disappoint them, he was obliged to work late into the night. If we include the four great violin sonatas (K. 376, 377, 379, 389), we find that this was a time of almost uncanny productiveness. For Aloysia Lange, née Weber, too, with whom he had now become reconciled, he composed an aria: *Nehmt meinen Dank, Ihr holden Götter*, and because it obviously recalls the style of the *Entführung*, the aria *Der Liebe himmlischen Gefühle* is also ascribed by a good many people to this period. It is a striking proof of the many-sidedness of Mozart's nature that in this summer, with its wealth of happy emotions, he should have composed the great C minor Serenade for wind instruments, which is inspired by such wild, indeed, hopeless grief.

Leopold was still, and with justification, doing his utmost to prevent this shocking marriage on the part of his son. Wolfgang was involved in a number of stormy scenes with Frau Weber, who, when Constanze took refuge in the house of Baroness Waldstätten, under whose auspices the ill-considered marriage was solemnised on August 4th, threatened to call in the police. Leopold's consent, which the infatuated Mozart had vainly sought, was only given after the event.

Mozart was now a married man, fettered, this time, by chains from which he was never to free himself.

It was an exultant young couple that set up house on the second floor of the house *Zum Roten Säbel,* Hohe Brücke, 387 (to-day 25).

In this house, where Mozart had once lived as a child, they stayed only until the autumn, and during the nine years that remained to him he was to make twelve more moves.

In the meantime he found in Constanze the relaxation that he needed. It may well have been balm to his spirit to turn to her after the ardours of creation, in which she had no part. A drawing of her by Joseph Lange of the year 1783 shows us a young woman in the first bloom of undeniable youthful charm. With her it was easy to be light-hearted. She had a zest for life—and this too was a quality he needed—she was glad to have escaped the disagreeable, quarrel-some atmosphere of her home, she was in love, and we are grateful to her for every hour that Mozart spent with her during this period. Arm in arm the merry couple could be seen walking through the Augarten in the early morning. On one occasion the Emperor happened to come upon them and gained a most favourable impression of their married life. To him they were just two little people. It was left to his brother Maximilian or Prince Kaunitz to place on record the fact that as regards rank they were poles apart; he himself, like his great mother, the Empress Maria Theresa in her time, did not give a thought to such things. Yet the new epoch was already approaching, and how cruelly was his poor sister Marie Antoinette, alone and utterly isolated, to be called to account for all such lack of sensibility on the part of the old epoch.

How long the Weber temperament remained dormant in Constanze we do not know. The honeymoon weeks, at any rate, were a time of unalloyed happiness. Leopold Mozart, who had now resigned himself to the inevitable, gave his belated blessing and consent to the marriage. There was food for thought, he felt, in the fact that a real Baroness had provided the wedding feast. Perhaps Constanze was not really so bad, after all, and did not take after that dragon of a Frau Weber.

Leopold was extremely curious about Baroness Waldstätten and wished to be told more about her. After all, she belonged to the highest nobility. But Wolfgang was evasive; he would have to reserve his description of her until his next letter, he wrote, and then never returned to the subject. In the meantime, in her eagerness to do him a good turn, she wrote on her own, or rather at Wolfgang's instigation, a most charming letter to his father. She must have read his replies not without a certain amusement. Her object, however, that of reconciling him to the marriage, was for the moment attained.

"Esteemed and Gracious Madame,

"I thank your Ladyship most sincerely for the particular interest she takes in my circumstances, and express my especial thanks for the exceptional kindness your Ladyship has displayed towards my son in providing so sumptuous a setting for his marriage . . . Indeed, my mind would be entirely at ease, had I not discovered a major failing in my son, which is that he is on the one hand too patient, too indolent, too easy-going, sometimes perhaps too proud, or whatever you may care to call that side of a man's character that renders him inactive; and on the other too impatient, too hasty and unable to wait for anything. There are two entirely contrary principles at work in his character—too much or too little and no mean. When he lacks nothing, he is forthwith content and becomes comfortable and inactive. But should he be forced to be active, then he is roused and bent on immediate success. Nothing must be allowed to stand in his way, and unfortunately it is precisely the most clever people, the outstanding geniuses, in whose path the greatest obstacles are placed. Who is there in Vienna to prevent his following the career he has embarked upon if he will but have a little patience? *Kapellmeister Bonno* is a very old man—Salieri will succeed to his post after his death, and is not Gluck also an old man? Your Ladyship, exhort him to exercise a little patience, and permit me to beg your Ladyship to let me know your opinion on this matter. Oh, would were we not so far from Vienna! I could wish to converse at length with your Ladyship on the matter—and if we could but steep ourselves first in music! Hope, may thou, the only consolation of our desires, calm my spirit!

"Your Ladyship's
"Most obedient servant,
"Leopold Mozart."

"Salzburg, August 23rd, 1782.

"My son wrote to me some time past to say that once he was married he would no longer live with his wife's mother. I hope he has really left her house by this. Should this not be the case, it will be to the great detriment of himself and his wife."

(To the Baroness von Waldstätten in Vienna)

" Highly Esteemed, Gracious Madame,

"I cannot hope to describe to your Ladyship the pleasure

with which I was filled when I read your Ladyship's very flattering letter to me. At that very instant Wieland's *Sympathien* lay open before me, and it is unquestionably true that some people are blessed with uncommon powers of imagination, and are bound unconsciously by a secret spiritual tie without ever having met or spoken to each other . . .

"May your Ladyship have a care for her health and peace of mind. It cut me to the heart to learn that your Ladyship had lost her peace of mind and health through great grief and agony. May the Good God keep you! I am deeply moved . . .

"Your Ladyship's
"Most obedient servant,
"Leopold Mozart."

Despite his son's warning "to be somewhat on his guard", Leopold eagerly kept up the correspondence with the grief-stricken Baroness, and sent a most unsuitable person to her with a letter of introduction. In the end the true character of the lady ceased to be a secret even to him, and Wolfgang then expressed himself on the matter. His words are dignified and admirable: " . . . she is frail, but I will say no more, and this much to you alone, for I have enjoyed too much kindness at her hands, and it is my duty to defend her wherever possible or at least to keep silence . . ."

How much better he himself knew the right tone to adopt with the woman who was "the friend of etceteras " the following droll epistle shows:

"Dearest, best, loveliest,
Gilded, silvered and sugared
Most estimable and precious
Gracious Lady
Baroness!

" . . . I can truly say that I am both a happy and unhappy man. Unhappy ever since the time when I saw your Ladyship so elegantly coiffée at the ball, for I am robbed of all my peace of mind, can do naught but sigh and groan! The rest of the time at the ball I no longer danced, I skipped. When supper was brought in, I did not eat, I gobbled . . . You smile? You blush? I am indeed happy. My happiness is assured. But alas! who is this that taps me on the shoulder? Who is this peeping at my letter? Woe, woe, woe is me—my wife! Well, she is mine now in God's name, and I must keep her. What else can I do? I must praise her, and pretend to myself that it is all true . . ."

Incidentally the Baroness seems to have been an uncommonly good-natured woman. Mozart had seen a red coat "that cruelly tickled his fancy"; he simply had to have it and he had made enquiries about the price. He already had some mother-of-pearl buttons that would just go with it; he had bought them in the Kolhlmarkt some time previously. "I should like to have everything," he confessed to her, "good, genuine and beautiful." The Baroness seems to have made him a present of this coat. ". . . I had a feeling all the time that I had something more to say . . . and that was to express my thanks to your Ladyship for having taken so much pains in the matter of the lovely coat—and for your kindness in promising me one like it . . . "

But she was just then on the point of leaving Vienna. Before her departure Mozart procured her a pianoforte to take with her, and ordered a tongue for her from Salzburg, "for I have incurred many obligations to her." For the moment he saw everything through rose-coloured spectacles. He was expecting to be appointed teacher to the young Princess Elizabeth of Würtemberg; indeed the appointment seemed a certainty. "Salieri, after all, is not competent to give her lessons. He would have some trouble to discredit me, and that he might try to do. Besides, the Emperor knows me, and on a previous occasion the Princess would have liked to take lessons from me. . . "His outward relations with Salieri were perfectly good; but the latter had no doubt realized his superiority and saw in him a dangerous rival. According to Jahn, he spoke to his confidants in very disaparaging terms of Mozart's s talents. He managed, after all, to prevent Mozart from being given the post of teacher to the Princess, and to have an obscure musician by the name of Summer appointed instead. But at first Mozart had every ground for expecting to obtain the post, and he boasted to his father of his connections, in order to dispel any impression that he had damaged his credit in high circles by his deplorable marriage. Unfortunately there were other things in this letter. Leopold had once more considered it expedient to warn his son expressly against Gluck and his favours. "As for Gluck, I feel just as you tell me you do in your letter . . . " And yet what a good thing it would have been for him to come into contact with the composer of *Alceste*, *Orphée*, and the two *Iphigènie*, a man whose influence might have been of such vital importance to him in his precarious position. Instead of Mozart, it was Salieri who was to belong to Gluck's more intimate circle and to be able to exploit all the advantages of that connection. If Mozart was a happy young husband, he felt on the other hand so isolated as an artist that, seized by a fit of profound depression, he conceived the plan, scarcely a fortnight after his marriage, of going to France and getting into touch with Le Gros in regard to the *Concerts Spirituels*. On August 17th he wrote to his father:

> " . . . These Viennese (by whom I mean principally the kmyolr[1]) must not imagine that I am in the world solely on Vienna's account. There is no monarch in the world I would more readily serve than the Emperor, but I will not beg for a

[1] Cipher for Emperor.

> post from anyone. I believe myself to be capable of doing honour to any Court. If Germany, my beloved fatherland, of which, as you know, I am so proud, will not have me, then, in God's name, France or England must become the richer for one more German of talent, to the shame of the German nation. You know very well that in almost all the arts it is the Germans who have excelled, but where did they attain fame and fortune? Certainly not in Germany? Even Gluck, was it Germany that made him the great man he is? Unfortunately not. Countess Thun, Count Zichy, Baron van Swieten, even Prince Kaunitz are all very dissatisfied with the Emperor for no longer prizing people of talent and letting them leave the country. The latter recently remarked to the Archduke Maximilian when my name came up that such people only came into the world once in a century, and should not be driven out of Germany, particularly if one were so fortunate as to enjoy their presence in the capital . . ."

But of what use was all this? Despite the success of *Die Entführung*, which very soon other German theatres, including that of his native Salzburg, were eager to put on, the Emperor did not even contemplate commissioning Mozart to write a new opera, and here Salieri's influence is unmistakable. Wolfgang had to be content for the moment to earn his living as a teacher. Since the few pupils he had paid him well, he managed to make as much as 100 florins a month, and his father did not find it difficult to dissuade him from his plan of moving to Paris. Vienna still held him far too much in thrall. He went on hoping, and possessed himself in patience. He had friends in Vienna, and his life was a full and rich one. Baron van Swieten, a former diplomat, a bachelor of forty-eight who was unfortunately as miserly as he was rich, arranged chamber concerts for him and other artists in his house on Sundays. Bach and Handel were the Baron's idols, and through him Mozart became really acquainted for the first time with these two masters. He studied their works thoroughly and for a time came completely under their spell. Once more he eagerly turned his attention to counter-point. As early as April, 1782, he had sent a fugue that he had composed to his sister with the words: "The cause of this fugue's coming into the world is really my dear Constanze." His bride had quite lost her heart to the fugue. "She will hear nothing but fugues, and then only Handel and Bach." We find him playing in delightful fashion with the fugue in the first of his quartets dedicated to Joseph Haydn. As to his compositions for the piano in fugal form, they may be said to be positively stilted. The pianoforte fugue was exhausted as a form, had become a foundation with no sub-soil. Just as in architecture, so in music, one style replaces another, and there is no looking back, except for the eclectic. It would be difficult for our store of symphonies to be enriched, and can we seriously expect anything like a revival of the sonata in its classical form? Modern exponents of these forms, be they, like Max Reger, never so important, can be no more than eclectics. Busoni has showed himself to be an innovator in archaising—if one may say such a thing—in so far as he "adapted" J.S. Bach, made him free for us; picked out for us all that is imperishable in him, many a treasure of his pianoforte music to which we should never have gained access without him.

Mozart arranged in an extremely fascinating manner a Bach fugue and incorporated it in one of his string quartets. The fugue which he originally wrote in 1783 for two pianos and rewrote for strings in 1788, adding a superb adagio for two violins, viola and violoncello, is a magnificent work of art. The prelude in which the themes represent the *dramatis personae* is not only superbly beautiful, but charged with almost poignant emotions.[1]

Name days played a great role in the Mozart family. A visit by Wolfgang, who wished to introduce Constanze to his father and the curious townsfolk of Salzburg, had been arranged for Leopold's name-day, which fell on November 15th. But the journey had to be postponed because Wolfgang could not afford to miss his lessons and because the concert season was just beginning. And so Wolfgang and his wife, then, took part in all the festivities of the Vienna Carnival, and the convivial side of Mozart, the clown, the dancer, now came into its own. How beautifully he must have danced! He himself gave a ball with Constanze, who could no longer get about much, for a child was already on the way. They went together to a masked ball, where in a harlequinade improvised by himself, he appeared as Harlequin, Joseph Lange as Pierrot and Aloysia as Columbine. The latter's marriage was generally considered to be unhappy. On the other hand she was no longer troubled by her husband's jealousy, and Mozart was able to see her again and write arias for her to his heart's content. Had he grown indifferent to her? Who, knowing how many selves dwelt within him, could say? Constanze took up an inordinately large share of Mozart's life, but she was mistress of only a fragment of his being. It is well known that a peculiar fate dogged the compositions which he dedicated to her. They were all provided with tender inscriptions but none of them, not even the delightful Bandl Trio, was finished. Even the magnificent C minor Mass remained a fragment. It was performed on August 23rd, 1783, in the Peterskirche in Salzburg, presumably supplemented by portions of his other Masses. Constanze sang the soprano part. It was for her sake—in fulfilment of a vow that "he had made in his heart" in the event of his marrying her—

[1] Adagio and Fugue for strings (K.546).

that he wrote the Mass; it is a thanksgiving Mass, a Mass of rejoicing, and its central feature is the *Qui tollis* which calls from the depths with all the solemnity of the psalmist and in almost intolerable accents of fear. How light and conciliatory are in comparison the choruses of the spirits, nay, even of the fiends of hell, in Gluck. In Mozart we find another realm than that of the shades. The realm of the impenetrable, the realm of dread in face of the all-devouring grave, the accusing, all-shattering hand of death. One understands only too well why Mozart reacted so violently to types such as the *Bäsle* and Constanze, became caught up in the very circumscription of their natures, their irresponsibility, found refuge and satisfaction in them. For he loved the world and life—it was in spite of himself that he was more experienced in ultimate things. His was less a demonic nature than one possessed by demons! Here, at any rate, lies the secret of his personality. We learn nothing as to his relations with women to whom he was bound by a more spiritual tie. It is indeed strange that not a single letter to the Countess Thun, not one to Josefa Duschek, is extant, not one to Frau von Trattner, to whom Mozart's *Appassionata*, the great C minor Fantasia, is dedicated, the only indication we have of this friendship or possibly love. Through many a chamber of his heart Mozart paced without ever again granting us a glimpse into them. The surrender he had once made of his feelings in the case of Aloysia, the trust he had reposed in her, had remained all too sore a point with him. How open in comparison lies the emotional life of Goethe, of Hölderlin, of Beethoven, of Wagner! In Mozart's case we have only the unambiguous letters to Constanze and the *Bäsle* to go upon. And at this point the latter disappears from the scene. To an enquiry on her part as to his betrothal, a rumour of which had reached Augsburg, he does not answer frankly, but by his failure to deny it says quite enough.

"Vienna, October 21st, 1781.

"Ma très chère cousine,

"I had been eagerly awaiting a letter from you, dearest *Bäsle,* and as I had imagined, so it turned out. For after having let three months go by I should never have written, even had the executioner with the naked sword been at my back, for I should not have known how, when, where, what and why. I had of necessity to wait for a letter.

"Meanwhile, as you doubtless know, many important things have happened to me, which have given me not a little to think about, and a great deal of vexation, trouble and worry, which also indeed may serve as an excuse for my long silence. As for all else in this connection, I must tell you that the gossip that people are pleased to spread about concerning me is in part true and in part false. More I cannot say at the moment, except, to set your mind at rest, that I take no step without reason, and, moreover, good reason. Had you shown more friendship towards me and confidence in me, and applied directly to me (and not to others)—if, I say, you had applied directly to me, you would certainly have known more than anyone, and, were it possible, more than—I myself! Nevertheless, I hope that our correspondence, dearest *Bäsle*, will now flourish all the more! If, as I hope, you will honour me with a reply, do me the favour of addressing your letter as before to *Im Auge Gottes*, in the Petersplatz, second floor . . .

"And now adieu, dearest and best *Bäsle*, and permit me to retain your friendship which is so precious to me. You are absolutely assured of mine. I am always,

"Ma très chère cousine,

"Your sincere cousin and friend,

"Wolfgang Amidé Mozart."

She does not appear to have complied with his request to write. It was one thing to retire in favour of the dazzling

Aloysia, but quite another to be put in the shade by Constanze, and she knew the Webers from the Munich days.

Only twice more does she find mention.

Mozart's letters to her, which, it is true, betray disparagement of her, but which constitute for us important documentary evidence, she kept and bequeathed to posterity.

Salzburg for the Last Time

IN AUGUST, 1783, THE YOUNG COUPLE PAID THEIR LONG deferred visit to Salzburg, and stayed with Leopold. Raimund Leopold, the child born to them on June 17th, was put out to nurse in the country, where he died during his parents' absence. Even apart from this, the visit turned out badly in every respect. Father and daughter joined forces in their mutual antipathy to Constanze; they realised only too soon with disappointment that she was no exception to the rest of her family. It may be that Mozart himself had ceased to have any illusions about her; there are many reasons for believing that this was so. But as a loyal husband he was bound to her for better or worse. Her well-being came before his own. He lacked that minimum of ruthlessness that men with a mission—and infinitely less important men than he—positively regard as a duty to themselves. He therefore pampered this far from modest or unassuming wife of his, while she for her part lived side by side with him in utter unawareness of his greatness; he was, in fact, thrown away upon her. The poor opinion that Leopold entertained of her and of which he may have let her be too plainly aware, did not make things any easier. He was determined not to hand over any of the costly presents that had been showered by emperors and princes on the child prodigy, Mozart. And Wolfgang took umbrage at this, particularly because of the effect it had on Constanze. It can be safely assumed that, having inherited her fair share of her mother's cupidity, she nagged him about these presents. We have, it is true, no stable picture of her, but contemporaries are unanimous in declaring that the greatest disorder and confusion reigned in her household. Mozart's remissness in financial matters in no way helped things, and from 1783 on, debts began to pile up. Of Constanze we are told:

"As the wife of Mozart, Constanze abandoned herself to her zest for life and frivolity. Very soon she came to regard, not her husband, but herself, as the focal point round which their poverty-stricken household revolved. She became capricious, discontented, coquettish and jealous. Every now and then she created the most impossible scenes. He, the infinitely peaceable, untiringly kindly, ever unselfish Mozart, who would have adapted himself to any woman, knew how to manage her skilfully, how to control and dispel the more vulgar elements in her nature. He did not remain faithful to her for long, but one can only say that Mozart loved his 'Stanzi' precisely as a Mozart can love a Constanze. He did everything to please her. He knew from long habit how to get round her. He always knew how to put her in a good humour. He liked to play the clown for her benefit, as he had formerly done for that of his parents and his sister, or, to put it more mildly, the role of the ever merry, jolly, light-hearted comrade, the protective, tender, doting husband. Many a friend and acquaintance of the modest Mozart household would come upon the high-spirited and merry young couple Singing and chattering and dancing about just like Papageno and Papagena in *Die Zauberflöte* . . .

"Wolfgang Amadé shared with her his earthly existence, the banal joys and sorrows of everyday life, but not the sacred and inviolate paradise of his dreams . . . "

We are told, on the other hand, that "Mozart was happy in his marriage with Constanze Weber. He found in her a kind and loving wife, who was admirably able to adapt herself to his temperament, thereby winning his entire confidence, and gaining a power over him that she only used in order to restrain him from rash actions. He loved her truly, confided everything to her, even his petty misdemeanours, and she rewarded him with affection and loyal solicitude . . ."

We get a glimpse of the depressed mood in which Mozart left his father and sister after this, his last, visit to Salzburg, in the letter of thanks that he wrote from Linz on the homeward journey, dated October 31st, 1783. The couple lingered there over four weeks, and stayed with the old Count Thun, an enthusiastic patron of Mozart's. There he wrote "pell-mell" the Symphony in C (K.425), which was performed as early as November 4th. Not until December 5th were the Mozarts back in Vienna.

❧

Life in Vienna-I

FROM 1782 TO THE SPRING OF 1786—IT WAS NOT UNTIL then that Mozart set to work on his next opera—he produced seventy-four compositions, for the most part chamber works. Joseph Haydn, of whom Mozart said that it was only through him that he learned "how to write a quartet", was the only friend of his own calibre at this period. This friendship became more and more cordial, despite the great disparity of age between the two of them. Leopold's usual warnings had come too late to interfere with this particular friendship. When he visited his son in 1785 he found it a *fait accompli.*

Hadyn, through his appointment as *Kapellmeister* to Prince Esterhazy, had, it is true, achieved some measure of security, but he too had not managed to convince the Emperor of his worth, and his enemies saw to it that the musical "jokes" of this outsider, as they regarded him, were not taken seriously. Haydn took the machinations of the "enviers" and "carpers", as he called them, very much to heart. All the more consoling, therefore, did he find the unstinted admiration of Mozart, whose greatness he for his part never wearied of proclaiming to all and sundry. "Could I," he wrote in 1787, in a letter to Prague, "make every lover of music appreciate the inimitable works of Mozart with the fervour and depth of feeling with which I understand and feel them, the nations would compete with each other to possess such a treasure within their frontiers. Prague should keep the precious man—but should also remunerate him; for without such remuneration the fate of great geniuses is a sorry one, and gives posterity little encouragement to make further efforts, wherefore, alas, so many promising geniuses languish." True words, preached to deaf ears! "Forgive me," he concludes, "for digressing thus; I love the man so."

Don Giovanni, produced in 1788, found him somewhat out of his depth, but his only contribution to the violent controversy that was raging round it in Vienna, was: "I do not rightly understand what the dispute is all about, but one thing I know, and that is that Mozart is the greatest composer that the world possesses to-day."

The two masters only saw each other during the winter months, which Prince Esterhazy spent in Vienna, for at other times he was very grudging in the granting of leave. When in 1790, Esterhazy died, Haydn, it is true, moved to Vienna, but that same year received an invitation to go to London, which, to Mozart's great distress, he accepted. On the day of his departure, Haydn felt himself constrained to proffer comfort to the friend who was so much younger than he but who was already overshadowed by a presentiment of death. The two, indeed, never met again. "For some considerable time," wrote Haydn from London in 1792 to Puchberg, "I was beside myself at his death and could not believe that Providence should summon so early to the other world a man who was irreplaceable."

He was unable to restrain his tears when recalling Mozart's playing of the piano. "Had he written nothing else," he once said, "but his violin quartets and the Requiem, they alone would have rendered him immortal."

"My friends often flatter me that I possess some genius, but he stood far above me," was his final verdict.

Mozart took enormous trouble, as he himself confessed to Haydn, on the six string quartets that are dedicated to him (K.387, 421, 428, 458, 464 and 465). Of the fifth quartet, Beethoven said: "It is indeed a masterpiece. In it Mozart says to the world: 'See what I could have done had your time come.'" He also greatly admired the magnificent Piano Quintet in E major (K.452), of which Mozart himself said on April 10th, 1784: "I consider it to be the best thing I have ever written."

An entire literature has sprung up on the subject of Mozart's music for strings. His twenty-four piano concertos have been much less thoroughly dealt with. There are some wonderful passages in them. Fifteen of these concertos can be obtained without much difficulty; the rest appear to be as good as unknown. Of the eight most famous ones the one in D minor—it is not the most interesting—is most often performed.

No matter how beautifully these radiant allegros open and die away, they often seem to suggest a runner who puts on a spurt far too near the tape, a vessel overflowing; and a profound melancholy broods over all the grace and charm; the slow movements, with the exception of those in the D minor and C minor concertos, are sheer elegies. It is not his true self that the master is allowed to give us here. What did it matter to him that he was becoming the fashion in Vienna, that opportunities were coming along thick and fast, and that any concert at which he was not billed to perform was unattended, boast as he might to his father, to whom he knew the news would be welcome, of all this. He wrote to him frequently at this period, and with the old affection.

Presumably by 1784 he had become a member of the Vienna Lodge of Freemasons, *"Zur Wohltätigkeit"*, and when the Emperor Joseph established the Lodge of *"Die neugekrönte Hoffnung"*, he became a member of that too. Both were nothing but a disappointment; neither lived up to its name. Apart from Masonic music he composed various other works for his Lodge, whereas it did nothing for him, either when he fell on evil days or when he died—did nothing to ensure that he was given a burial worthy of him.

Of Mozart's outwardly very troubled life at this period we shall learn from Leopold's letters to his daughter. Not until February, 1785, did he return his son's visit, and when he did so he was unaccompanied by Nannerl, who in the summer of 1784, had married Reichsfreiherr Berchtold von Sonnenburg, a widower with five children, and now lived in St. Gilgen. In Leopold's presence even the Webers pulled themselves together, and he learned nothing of the true state of affairs.

(To his daughter in St. Gilgen.)

"Vienna, February 14th, 1785.

" . . . You may gather that your brother has fine quarters with all suitable appointments when I tell you that he pays a rent of 460 florins . . . On Saturday evening Herr Joseph Haydn and the two Barons Tindi visited us, and the new quartets were played, but only the three new ones that he has composed in addition to the other three which we already have.

They are somewhat easier, it is true, but admirably composed. Herr Haydn said to me: '*I swear to you before God, as a man of honour, that your son is the greatest composer that I know, either personally or by repute: he has taste, and beyond that a very great knowledge of composition.*'

"On Sunday evening Madame Laschi, the Italian singer who is about to return to Italy, gave a concert at the theatre. She sang two arias. A violincello concerto was performed, a tenor and a bass each sang an aria and your brother played a magnificent concerto that he had composed for Madame Paradies in Paris.[1] I was only two boxes away from the truly beautiful Princess of Würtemburg, and was so fortunate as to follow so perfectly the varied use of the instruments that tears of delight sprang into my eyes. When your brother left the stage, the Emperor stood hat in hand, bowing to him from his box, and shouted: 'Bravo, Mozart!' When he came on the stage to play, he was greeted, moreover, by a storm of applause . . ."

(To his daughter in Salzburg.)

"Vienna, February 21st, 1785

". . . This evening your brother is to perform at a big concert at the house of Count Zichy. . . . It will, no doubt, be one o'clock, as usual, before we get to bed. On Thursday, the 17th, we dined at the house of your brother's mother-in-law, Frau Weber; there were only the four of us, Frau Weber and her daughter Sophie, for the eldest daughter is in Gratz. I must say that the food was neither too abundant nor too little, and, moreover, was incomparably cooked: the roast was a fine large pheasant, and everything, altogether, admirably prepared. On Friday, the 18th, we dined with the younger Stephani, where there was no one but the four of us, Father Le Brun, his wife, Carl Cannabich and a priest. Well, as I have said, fast days are not to be thought of here. None but meat dishes were served, and the pheasant was garnished with greens; the rest was princely, oysters even, and the most marvellous sweetmeats,

[1] Marie Theresa von Paradies, a Viennese pianist.

not to mention a great many bottles of champagne. And, to crown all, coffee—that goes without saying . . .

"You can well imagine what has become of the *Bäsle* in Augsburg; a prebendary of the Cathedral has bestowed his affections on her. I intend shortly to write the very devil of a letter to Augsburg, as though I had come to hear of it in Vienna. The most diverting thing about it is that all the presents she received, thereby attracting everyone's attention—all of them, she said, were sent to her by her revered uncle in Salzburg. What an honour for me!"

So the *Bäsle* had strayed from the straight and narrow path.

(To his daughter in Salzburg.)

"Vienna, March 12th, 1785.

" . . . We never go to bed before one o'clock, and never rise till nine, and dine at half-past two. Abominable weather! A concert every day, constant study, music, writing, etc. where is there for me to go? If only the concerts were over! The fuss and bother are indescribable. Your brother's fortepiano has been carried to the theatre or to some other house at least twelve times since I have been here. He has had a huge *fortepiano pedale* made which stands under the instrument, and is about three spans longer and astonishingly heavy; it is taken to the Mehlgrube every Friday, and also to Count Zichy's and Prince Kaunitz's."

Mozart was in the very centre of the musical life of Vienna, and purely superficially his position was not devoid of brilliance. "I believe," wrote Leopold on March 12th to his daughter, "that my son, *if he has no debts to pay*, should now be in a position to deposit 2,000 florins in the bank." Was it because he did not entirely believe this himself that he underlined the words? And the longer he stayed the more did his aversion to Constanze gain ground. True, she was on her guard in the presence of her dreaded father-in-law, but she could never control herself for long. Leopold's visit was extended for longer than he himself cared for. The winter of this year was exceptionally severe . . . Frost and snow made the streets impassable right into the month of April. Leopold was threatened by his old enemy, rheumatism, the rooms in the young Mozart's house were poorly heated, and there was too much coming and going and bustle for the old man. Almost every day they dined out; and the Mozarts were once more on lively visiting terms with the Langes. "I have seen Mdme Lange (Weber) . . . she sang both times and played admirably. We all dined at Herr Lange's . . . and to-morrow they dine with us. On Easter Sunday we are to dine with a banker, on Monday with Herr Dr. Rhab, Tuesday with Herr von Ployer . . . " On April 8th Leopold believed himself to be on the point of departure; he intended, he wrote, to go first to Munich, did not yet know what his address would be, and exhorted Nannerl to write a letter that would be sent on to him, and *"that your brother too can read"*. So little frankness now obtained between him and these children of his. The weather was so inclement that it was April 25th before he could set out. "Your brother and sister-in-law were firmly resolved to accompany me on the journey," he wrote on April 16th, "but now there is a hitch again and I expect nothing will come of it, although they have each had six pairs of shoes made, which have already been delivered."

In the end the young couple did after all accompany him as far as Linz.

"We left Vienna at last at half-past ten on the 25th in the company of your brother and his wife, ate a midday meal together in Burgersdorf, after which they returned to Vienna." That is all. The parting was no doubt a relief to all concerned.

But scarcely was Leopold back at home than he was bored to death. An everlastingly discontented man, Hasse called him. "I cannot deny," he was writing from Salzburg as early as May 27th, "that time hangs heavy on my hands and will hang ever heavier in the coming week when the theatre closes. For I went for some four months to all sorts of places and met a great many people.

"And where is there for me to go now? Is there anyone with whom I can converse intelligently? I do not know whether it is that I am too clever for many of them, or that some of them are too stupid for me! In short, I feel a sorry deprivation of the company that I enjoyed in Vienna, Linz and Munich. The Corpus Christi procession went off well yesterday; only during the last salvos at Court did it begin to rain a little. Count Arco sent an umbrella for me . . ." He cannot refrain from mentioning this.

At Linz he had taken leave of Mozart for ever. Whether because he had no time to write oftener, or because he had less and less to say to him, Wolfgang's letters to his father are from now on more and more infrequent. The pecuniary difficulties that had been so carefully hidden from him, continued to increase. All in all, he earned no less, and at times a great deal more, than other musicians; but as a result of his incompetence in managing his household affairs, and his open-handedness, which was often so ruthlessly exploited, his modest income melted away, and in the meantime his prospects as a composer, instead of improving, dwindled. In spite of the success of *Die Entführung*, his reputation as a composer was not high; he did not manage to get his *Idomeneo* put on in Vienna, while both his church music and his early operas were practically unknown. He abandoned all work on the drafts of operas such as *Zaide, l'Oca del Cairo*, and *Il Sposo deluso*, for he was constitutionally unable to complete a composition unless there were definite prospects of its being performed and unless it had been officially commissioned. He was devoured by impatience, and often the patience which he nevertheless summoned up gave way to moods of profound discouragement. A dramatist by the name of Anton Klein, from Mannheim, who had sent him the libretto for an opera entitled, *Rudolf von Habsburg*, received from him the following letter:

"Highly esteemed Herr Geheimrath,

" . . . I can as yet give you very little news of the proposed German Opera, since, apart from the reconstruction work which has already been begun on the Kärntnerthor Theatre, which has been set apart for the purpose, everything is proceeding very slowly. It is to be opened at the beginning of October. I for my part do not anticipate it will have much success. To judge from the present plans, it would seem that they are attempting rather to deal a death-blow to German opera, which is perhaps only temporarily on the wane, than to restore it once more and foster it. My sister-in-law, Madame Lange, is the only one who has been given permission to sing at the German opera. Madame Cavallieri, Adamberger, Madame Teuber, all German singers, of whom Germany may well be proud, are to remain with the Italian opera, as rivals of their own fellow countrymen! The number of German singers, male and female, at the present time, can easily be counted, and even should there be any as good as those I have named, or even better, and that I greatly doubt, I yet think that the directors of the theatre here are too cheese-paring and not sufficiently patriotic to dream of paying large sums to get singers from elsewhere to come here when better, or at least as good, singers are to be had here in Vienna— and for nothing; for the Italian company does not require them; as far as numbers go, it is self-sufficient. The present plan is for the German opera to make shift with actors and actresses who will only sing when required. Most unfortunately, the directors both of the theatre and of the orchestra, who by their ignorance and apathy have contributed most of all to the failure of their own project, are to continue in office. Were there but one single patriot among them, the matter would take on quite a different complexion! Then, after all, perhaps the budding National Theatre would burst into blossom, and what an everlasting disgrace it would be to Germany if we Germans once seriously began to think in German, to act like Germans, to speak German, and above all, to sing in German . . . "

But how wholeheartedly are we ready, at all times and in all circumstances, to declare our undying allegiance to a German cultural tradition such as *he* personified!

❧

Figaro

IT WAS ALMOST FOUR YEARS SINCE MOZART HAD COMPOSED *Die Entführung*. A *Singspiel* entitled *Der Impresario (The Impresario)*, a trifle composed for a special occasion, was the only dramatic task with which he found himself confronted. It was performed for the benefit of the Imperial Court in the orangery at Schönbrunn, with Adamberger, Aloysia and Madame Cavalieri as the principal singers. It must have been with secret fury that Mozart acknowledged the polite compliments of the evening, and can we not once more almost glimpse in a flash the fire and pallor of his countenance. With his carefree, mercurial temperament, he was able, indeed, to make light of all his troubles except one: the consuming bitterness at not being able to put his now mature powers to a test worthy of them, at seeing them, whenever they were manifested, over and over again disregarded or discredited.

Yet in one respect the frustrations of his existence were

now nearing their end. He was already contemplating the composition of *Figaro*, and was able, as though with outstretched wings, to abandon himself to his genius. His time had come. Happy Mozart, despite all the sufferings that lay ahead of him!

In consequence of the collapse of the German *Singspiel,* which had at first been taken up and afterwards dropped by the Emperor, Italian opera—in particular *opera buffa*—received fresh and vigorous impetus. Mozart was passed over in both fields. Not only did Salieri, the Emperor's favourite composer, and musicians like Cimarosa and Paisiello, bar his path; but celebrities who are as unknown today as Bonno, Martini,[1] Neumann and so on, were his favoured rivals. Not for ever could things continue thus; a turning point in Mozart's life was bound to come. Otherwise one would be convinced of the utter pointlessness of all things, even of a life such as his.

As early as 1783 he had made the acquaintance of the librettist Lorenzo da Ponte. Da Ponte was born at Ceneda, near Venice. By birth a Jew, he had been baptised a Christian at the age of fourteen, and received into the priesthood in 1773, later assuming the title of Abbate da Ponte. He came to Vienna in the year 1781 with a letter of recommendation to Salieri. He was eccentric, clever, and adventurous, and was reputed to be as vain as he was cunning. The legend of his cunning is contradicted by the fact that, later in life, he was to be reduced to dire poverty and to die in penury. However that may be, he has an eternal claim on our gratitude for the services he rendered Mozart. He was fully alive to real greatness, was possessed of exceptional critical faculties, and instinctively recognised Mozart's genius; a fact which did not prevent him from first coming

[1] Vicente Martin y Soler.

to an understanding with Wolfgang's more successful rival. He started off brilliantly with a libretto after a piece by Goldoni, but then had bad luck with Gazzaniga, Righini, and above all Salieri, after which he got into touch with Mozart. It was Mozart who asked him, so he relates, whether he would write a libretto on the sensation of the day—Beaumarchais' *Figaro ou la folle journée*. The libretto was completed by July, 1785, and Mozart, although he had received no official commission, was now able to set to work with more confidence. Da Ponte, although he had not managed to succeed the late Metastasio as *poeta Caesareo*, was highly esteemed by the Emperor Joseph, who set some store by his judgment. In his memoirs, which, it is true, he only wrote at a much later date, he describes the whole story as follows:

"I set to work, and while I wrote the libretto, Mozart composed the music to it. In six weeks the whole thing was completed. Mozart's lucky star ordained it that operas were the very thing the theatre lacked. Without saying a word to anyone, I took the first suitable opportunity of submitting Figaro to the Emperor himself. What did he say? 'You know that Mozart, excellent as he may be as a composer of instrumental music, has up to now written but one single opera (*Die Entführung*)—and that was no great matter. And besides, I have forbidden *Die Hochzeit des Figaro* in the Kärtnerthor-Theatre.' 'Yes, Sire,' I said, 'but since my task was to write an opera and not a comedy, I had to omit several scenes and shorten most of them, with particular reference to anything that might offend the decorum of a Court theatre. As for the music, it is, in so far as I can judge, very fine.' 'Good,' replied the Emperor; 'if that is so, I shall rely on your good taste for the music, and on your skill for the propriety, of the opera.'" Da Ponte's skill consisted in despoiling the character of the hero of its bold outlines; he was not by nature a creative artist, and furthermore he was inhibited by considerations which he could not afford to ignore. Thus his attenuated Figaro had at most a certain gaiety and versatility in common with that of Beaumarchais' hero, and was for the rest a true servant of his master, in accordance with the prevailing tradition. But what did Mozart care? The feminine vein in his artist's nature invariably triumphed over all questions of theory; political standpoints, political considerations, were all too prosy matters to fetter his genius. It was purely *instinctively* that he had by his attitude championed the principles of true equality. He threw a perfectly natural light on Figaro's challenge to the Count. But as for slogans, programmes, ideologies, oh, how inconceivable is a Mozart in our mechanised world! Is not to make the recluse gregarious really to place him all the more in solitary confinement? Mozart's becoming a mason was in itself an anomaly. One has only to try to imagine him as a conscript, as a recruit, as a member of a party, to realise this. The utter incongruity of such absurd contingencies characterises him more clearly than anything else.

Figaro was entered in the catalogue of his works on April 29th, 1786. Three days later the first performance took place. Despite all the machinations that were on foot to prevent it. The Emperor was not the man to go back on his word. He was present at the dress rehearsal, and the Irishman Michael Kelly, who took the role of Basilio—an enthusiastic devotee of Mozart, who left behind so many interesting reminiscences of him—describes the ovation accorded the composer by the members of the orchestra. Mozart's collaboration with da Ponte had been of the happiest nature, and he was also fortunate this time in his singers. The five-and-twenty-year-old Nancy Storace, who was as beautiful as she was talented, captivated everyone in the part of Susanna. The material was so rich and so diverse that nothing could spoil it for him; it offered him inspiration in full measure; its shortcomings vanished in the consuming flame of his music. Even in its lesser moments it is winged; at no point is it bombastic. It is the light cloud in the summery sky; not a leaf is as yet withered and even the night is clear. It is not the ocean-blue, luminous in the shade, of Bach, nor the sculptured stateliness of Gluck, nor the metallic splendour of Handel's rhythms, nor is it any longer the clear note, almost Arcadian in its limpidity, of Haydn's reed. His music might be symbolised by the serene shimmer of pearls. The arias, duets, and finales in *Figaro* are strung together like pearls on a silken thread, and it was inevitable that such magic, so much perfection, should charm only a small band of devotees and in general should nonplus its hearers. Count Zinzendorf, a dilettante, who wrote a "Musical Diary" held in great esteem at that time, and who had already remarked with regard to *Die Entführung* that "the music was plagiarised", was undoubtedly expressing the feelings of the public when, after the première of *Figaro*—Zinzendorfs never miss a first night—he pronounced the following verdict: "May 1st, 1786, at seven o'clock in the evening, at the Opera House, *Die Hochzeit des Figaro*. The libretto is by da Ponte, the music by Mozart. The opera bored me." In his diary of July 4th, he notes: "Mozart's music is strange; hands without a head."

But let us listen to other, more appreciative opinions of it: *"Mozart n'amuse jamais. C'est comme une maîtresse sérieuse et souvent triste, mais qu'on aime davantage, précisément à cause de sa tristesse,"* wrote Stendhal, who swept away, even before it arose, the legend of Mozart's "gaiety". How underpinned is that gaiety, indeed, by suffering! And how well did Mozart, allegedly so poor a judge of human nature, see through the human heart. It is his "*tristesse*" on which Stendhal constantly insists. It was only by slow degrees that he found his way to him. So wedded to Italian music that he desired to be Paisiello's lackey, he hesitated for a very long time between Cimarosa and Mozart before finally pledging himself to the latter: "*Je ferai dix lieues à pied par la crotte, la chose que je déteste le plus au monde, pour assister à une répresentation de Don Juan bien joué.*" "*Bien joué,*" he felt constrained to add; a mediocre performance of this opera is torture. Stendhal's judgment was unerring, a thing by no means so common in the case of great writers as one might imagine; the lack of it, it is true, detracts considerably from their greatness. So keen were Stendhal's powers of discrimination that he could even afford to play the prophet—both as regards himself and others. It is interesting to note how he records the fluctuations in the reception of Mozart's music on the part of the Latin public: "*Mozart . . . comme tous les grands artistes, n'ayant jamais cherché qu'à se plaire à lui-même, et aux gens qui lui ressemblaient . . . ne pouvait se flatter de prendre la société que par les sommités; ce rôle est toujours dangereux.*" Years after his death Mozart was looked upon by the Romans as a barbarian and his work was considered to have been over-estimated. "*Mozart n'aura jamais en Italie le succès dont il jouit en Allemagne et en Angleterre,*" Stendhal predicts. In the year 1823 he writes: "*Mozart est à la mode dans la haute société, qui, quoique necessairement sans passions prétend toujours faire croire, qu'elle a des passions, et qu'elle est éprise des grandes passions. Tant que cette mode durera, l'on ne pourra pas juger avec sûreté du véritable effet de sa musique sur le cœur humaine.*" Then the Rossini craze set in. Mozart was once more thrust into the background. In Germany, about the middle of the century, Richard Wagner was lamenting that "the infinite charm and subtlety of Mozart's tonal structures appear dull and tedious to the grotesquely pampered public of to-day."

We shall see how Prague reacted to *Figaro*. In the year 1786, it was performed nine times in Vienna, and then not put on again until August, 1789. In the Emperor Joseph's eyes Mozart remained a brilliant virtuoso and a mediocre composer, who considerably over-estimated his own talents. Now as ever he was not taken seriously.

❧

Life in Vienna —II

THE SUCCESS OF *FIGARO* HAD THUS BROUGHT ABOUT no external change in Mozart's life, though it must have effected a spiritual change in him, for he had stood the test in his own eyes, and in the face of his consciousness of his own greatness such things as success or failure no longer carried weight. His attitude, too, to the world around him was no longer what it had been. This world had ceased to be his native element; he had shaken off all his illusions with regard to its constitution, and no longer buoyed himself up with sanguine hopes as in the Munich days during the production of *Idomeneo*. He no longer visualised himself as the owner of a splendid house and garden. Such dreams were now replaced by premonitions of early death.

He continued to follow the hated profession of a music teacher. 'You happy man! Oh, how happy should I be could I but accompany you,' he said to Gyrowetz,[1] who was set-

[1] Gryowetz, Autobiograhy.

ting out for Italy. 'You see, I have now to give another lesson so as to earn something.' No wonder that he appeared to his pupils on first acquaintance to be so cold and aloof. This was what the young Beethoven[2] found him, and the famous Dr. Frank, who in the year 1790 took lessons from him, describes him in the following terms: 'I found Mozart to be a small man with a large head and fleshy hands, who received me somewhat coldly. Well, he said, play me something. I played him a fantasia of his own. Not bad, he said, to my great astonishment, now I shall make you listen to it. Beneath his fingers the piano became a completely different instrument. He had reinforced it with a second instrument, which served him as a pedal. Mozart then made some observations as to the manner in which his fantasia should be executed, and I had the good fortune to understand him. Can you play any other of my compositions ?—Yes, sir, I replied. Your variations on the theme, *Unser dummer Pöbel meint* and a sonata with violin and violincello accompaniment.—Good, I shall play you that. It will be of more profit to you to listen to me than to play it yourself.' God knows it must have been.

Nevertheless he took the lad Hummel (born 1778), who so ardently worshipped him, into his house. Hummel was permitted, moreover, to play with him at Court and left him only at the end of 1787 in order to go on a concert tour with his father.

Sometimes a pupil who turned up, armed with his music, would be asked to join in a game of billiards instead

[2] The seventeen-year-old Beethoven went to see Mozart in the spring of 1787, and made a great impression on the Master, who, moreover, gave him one or two lessons in composition. Beethoven complained later that Mozart had never played to him. He had, he is said to have declared to Czerny, a subtle but disjointed touch, no *legato*. We know nothing definite about this interesting encounter between the two composers.

of playing the piano, or be given his lesson in the intervals of a game of skittles.

The reasons for his being unable to stave off financial ruin are perfectly clear, though it remains unexplained just why it should have overtaken him at a time when such considerable sums of money were pouring in that even his father was impressed, when his concerts were the very centre of public interest, the nobility only subscribing to those announced in his name, and when the proceeds from them sometimes amounted to 1,600 florins or more. On one occasion also he gave a concert with Aloysia Lange. To the aria *Non so d'onde viene,* composed for her in the days of his infatuation, he had added a set of fresh variations. We wonder what she must have felt as he accompanied her. And he, whom she had so spurned, who was now the darling of all the women and had won all their hearts, what was his attitude to her? We do not know. At this concert he also conducted the symphony composed for the *Concert Spirituel* in Paris, and once more, as he relates to his father, Gluck made overtures to him. 'Gluck had the box next to that of the Langes, in which my wife was also seated. He could not praise the symphony and the aria enough, and invited us all four to dine with him next Sunday.'

The numerous private concerts, already mentioned, arranged at the house of the Russian Ambassador, Prince Galitsin and in the Palais of Prince Auersperg, who also arranged for a performance of Mozart's child of sorrow, *Idomeneo*, also proved very lucrative. This was the period of a still hopeful, usually cheerful, and extremely sociable Mozart. His easy manner, his aristocratic lack of constraint, his amiable and chivalrous nature, combined withal with a profound sense of his own worth, at once impressed and charmed. No details of his friendship with

Prince Carl Lichnowsky have been recorded. His relations with Count August Hatzfeld, whose early death he took so much to heart, developed into a more intimate friendship. The thing that had charmed people about Mozart as a child had been, even more than his playing, his improvising. And now it exerted an indescribable spell. 'If I might ask of God one more earthly joy,' said Niemetschek as an old man, 'it would be once more to hear Mozart improvising on the piano; no one who has not heard him can have the remotest idea of what he could do.'

In the year 1851 there died an eighty-year-old choirmaster who could still remember his playing. "As a young man I admired many a virtuoso both on the violin and on the piano, but picture my amazement when I was privileged to hear the immortal and great W. A. Mozart not only play variations but also improvise on the piano before a vast audience. To me his playing was creation of quite another character from any that I had hitherto been accustomed to hearing and seeing. Even the most accomplished master of music could not sufficiently admire and marvel at the way his fantasy soared up to the heights and then swooped down again into the depths. I can still, now that I am an old man, hear those heavenly, incomparable harmonies resounding in my ears, and shall go to my grave in the fullest conviction that there has been only one Mozart." In the year 1799 the following paragraph appeared in a notice about Beethoven: "He shows himself to the greatest advantage in his improvising. Since the death of Mozart, who in this sphere still remains for me the *ne plus ultra*, I have never experienced this pleasure to such a degree as when listening to Beethoven."

Mozart also gave concerts on Sunday morning at his own house, not only to friends, but to a paying public; and costly presents, as we know, were showered on him. How did it come about that he was already in such serious financial straits that first the Baroness Waldstätten had to help him out, then Hofmeister, the publisher? Some have blamed his extravagance, his penchant for fine clothes, choice laces, trinkets and watch-ribbons, others his undisciplined mode of life, which was entirely lacking in solidity. Mozart always gave occasion for a great deal of gossip. That he did not waste much time in keeping of accounts or budgeting we can well believe. And yet in the year 1784, when he was beginning to be very well off, he made a beginning by opening a book in which for a whole year he noted down all his expenses and receipts, even entering with gusto one kreutzer for "two sprays of lily-of-the-valley" and 34 kreutzer for the bird-seed for his beloved "Stahrl". Then of course he lost patience, and confined himself to keeping a careful catalogue of his compositions until the day of his death, leaving the task of entering up the housekeeping book to Constanze. Very soon, however, she too ceased to bother about it. It was her negligence and slovenliness that were mainly responsible for the decline in the family fortunes. She was often ailing—although always very much alive and kicking when some diversion or a journey was contemplated—and was always demanding to be sent to a spa, even at times when Mozart did not know where to turn for money. But she left that to him. She, who was one day to prove herself to be such a capable business woman, rivalled him in one point alone: her fecklessness. Was she to pinch and scrape whilst he kept open house and entertained buffoons? His sister-in-law, Sophie Haibl, complained of the "false friends, blood-suckers, although he did not realise it, worthless people, who only served to amuse him and association with whom injured his reputation". True, he was an easy prey for such people, and, too, he was shamelessly swindled in many other respects; by publishers, for example, who infringed his copyright. Yet even more than all this, than his alleged debauchery, his helplessness in practical matters, it was a certain princely open-handedness, to the tragic side of which we shall return, that prevented him from ever placing his financial affairs on a sound basis.

An acute crisis set in soon after the production of *Figaro*. He may well have lost all desire to shine before a public that acknowledged in him the virtuoso and improviser, but not the creative musical genius. Following his own inclination, he now went his ever more lonely way. Not that he lacked friends and admirers, even though increasingly few in number, who completely and entirely appreciated his importance. Amongst these was his family doctor, Dr. Sigmund Barisani[1] of Salzburg, who twice nursed him through a violent attack of influenza, and who looked upon him as his protégé.

Since Mozart was in the habit of working late into the night and starting again early in the morning, but had

[1] Interesting in this connection are some verses written in an album by Barisani, the following lines of which we quote:

> If that thine art, in which none else with thee
> Save but a Bach or Haydn can compare
> Should one day bring its long deserved reward
> Forget not then thy faithful friend
> Who ever will with pleasure and with pride
> Remember 'twas his happy lot to tend
> Thee twice, and as physician to preserve thee
> For the world's great delight; but who is prouder far
> To know thou art his friend, as he is ever
> Thy friend Sigmund Barisani.

Vienna, April 14th, 1787.

On the day of Barisani's death Mozart wrote the following lines at given up his morning ride, Barisani advised him to compose in a standing position or to get some exercise by playing billiards and skittles; particularly since the latter occupation did not interfere with his work of composing. It was thus that he wrote part of *Don Giovanni* when staying with the Duscheks in Prague. When his turn came along, he would get up to throw the ball, and then immerse himself once more in work.

In the autumn of 1786 Mozart for the second time conceived the plan of leaving Vienna and travelling via Germany to London, and he asked his father to take charge of his two children, the youngest of whom was only some weeks old. Leopold had taken Nannerl's baby son to live with him, without informing Wolfgang's family, but they had nevertheless come to hear of it. Reason enough for the greedy Constanze to try to procure a similar advantage for her own children! It was without doubt under pressure from her that the request was made to Leopold. But the old man's refusal was cold and resentful, and revealed the full extent of his aversion to the marriage of his son. He writes to his daughter in St. Gilgen on November 17th, 1786, from Salzburg:

> "I have to-day been obliged to answer a letter from your brother that has cost me a great deal of effort; and hence I can write but little to you . . . that I was obliged to write a very emphatic letter you may easily imagine when I tell you that he proposed nothing less than that I should take care of his two

at the bottom of this page of the album: "To-day, September 2nd of this year, I was so unfortunate as to lose quite unexpectedly by death this noble man, good friend and saviour of my life. It is well with him! But with me—with us, and all those who really knew him—it will never be well until we are so happy as to meet him again, never more to part, in a better world."

children, since he wished half way through the Carnival to make a tour through Germany to England; I, however, wrote firmly and promised to write to him further by the next post. . . A fine thing, I must say! They can set out on their travels without a qualm and remain in England, while I can go running after them with the children, or after the payment he offers for servants and children. Basta! My excuses are emphatic and, if he will take them to heart, instructive . . ."

For all his embitterment Leopold's interest in the fortunes of Mozart remained as keen as ever. A meeting was no longer contemplated, either in Vienna or in Salzburg. Yet the day was not very far off when in the face of death the old harmony and love between them would once more spring to life.

Meanwhile this refusal on the part of his father put an end to Mozart's plans for going to England, and did not exactly serve to enliven their correspondence.

'. . . I have not up to the present had a letter from your brother,' he writes to his daughter in St. Gilgen, Munich, on February 13th, 1787, 'and therefore do not know where he is . . .' For Wolfgang things had at last taken a turn for the better. At Christmas, 1786, he was requested to be present at a performance of his *Figaro* in Prague, and this Prague performance was an enormous success. In Prague, the true Mozartian town, he was to spend several happy weeks, and was there to enjoy most fully the rewards vouchsafed to a creative artist.

❧

Mozart in Prague

THE SINGER JOSEPHA DUSCHEK, WHOM WE KNOW FROM Salzburg, where in 1776 she won Mozart's enthusiastic admiration, lived in Prague in the most delightful circumstances; she was one of his most loyal friends and was untiring in her efforts on his behalf. Four years previously she had worked hard to ensure the success of *Die Entführung*, and more recently that of *Figaro*, which now, triumphant and unimpeded by cabals, reigned supreme on the Prague stage. Mozart, accompanied by Constanze, set out in high spirits for Prague, arriving there on January 11th. Hope—of a fresh commission for an opera—buoyed the heart that was so often cast down but was always so ready to rejoice.

Unlike many, possibly most, musicians, Mozart lived intensely through his visual senses, and his new surroundings, the Palais of Count Johann Thun, a great patron of music, whom he had known in Vienna, and by whom he and Constanze were welcomed as honoured guests, were in themselves calculated to raise his spirits. Once more the gay, worldly Mozart came to the fore, and all the tiresome money worries were relegated for a while into the background. In a letter written on January 15th to his friend, Gottfried von Jacquin, he describes a grand ball, at which he himself had not danced, it is true, because he was too tired.

"It gave me intense pleasure, however, to watch all these people hopping about so delightedly to the music of my *Figaro*, which was transformed into quadrilles and waltzes; for nothing is talked of here but *Figaro*, nothing played, whistled or sung but *Figaro*, no opera attended but *Figaro, Figaro*, everlastingly *Figaro*—very flattering to me, I am sure. Well, to return to the catalogue of my doings. Since I came home very late from the ball, and was, besides, very weary and sleepy after the journey, nothing in the world could be more natural than that I should sleep very late, which was precisely what I did do, and in consequence the whole of the next morning was again *sine linea*. After dinner there is always the Count's music, and as on the same day an excellent pianoforte was taken up to my room, you may well imagine that I did not leave it untouched and unplayed-upon for a whole evening; it went without saying that we should play a little *quatuor in cantatis camera* and the lovely *Bandl hammera*[1] and that the whole evening should be frittered away, again *sine linea*, in this manner. And that is precisely what did happen . . . Well, farewell, dearest friend, dearest Hikkiti Horky!—that is your name, you may like to know; we invented names for all of us on the journey, and that is yours. I am Punkitititi, my wife Schabla Pumfa; Hofer Rozka Pumpa, Stadler Notschibikitschibi, my man Joseph Sagadarata, Goukerl, my dog, Schomanntzky, Madame Quallenberg Runzifunzi, Mlle. Crux Ps, Ramlo Schurimuri, Freystädtler Goulimauli; have the kindness to inform the worthy latter gentleman of his new name. And now, adieu. Next Friday, the 19th, my concert is to be given in the

[1] K.441.

theatre; I expect to have to give a second, which will, I fear, prolong my stay here. Pray present my respects to your esteemed parents and your brother (whom we may as well call Blatterrizzi). Tell your sister (Signora Diniminiriri) I kiss her hand 100,000 times, and implore her to practise diligently on her new pianoforte, though such an admonition is unnecessary, for I must admit that I have never yet had a pupil who has shown herself to be so diligent and so zealous, and, indeed, I positively rejoice at the prospect of giving her further lessons, according to my humble capacity. *Á propos* if she would care to come to-morrow I shall most certainly be at home round about eleven o'clock . . .

"P.S. Address the letter that you may *possibly* write to me to the Palais Thun."

When, on January 17th, he entered the auditorium to attend a performance of his *Figaro*, he was given an unprecedented ovation, and when, on the 29th, he himself conducted, there was no end to the applause. Between these two performances he gave a concert. What would we not give to have been present on those occasions! How many evenings of our lives, how many years!—Niemetschek writes of it: "Never have I seen the theatre so full of people, never witnessed such intense and general delight as that aroused by his divine playing."

"At the conclusion of the concert," relates another contemporary, "Mozart improvised for a full half hour on the piano. His features glowed with inward satisfaction at the enthusiastic reception accorded him by the public. He was beginning for the third time with heightened enthusiasm and was playing miraculously, when suddenly someone called out in a loud voice from the deathly-silent audience: 'Something from *Figaro*!' Mozart thereupon began with the theme of the favourite air *Non piu andrai*, extemporised a dozen wonderful variations on it and finished amidst deafening applause."

The concert brought him in 3,000 florins, and the hoped-for contract with Bondini, the Director of the theatre, to write a new opera for the customary honorarium of 100 ducats was fixed up there and then. He now loved Prague more than ever. During this first visit he was actually to compose but little, owing to the innumerable distractions and festivities, but the Contredanses for Count Pachta and the six *Allemandes* (K.509) are dated February 6th, 1787.

About the middle of the month he was back again in Vienna. This year, which had begun so auspiciously, was to rob him of his best friends. Nancy Storace, Kelly and Attwood were the first to leave him, and he relapsed into such depression that he seriously contemplated following them to England so soon as they should have secured an appointment there for him. Indeed he wanted to go with them there and then.

Then on May 28th his father died. Wolfgang's last letter to him was dated April 4th.

"Mon très cher père,

"I am very annoyed that, owing to the stupidity of Mlle. Storace, my letter never came into your hands. Amongst other things I expressed the hope that you had received my last letter. Since, however, you make no mention of this letter (it was the second I wrote from Prague), I am at a loss what to think. It is very possible that one of Count Thun's servants thought fit to pocket the postage money. I would far rather pay double the postage than know my letters to be in the wrong hands. . . I have this moment received some news which greatly disturbs me, the more so as your last letter had led me to suppose that you were, God be praised, in excellent health. And now I hear that you are really ill! I need hardly say how ardently I hope for reassuring news from you yourself, indeed I confidently expect it, although I have accustomed myself in all things to anticipate the worst; for since death (strictly speaking) is the true goal of our life, I have during the past few years made myself so well acquainted with this true and best friend of mankind that the prospect of it no longer holds any terrors for me, but much that is soothing and comforting, and I thank God that He has blessed me with the opportunity (you will understand my meaning) of recognising in death the *key* to our true happiness. I never lie down to sleep without reflecting that (young as I am) I may never see another day; yet no one who knows me can say that I am morose or gloomy in company, for which blessing I daily thank my Creator and with all my heart wish the like happiness to my fellow men. In the letter (the one which Mlle. Storace despatched) I explained my sentiments on this point, when referring to the sad death of my very dear and good friend, Count von Hatzfeld.[1] He was just thirty-one—my own age. I do not grieve for him, but grieve profoundly for myself and all those who knew him as well as I did. I hope and trust that even as I write you may be much recovered; but if; contrary to my expectations, you are no better, I entreat you by . . . not to conceal it from me, but to write me, or have someone else write me, the honest truth, so that as soon as is humanly possible I may be in your arms. I conjure you-by all that we hold sacred. But I hope soon to receive comforting news from you, and in this agreeable hope, I and my wife and Carl[2] kiss your hands a thousand times, and am ever

"Your most obedient son,
"W. A. Mozart."
"Vienna, April 4th, 1787."

"To Gottfried Freiher von Jacquin in Vienna.
"Vienna, May 29th, 1927.

" . . . I write to tell you that on my return home to-day I received the sad news of the death of my very dear father. You may picture my state of mind."

[1] Count August Hatzfeld (born in Bonn, 1787).
[2] His son, born in 1784.

The slights that he had to endure in Vienna were doubly galling to him after his triumphs in Prague. Dittersdorf, with his *Doktor und Apotheker,* his *Betrug durch Aberglauben*, and his *Liebe im Narrenhause*, had in the meantime become the man of the moment, having secured the patronage of the Emperor, the hearts of the Viennese went out to him; and commissions poured in. It was fortunate for Mozart, indeed his salvation, that he had not come home empty-handed, and was able immediately to apply to da Ponte for a libretto for a new opera. The latter, according to himself, already had his work cut out to write the *Tarare*, after Beaumarchais, for Salieri, and the *Baum der Diana* for Martini. As a special favour to Mozart, for whom *Don Giovanni* was reserved, he sacrificed his nights' rest. Mozart himself no doubt suggested *Don Giovanni*, at this time a favourite and much-adapted libretto, as he had suggested *Figaro*. Mörike, with true poetic imagination, has credited him with the lion's share in the composition of this perhaps most inspired of all librettos; in his short story "Mozart auf der Reise nach Prag," he describes, convincingly enough though there is no historical evidence, the little scene in which Mozart late one evening—all is still around him—finds on his writing table a sealed envelope "from the Abbate . . . yes, indeed! sending me the remainder of the libretto, now revised, which I had not expected to set eyes on before the end of the month. And so I immediately sat down eagerly to read it and was delighted to find how well the odd fish knew what I wanted. It was all far simpler, terser, and at the same time richer . . ."

During this visit to Prague Mozart lodged in the Kohlmarkt, in the house "*bei den drei goldenen Löwen*", but spent most of his time with the Duscheks at their lovely vineyard, and there completed his *Don Giovanni*; more often than not surrounded by friends. He had no need to flee from them in order to preserve his solitude. Wherever he went, no matter how much bustle there was about him, he was secure within the hermetically-sealed walls of his ivory tower. Such men as he do not like being alone. Nissen relates of the composition of the overture, basing his story on Constanze's recollections: "Two days before the première, and when the dress rehearsal was over, Mozart told his wife in the evening that he proposed to write the overture overnight, and asked her to brew him some punch and stay with him to keep up his spirits. This she did and, in compliance with his request, told him amusing stories, the story of Aladdin's lamp, of Cinderella, and so on, at which the master laughed until he cried. The punch, however, made him so drowsy that whenever she stopped he began to nod, and only set to work again when she embarked on a fresh story. Since, however, the work was not making much progress, his wife begged him to lie down on the sofa and have a nap, promising to wake him in an hour's time. Mozart slept so soundly, however, that Constanze had not the heart to wake him, and did not do so for two hours, by which time it was five o'clock in the morning. The copyist was due at seven, and at seven the overture was written out. The copyists only just managed to complete their work in time for the performance, and the orchestra, whose capacity Mozart already knew, performed it excellently *a prima vista*."

Without a rehearsal? Here Constanze's memory must have been at fault. Otherwise this interesting account has a very credible ring about it. And it is in such little anecdotes that Constanze always comes off best, although one must always bear in mind the fact that they emanate from her. It is difficult to be fair to her, so fluctuating is the picture we get of her. She possessed, when in a good mood, one quality that for Mozart was very important, sociability, and for that reason her presence at moments of high tension held for him an element of homely security.

The première of *Don Giovanni* was fixed for October 14th, as a gala performance for Prince Anton of Saxony and his young wife, the Archduchess Maria Theresa, sister of the Emperor. But all was not yet ready; in the production of an opera like *Don Giovanni* there were difficulties enough to be overcome even without the added stumbling block of machinations and intrigues, and so *Figaro*, conducted by Mozart in person, was given in its stead.

> "You will no doubt imagine," he wrote on October 15th to the young Gottfried von Jacquin, who at this period seemed to be his closest friend, "that by now my opera (*Don Giovanni*) is over, but there you will be somewhat mistaken. First of all, the personnel of the theatre here is not as capable as that in Vienna of studying such an opera in such a short time. Secondly, on my arrival I found that so few preparations and arrangements had been made that it would have been a sheer impossibility to get it put on by the 14th, that is, yesterday. So yesterday my *Figaro* was performed in a brilliantly illuminated theatre, and I myself conducted."

> "Dearest friend," wrote Mozart to Gottfried von Jacquin on November 4th, "I hope that you will have received my letter. My opera *Don Giovanni* was given on October 29th, and scored a most brilliant success. Yesterday it was performed for the fourth time, and it was my benefit night . . . I expect to leave here on the 12th or 13th. As soon as I get home you shall have the aria to sing—N.B. strictly between ourselves. I only wish, my dear friend, that you could be here just for one evening to share in my pleasure. Perhaps it will be performed in Vienna after all. I hope so. Every possible argument is being put forward to persuade me to remain here a few months longer and write another opera. Flattering as is this proposal,

I cannot agree to it. And now, dearest friend, how are you? I hope that you are all as well as we are. Happy you cannot fail to be, my dear friend, for you possess everything that you can wish for at your age and in your station in life, more especially since you seem to have abandoned your former somewhat restless mode of life. You are every day becoming convinced, are you not, of the truth of my little sermons? Is not the satisfaction to be derived from an unstable, transitory, capricious love affair a vastly different matter from the bliss that true, rational love can give? I am sure that in your heart you often thank me for my sage counsel. You will be a credit to me yet! But, joking apart, you owe me some little gratitude if you have become worthy of Fräulein N . . . for I have played no insignificant part, after all, in your reformation or conversion. My great-grandfather used to tell his wife, my great-grandmother, and she her daughter, my grandmother, and she again her daughter, my mother, who again told her daughter, my own sister, that it was a great gift to talk well and eloquently, but a no less great gift, perhaps, to know when to stop. I shall therefore follow the advice which my sister, thanks to my mother, grandmother and great-grandmother gave me, and bring not only my moralising, but my whole letter to an end . . ."

Da Ponte had to return to Vienna before the première of *Don Giovanni*. Guardasoni, the assistant director of Bondini's theatre, wrote to him enthusiastically: "*Evviva da Ponte, evviva Mozart. Tutti gli impresari, tutti i virtuosi devono bene dirti! Finché essi vivranno, no si saprà mai, cosa sia miseria teatrale !*"[1]

On Monday, October 29th, the opera was performed for the first time. The Prague "Oberpostamtszeitung" of November 3rd announced that *Don Giovanni*, or *Das Steinerne Gastmahl*, the opera by the great master, Mozart, so eagerly awaited, was performed in Prague by the Italian

[1] "Bravo da Ponte, bravo Mozart! Every impresario, every singer must sound your praises. So long as you are alive, there will be no more talk of the wretched state of the theatre."

Opera company. "Connoisseurs and composers say that its like has never before been heard in Prague. Herr Mozart himself conducted, and when he took his place in the orchestra he was accorded three rousing cheers. The opera is an extremely difficult one to produce; nevertheless everyone was astounded at the excellence of the performance after so few rehearsals. Everyone concerned, both actors and orchestra, did his utmost to repay Mozart by performing to the best of his ability. A considerable sum, moreover, has been spent on the numerous choruses and on the decorations, all of which Herr Guardasoni has carried out brilliantly. The exceptionally large audience is proof of the general approval."

"Crown of operas." Who would venture to repeat this epithet that has been applied countless times to Mozart's *Don Giovanni!* And yet, whether he has heard it before or not, it leaps to the mind of the listener, who at the first notes, when the curtain has scarcely risen, is carried breathlessly and irresistibly away by the incomparably noble, flawless music, which, like a divine element, pours forth in one harmonious stream. To have produced within the space of two years two such masterpieces as *Figaro* and *Don Giovanni* is surely to have reached a pinnacle of human creative achievement. Goethe recognised in Mozart a universal genius of his own stamp, and when in 1797 he first heard *Don Giovanni*, he wrote to Schiller: "The hopes that you had of the opera you will lately have seen to a considerable degree fulfilled. And yet this piece stands all alone, and by Mozart's death all prospect of anything like it is shattered."

Mozart held the mean between Goethe and Molière. He had Molière's spiritual sparkle, his clouded gaiety, his vivacity, his impatience and irony. Beethoven, himself a musical pioneer, was too near him in point of time; but between Mozart and Richard Wagner, who was born twenty-two years after his death, there was just the right distance; Wagner perceived in Mozart a musical miracle, and was never weary of returning to him in his writings. He looked upon the Mozart slump of the period as a melancholy proof of the spiritual poverty of the public, whereas Busoni, who was constantly insisting on his enthusiasm for Mozart, was one day to be exasperated to find that he had created a Mozart boom among this very public. Indeed both boom and slump have their disagreeable sides. Busoni wrote to his wife on August 2nd, 1907: "This summer I have become aware of one of the biggest advances in my development. As regards my musical taste, I first of all, as you know, developed beyond Schumann and Mendelssohn. Liszt I first misunderstood, then worshipped, then more soberly admired; Wagner I maligned, then marvelled at, and then again, Latin that I am, turned from; I let myself be taken by surprise by Berlioz and—one of the most difficult tasks of all—learned to distinguish between good and bad Beethoven. More recently I discovered for myself the latest French composers, and when they became too rapidly popular, dropped them again. Now at last I have made spiritual contact with the older Italian operatic composers. These are metamorphoses extending over a span of twenty years. All through these twenty years, like a lighthouse in a burning sea, the music of *Figaro* has kept its unchanging place in my regard. But when, a week ago, I looked at it again, I perceived in it for the first time certain human weaknesses; and my heart leaped for joy at the discovery that I was no longer so inferior to Mozart as I had been, although on the other hand this discovery not only signifies a real loss, but points to the transitoriness of all human effort (and how much more of my own!)"[1]

There is hardly anything so stimulating as to hear a judgment passed which we ourselves are neither competent nor qualified to make, but the truth of which immediately impresses itself on us. Which Beethoven did Busoni mean? We can only guess; although we too, from time to time, have suffered from Beethoven, as from the inaccessibility, the harshness, of bare slopes. Even the greatest musician has his rocks! Bach his insistence, Mozart his trimmings, Beethoven his wintry gleam, Richard Wagner his hackneyed moments. Each of these musicians raised himself to final perfection: there was no such thing for any of them as completely static perfection; would they else be mortal?

How much ink has flowed in the effort to portray the Don Juan type! A vast mass of prosaic verbiage and a plethora of philosophical and psychological essays have been employed in the endeavour to bring down the firebird. Can he be portrayed except by implication? Again it is a writer of imagination who has grasped this—E. T. A. Hoffman, who suggests Donna Anna's love for her father's murderer. They are searchlights in their splendour, the accents which Mozart lent to her hapless and monstrous passion. It is only because he drew her in such bold outlines that we feel the irresistible power of his Don Giovanni. Wherever she remains indefinite, Don Juan (even Molière's) scarcely rises above the level of the upstart and trickster. The hundred and one others, the Charlottes, the Mathurinas and Zerlinas, even the Elviras, are not enough. It is only in the light shed by Donna Anna that Mozart, the

[1] Busoni: "Briefe an Seine Frau". Rotapfel-Verlag, Zürich. One of the most interesting books of our day.

connoisseur of women, is himself caught up in the spell of his own Don Giovanni. Each of his gestures, his expressions, he decks out as those of the seducer for seduction's sake; stamps him, even in the face of death, a gallant. And it is not as a "justly-punished" profligate—the usual concession to the morality of the day—but as a phoenix that he consigns him to the flames. This partiality contains, surely, more seriousness and a loftier morality than the heavily ironical finale which is retained out of piety and respect for Mozart's memory; so little does it add to the work that one may be permitted to ask whether on those very same pious grounds it could not be omitted.

Refreshed, and fêted on all sides, Mozart stayed on in Prague for some weeks after the production of his *Don Giovanni*. When at night, relates a contemporary, he returned from the old town to the Duscheks in the Villa Bertramka, the true Mozart house, he would often drink a final cup of coffee at the Steinitzer coffeehouse. It might happen that, arriving after the place was closed, Mozart would knock on the window and the landlord would himself make coffee for him. The coffee had to be as Mozart liked it, very strong. As a rule he wore a blue coat with gilt buttons, nankeen knee-breeches, stockings and buckled shoes.

As a parting gift he wrote for Josepha Duschek the *scena, Bella mia fiamma,* and the lovely concert aria associated with it, *Resta o cara*, which so vividly recalls his early love for her. In the middle of November he set out on his homeward journey to Vienna, where Gluck had died on November 15th, 1787. The Emperor Joseph, who, after the production of his new opera, was more firmly convinced than hitherto of Mozart's worth, had no hesitation in appointing him Gluck's successor. By December 7th, the decree was published appointing him Chamber-musician to the Court, at a much lower salary, it is true, than that paid to Gluck: 800 instead of 2,000 florins. All the same, according to the standards of the day it was a considerable sum, sufficient to fill a good many gaps. And so this year that had been for Mozart's career so eventful, so rich in fulfilment, drew to a more auspicious close; for the first time since his marriage he could look forward with less anxiety to the future.

❧

1788

NOTHING HAD PREPARED MOZART FOR THE FRUSTRAtions and the bitter experiences that now engulfed him. As though in response to a secret signal, the descent began, and at the very height of his creative powers he was to sink into oblivion. It was not merely that the public turned its back on him; he himself withdrew further and further from it. He put from him with repugnance, nay, disgust, all thought of courting its favour, which in his first few years in Vienna had been so inseparable a part of the joy of creation; he now grudged it the slightest expenditure of energy. He was still to be obliged, alas! to do only too much "bread-and-butter" work; nevertheless, it was a case of mutual desertion.

In his piano music, too, a certain austerity, a certain aloofness, are clearly perceptible. We need only consider the Rondo in A minor (K.511), its soliloquising along tortuous paths, its light, its shade, its smiles. To this year belong a new piano concerto (K.537) and two piano trios; and above all the last three great symphonies. They were intended for performance at subscription concerts, which, owing to lack of subscribers, had several times to be postponed, and appear finally to have been abandoned. Even the concerts arranged in his own house proved a failure. Mozart was no longer a "draw". However little he might value his public, this was a dire discovery for him, for he was now cut off from his chief source of income. And so it was that he began writing those pitiful letters to his Lodge Brother, Michael Puchberg, which today we read with such a catch in our throats.

In Vienna there was so little curiosity to hear *Don Giovanni* that it took an Imperial Command to bring about a performance. Mozart received 225 florins, da Ponte 100 florins, for making certain changes and additions, among them a scene between Zerlina and Leporello which was later dropped. The première, with Aloysia Weber as Donna Anna, took place on May 7th, 1788, and went off somewhat unimpressively. "The music is by Herr Wolfgang Mozart, Imperial Chamber Musician in Ordinary," was the only notice accorded it by the "Wiener Zeitung." There were those, it is true, who expressed unstinted admiration of it, but the libretto aroused unanimous indignation. "Oh that you," one critic concluded his remarks, "had not been so prodigal of the strength of your spirit! That your feeling had been on more familiar terms with your imagination, and that the latter had not directed you to take such impure steps towards greatness. What could it avail you were your name to stand in diamond letters on a golden tablet—if that tablet were affixed to a pillar of shame!" For Joseph Haydn alone was Mozart's *Don Giovanni* sacred.

Despite the failure of the opera it was repeated, as a

result of da Ponte's efforts, fourteen times. The librettist, always heart and soul for Mozart, records that the Emperor thought the opera superb. "But it is no food for the teeth of my Viennese." Even before the end of the year it was relegated to oblivion for the rest of the composer's lifetime, and it was only gradually that it found favour in other theatres, even that of Prague, where it had, after all, been accorded so enthusiastic a reception. With it, and the three last great symphonies, "Mozart's second romantic period," according to Saint-Foix, came to an end. These symphonies betray no hint of the strain under which Mozart was now living: no prospect of a commission to write a fresh opera, insufficient subscribers to his concerts, indifference wherever he turned. But he had established another home for himself, beyond the reach of everyday cares. Tranquillity, delirious happiness, nay exuberance, pervades the E flat major Symphony (K.543) which he completed on June 26th. In the intervals of composing it he had written to Puchberg.

The so-called Jupiter Symphony in C major (K.551), finished on August 10th, is imbued with a note of triumph, of blissful reverie, of heroic composure. Between these two works, on July 25th, the G minor Symphony was completed. But just as little now as in 1776 does Mozart afford us a glimpse into what was going on within him. This symphony, for all its passion, seems to be charged with resignation; it is as though his heart were palpitating, and as though a storm were brewing; a storm that bursts forth in music so penetrating, of such inspired form and of such airy grace, that in its light the futility of all things fades away like a spectre.

It is thus that the suffering of the poet, bearing within it its own healing balm, is poured forth in Goethe's lines:

"Ist denn die Welt nicht übrig? Felsenwände
Sind sie nicht mehr gekrönt von heiligen Schatten?
Die Ernte, reift sie nicht? Ein grün Gelände,
Zieht sich nicht hin am Fluss durch Busch und Matten?
Und wölbt sich nicht das überweltlich Grosse,
Gestaltenreiche, bald Gestaltenlose . . ."[1]

In June then, while he was busied on the F flat major Symphony, he wrote the following letters to his fellow Mason, Michael Puchberg, a Viennese merchant:

"Vienna, beginning of June, 1788.

"Dearest Brother,

"Your true friendship and brotherly love embolden me to ask you a great favour. I still owe you 8 ducats; but in addition to the fact that I am at the moment not in a position to pay you this back, my trust in you is so great that I venture to ask you to help me out only until next week, when my concerts begin in the Casino, with 100 florins. By that time I shall be bound to have the money for the subscriptions in hand and will then easily be able to pay you back 136 florins with my warmest thanks.

"I take the liberty of placing at your disposal the two tickets enclosed, which I beg you, as a Brother, to accept without all payment, since I shall in any case never be able sufficiently to return the kindness you have shown to me.

"I ask you once more to forgive me for my importunity, and presenting my compliments to your esteemed wife, remain in all friendship and brotherly love,

"Your most devoted Brother,
"W A. Mozart."

[1] Is there a world no longer? Towers of rock,
Are they no longer crowned by mystic shadows?
Does not the harvest ripen, verdant landscape
Follow the river's course through bush and meadow?
Broods not o'er all the vault of infinite vastness,
Now charged with form, now formless . . .

"ESTEEMED O.B.[1], DEAREST AND BEST OF FRIENDS,

"The conviction that you are a true friend, and that you know me to be an honourable man, gives me courage to open my whole heart to you and make the following request. Without further preamble and with the frankness natural to me I shall come straight to the point.

"If you would have the kindness, the friendliness, to assist me by the loan of one or two thousand florins for one or two years, at a suitable rate of interest, you would enable me to keep body and soul together. You yourself, no doubt, will realise and appreciate how difficult, nay impossible, it is to live when one is obliged to wait for the receipt of one sum after another, for without a certain, or at all events, the necessary, amount of ready cash, it is impossible to put one's affairs in order. With nothing one can do nothing. If you do me this service, I shall in the first place, having something in hand, be able more easily to meet certain necessary expenses at the right time, whereas as things stand I am obliged to postpone payment, and then when I receive any money to pay it out all at once and just at the most inconvenient moment. In the second place, I shall be able to work with a less troubled mind and a lighter heart, and thus earn more. As to security, I do not imagine that you will have any doubts. You know pretty well how I stand, and you know my principles. You need not be uneasy with regard to the subscriptions; I am only extending the time for a few months, in the hope of finding more lovers of music elsewhere than here.

"I have now opened my whole heart to you in a matter which is of the greatest moment to me, and thus treated you as a true Brother, but it is only to a true Brother that one can unburden oneself frankly. I now eagerly await a reply from you, and indeed a favourable reply. I do not know, but I take you to be a man who, like myself; will, if possible, help a friend, if he is a true friend, a Brother, if he is a true Brother. If you should find it inconvenient to part with so large a sum at such short notice, I beg you at all events to lend me a few hundred florins until to-morrow, for my landlord in the Landstrasse was so pressing that, in order to avoid unpleasantness,

[1] O.B. Ordens Bruder—Lodge Brother.

I was obliged to pay him on the Spot, and this put me in great difficulties . . .To-night we sleep for the first time in our new lodgings, where we shall remain for the summer and winter. I think this quite as good, if not better, than our former arrangement, for I have not in any case much to do in the town, and since I shall not be likely to receive so many visits, I shall have more time for work. And should I have to go into the town on business, which is not often likely to be the case, a fiacre will take me there for 10 kreutzers. These lodgings, moreover, will be not only cheaper, but pleasanter during the spring, summer and autumn, particularly as I have a garden. They are in the Währingergasse, bei den Drei Sternen, No. 135. Pray regard my letter as a proof of my sincere trust in you, and remain ever my friend and brother, as I shall be yours till the grave.

"Your true, most devoted friend and Brother,

"W. A. Mozart.

"P.S. When are we to have a little music at your house again? I have written a new trio!"

But why Herr Puchberg? one is constrained to ask oneself. His relations with Mozart were not particularly intimate; the assurances of friendship, the invitations, which Mozart feels he owes him, sound forced enough; and this is the very first we hear of him. Would not the Jacquins, the Auernhammers, the Duscheks, the Countess Thun, scattered though they were, have combined to help him? But this was precisely the sore point. Mozart must have found it less difficult to admit his impoverishment to this stranger than to the friends who knew him from so different an angle: an elegant young man of the world who charmed everyone by his playing and enhanced the brilliance of their parties. Rich people like discussing their financial difficulties; those who have nothing prefer to keep the fact dark. Who moreover would not have been deceived by Mozart's generosity? A generous spirit—for it is more blessed to give than to receive—never feels happy in taking, however good a face he may put on it. The fact that he himself gave so unhesitatingly, that giving was second nature to him, was no consolation to him in his role of pauper, but rather doubled or trebled his discomfiture and depression.

Constanze, of course, lacked the most elementary understanding of a person with his mental make-up. And indeed, in Mozart's case, it would have been no easy matter to set things right. He spent a great deal; nevertheless he now had at least a regular, if somewhat modest income. And according to the accounts of his contemporaries his philanderings and his lavish hospitality by no means accounted for the rapidly declining State of his finances.

But his innate good nature played him even worse tricks. In Leipzig he not only allowed the choristers to attend his concert free of charge, but he also Secretly made a double-bass player who had particularly pleased him a handsome present. On another occasion a poor old piano tuner who stammered out an embarrassed request for a thaler, received several ducats from him. Whenever he had money, he found it impossible to refuse it to any needy wretch, even if he brought himself and his family into difficulties. And so it was inevitable that he should be shamefully fleeced. Take for example, the case of Anton Stadler. Stadler was an excellent clarinettist, a jovial and easy-going fellow, and furthermore a Freemason; he therefore soon became a regular guest at Mozart's table. On one occasion, discovering that Mozart had received 50 ducats from the Emperor, he pretended to be in straitened circumstances and declared that if Mozart were not to lend him this sum, he would be a lost man. Mozart, who himself needed the money, gave him two heavy repeater watches to pawn, asking him to bring him the tickets and also to redeem the watches in good time. Since he failed to do this, Mozart, in order not to lose the watches, gave him 50 ducats and the interest. Stadler neglected to redeem the watches and kept the money. But Mozart was not a whit the wiser for the lesson. After his visit to Frankfurt in 1790 he asked Stadler to redeem certain articles of silver that he had pawned and to renew the terms of the rest. Stadler was seriously suspected of having purloined the pawnticket from an unlocked cabinet, but in spite of this Mozart furnished him with money for a concert tour in 1791 and even with a new concerto (K.622) which he composed for him a few months before his death.

Mozart's naturally delicate constitution, undermined from childhood up by illness and over-work, could not long withstand the cares and worries that from now on were his portion. He had but another three years to live. We have now come to his last symphonies, which Saint-Foix calls "la grande trilogie finale", his last *Kleine Nachtmusik* (K.525), his last sonata for piano and violin (K.526), his last two piano compositions, the so-called Coronation Concerto (K.537), and the moving Adagio in B minor (K.540) with its delicate and intricate pattern of tranquilly reflected grief. In the Divertimento in E flat major for violin, viola and violincello (K.563), however, which he wrote in September for Michael Puchberg, he soars far above the miseries of his life, forgets them one and all, dreams and exults.

We do not know whether the excellent Herr Puchberg, who proved himself to be a true friend of Mozart's, but whose right hand knew exactly what his left hand was doing, was musical or not. There is a great deal to suggest that he was not, in which case he must have regarded the gift and the dedication, and also the inestimable advantage of being able to hear Mozart as often as he pleased, as scarcely a fair exchange for his good, profitable money. He must have been taken aback at the gay character of this trio. Were things, after all, going so badly with Mozart?

In November Mozart at last set to work, at the request of Baron van Swieten, on the reinstrumentation of Handel's oratorios. Thus this year, so poor in events, so rich in work, drew to a close.

❧

1789

EVERY JOYOUS EXPERIENCE, EVERY GRATIFICATION, that is to come Mozart's way from now on, we note with a sigh of relief, as though they had not, even as his sorrows, faded into nothingness.

In March his pupil and admirer, the young Prince Carl Lichnowsky, suggested that he should accompany him on a trip to Berlin, where he would introduce him to King Friedrich Wilhelm II, a lover of music, who might perhaps take him into his service. Here, then, was a fresh hope. Mozart loved change. He glowed at the thought of escaping for a while from the hampering cares and worries of his situation, and joyfully accepted the invitation, which was for him alone, and did not include the disappointed Constanze. Whenever there was any question of having a good time, it never occurred to her to worry over the children, nor did she bother about such urgent and practical considerations as the fact that Mozart would have to borrow in order to scrape together the money necessary for the trip. Such things simply did not enter into her calculations. On April 8th the Prince set out, accompanied only by Mozart, who sought to placate the sulking wife he had left behind by writing her letters full of endearments and entertaining nonsense. By the 10th he was in Prague. He rushed off to the Duscheks, only to find that Josepha had left for Dresden some days before; he then got into touch with Guardasoni and wrote home that the contract for a new opera was "almost settled". In the evening he took the Prince to visit Herr Duschek in the Villa Bertramka. And the day following they both travelled on to Dresden. Josepha was staying at the house of Johann Leopold Neumann, Secretary to the Military Council and a very distinguished man; Mozart dined there every day and once more found himself living a gay life. On the 13th, after a merry breakfast, they all went off in a body to the Catholic church, where the *Hofkapellmeister* conducted a Mass in Mozart's honour, after which the whole company were entertained at the Hôtel de Pologne as guests of Prince Lichnowsky. At half-past two Mozart was due to wait upon the Elector and to play to him and his family; later in the day they assembled again in the hotel for a private concert, at which Josepha sang airs from *Figaro* and *Don Giovanni*, and Mozart played the Divertimento in E flat major (K.563) which he had composed for Puchberg. On the 14th a concert, at which Mozart played, was given at Court, and on the 15th he and Lichnowsky dined with the Russian Ambassador, after which Mozart played on the famous Silbermann organ in the Catholic church and then returned to the Russian Ambassador's. In the evening they went to an opera, which Mozart found "wretched". Afterwards they all sat about until the small hours at the hotel. On the 16th he was invited to dine with Körner, a Counsellor of the High Court of Appeal and friend and patron of Schiller. He took a fancy to his hostess's unmarried sister, Dora Stock, who was twenty-nine years old and a skilled etcher. On this and presumably the following day he sat for his portrait. It was to be his last: a silverpoint, which has been much admired, but which represents him so differently from all his other portraits that one is less than ever able to imagine what he really looked like; it portrays him with the large eyes of a sick man, sunken temples, strikingly fragile and delicate features.

On the 18th they resumed their journey. From the Elector, who was given as a rule to ignoring foreign artists, Mozart had received a present of a gold snuff-box containing 100 ducats. He wrote to Constanze of the "really lovely box", suppressing all mention of the 100 ducats. He had every right to do so, but was it because he knew that he would need them, or because she was so greedy, or because he wished after all this long time to spend, to lavish and to squander money to his heart's content? All three, perhaps. How significant is it, nevertheless, that he did not take her into his confidence! How little must she have understood him for frankness to be no longer possible between them!

On April 18th they continued their journey to Leipzig, where Mozart immediately looked up Johann Friedrich Doles, a pupil of J. S. Bach and now Cantor of the Thomaskirche, who received him with every possible mark of esteem. In Leipzig, too, he played a great deal. "On April 22nd,"writes a contemporary, "without any preliminary announcement and without making any charge for admission, he played the organ in the Thomaskirche. He played beautifully and with consummate skill for the space of a whole hour to a large audience. Görner, who was the organist at the time, and Doles, the Cantor, since deceased, stood by him and pulled out the stops. I myself saw him—a young, fashionably-dressed man of middle height. Doles was quite enchanted by the artist's playing and almost imagined that his teacher, old Sebastian Bach, had come to life again. With very great dignity and ease Mozart employed all the arts of harmony and executed the themes, among others the chorale '*Jesu meine Zuversicht*', admirably and impromptu."

Mozart, who in his own country saw himself more and more obviously neglected and forgotten, now had the satisfaction, many hundreds of miles away, of perceiving, in every town he visited, that he was a tremendous and unique attraction, and that all connoisseurs and music-lovers rallied round him. It was the same in Potsdam, where the Court was in residence and where he and Lichnowsky arrived on April 25th. On May 4th he was back again in Leipzig; this time for a longer stay, allegedly to accompany the Prince, who was setting out on his homeward journey; in reality because there were a great many things to draw him back to that city, and because, too, he had arranged to meet Josepha Duschek and his other Dresden friends. On May 12th they gave a concert there, Frau Duschek singing the air composed in 1786 for Nancy Storace, *Non tener, amato bene* (K.505), and when, at the end, the audience clamoured to hear Mozart alone on the pianoforte, although he had already played for two hours, "he began", writes Rochlitz, "simply, freely and solemnly in C minor, swooped down and down, on the wings of his fantasy, and concluded with the E flat major variations, which were later published."

That same evening, we are also told, he drew one of Leipzig's best violin soloists, by the name of Berger, aside.

"Come with me, my dear Berger! I want to play to you for a while longer. You understand my playing better than all these people who have applauded me here." He took him along with him and improvised to him until midnight, when he jumped up, saying, "Are you pleased? Now you have really heard Mozart. Others can play as well as I in public."

At the concert, which had been poorly attended, half of the audience had had free tickets. Others, crowding behind, clamoured also to be allowed in free. When the official in the box office turned to Mozart for instructions, the latter said: "Oh, let them in. Whoever would make a fuss about such a trifle!"

No wonder that he was obliged to write to Constanze: "You will have, on my return, to find your pleasure in *me*, rather than in any money that I shall bring."

Rochlitz describes how, at a rehearsal, Mozart took the first allegro of one of his symphonies unusually fast, and when the orchestra failed to keep up with him, he beat time with his foot on the floor so vigorously that one of his steel buckles flew off. Not until the musicians, now thoroughly incensed, started off at a brisk pace did he register his satisfaction. Later he remarked that he was, indeed, an avowed enemy of over-hurried tempi, but in this case, having regard to the advanced age of most of the members of the orchestra, he had feared there would be too much "dragging"and had been therefore obliged to "put some fire into them", whereupon from sheer annoyance they had done their utmost.

Rochlitz gives us still further interesting details of Mozart's stay in Leipzig:

"In Leipzig Mozart paid frequent and very enjoyable visits to the house of Friedrich Doles, Cantor to the

Thomaskirche, and his musical son. Here he let himself go completely and took nothing amiss, convinced that those present would for their part also take no exception to his behaviour. He was on his way from Leipzig to Dresden, and contemplated returning to Leipzig for a few days. The evening before his departure he dined with Doles and was in high spirits, and his hosts were all the more melancholy, therefore, when the time came for his departure. 'Who knows if we shall ever meet again!' they said. 'Will you leave us a line or two in your hand.' Mozart, whose entire life, almost, had been a succession of arrivals and departures and who had therefore become indifferent to both, rallied them on their moaning and groaning, as he called it, and was rather more inclined to go to bed than to start writing. At length he said: 'Well then, Papa, give me a sheet of music-paper.' He took it and, tearing it in half, sat down to write—for no more than five or six minutes at the most. He then gave one half to the father, and the other to the son. On the first piece there was a three-part canon in breves, without words. We sang the notes; it was an admirable canon and very solemn. On the second sheet was a three-part canon in quavers, likewise without words. We sang the notes; this canon, too, was admirable and very droll. Only now did we remark that both could be sung together, thus forming a six-part whole. We were delighted. 'Now for the words,' said Mozart, and wrote under the first: '*Lebet wohl wir sehen uns wieder*!' (Farewell, we shall meet again), and under the second: '*Heult gar nicht wie alte Weiber*' (Do not squawk like poor old women). We now had to sing it through again and again, and it is impossible to describe how ridiculous and yet profoundly, almost bitterly scathing, one might say sublimely comic, it sounded to us all. . . At this same house, one evening after Mozart's return, an argument took place as to the merits of certain living composers, with particular reference to a man who was possessed of obvious talent for writing comic opera, but held a post as composer of church music. The elder Doles, who held rather more than was right and proper by the operatic style in church music, always took this composer's part in very lively fashion against Mozart's constant, 'It all amounts to nothing.' 'And I'll wager you've not heard much of his,' Doles interposed with some heat. 'You win,' replied Mozart, 'but there's no need; such a man can do nothing in this genre. He has no conception of it. Heavens, if God had placed me in such a post in the church and before such an orchestra!' and so on. 'Well, to-day you shall see a Mass of his that will reconcile you to him.' Mozart took it away with him, and brought it back the following evening. 'Well, what do you think of —'s mass?' 'It's well enough, but it's not suitable in church. I hope you will not take it amiss, but I have written new words to the credo; it will go much better thus. No! No one is to read them beforehand. Let us sing it straight away.' He sat down at the fortepiano, and distributed the four vocal parts; we had to do as he wished, and so we sang whilst he accompanied. Never, I fancy, has there been such a droll performance. The principal characters: Father Doles the tenor, who, despite grave and perpetual head-shakings over the scandalous business, yet sang so admirably; Mozart, all ten fingers kept fully occupied with the movements, which made such free use of trumpets and drums, exclaiming every now and then, with boisterous glee: 'Well—doesn't it go better thus?' And then the mischievous and yet admirably apt words—the brilliant allegro to *Kyrie Eleison*, for example: *Hols der Geier, das geht flink!* [Devil take us, this goes nimbly.] And, finally, the fugue, *Cum sancto spiri-*

tu in gloria Dei patris; Das ist gestohlen Gut, ihr Herren, nehmts nicht übel [He's stolen every note, my friends, take't not amiss] . . .

"Having thus, as so often, expressed himself in doggerel, he went over to the window, strummed on the cushion of the window-seat as was his habit, and plunged into a reverie, paying no more attention to the conversation and returning almost absent-minded and apathetic replies to the questions addressed to him. The discussion on church music had become more general and more serious. 'A thousand pities,' he said, 'that so many great musicians, particularly in the past, fared like the old painters in having almost always to expend their vast energies on not only barren, but soul-destroying ecclesiastical subjects.' At this point he turned to the others and in a quite altered and gloomy mood, added in effect, though not precisely in these words : 'Here am I again prating on about art! You enlightened Protestants, as you call yourselves, whenever you bethink yourselves of your religion, there may be something real in it, I don't know. But with us it is different. You have no idea what one feels when one hears the words, *Agnus Dei, qui tollis peccata mundi, dona nobis pacem*, and the like. But if a man has, like myself, been initiated in early childhood into the holy mysteries of our religion, if, at an age when he did not yet know what to do about his obscure but thronging emotions, he went to Mass, without really knowing what he wanted, and came away lighter in spirit and exalted, without really understanding what it all meant to him when he called them blessed who knelt to the moving strains of the *Agnus Dei* and received the Eucharist, pouring out their hearts, as they knelt, in the sweet, joyous notes of the *Benedictus qui venit*, and so on, then it is quite different. Well, of course, you lose all that through living in the world, but—at least in my case—when you take the words you have already heard a thousand times to set them to music, it all comes back to you and is real and vivid and stirs the soul.'

"He went on to describe one or two scenes of this kind from his early childhood, first in Salzburg and then during his first journey to Italy, and dwelt with particular interest on the story of how Maria Theresa had commissioned him, as a fourteen-year-old lad, to compose a Te Deum for the dedication ceremony of a—I don't remember—a big hospital or some institution of the kind, and to conduct the whole Imperial Orchestra himself. 'What days those were for me! What days those were!' he exclaimed again and again. 'But they will never return! One loses oneself in the emptiness of everyday life,' he continued, grew bitter, drank a great deal of strong wine and did not utter another sensible word.

". . . That Mozart was richly endowed by a kindly Providence with wit is well known. That he often revealed this gift in strange and not exactly discreet ways could not but be, since, apart from his art and things closely connected with it, his ideas were not varied enough, and thus he had too little material on the elaboration of which he could have practised and vented his wit. But, in his art, what a rich and joyous source was at his disposal! When, for example, he improvised on the fortepiano, how easy it was for him to work up a theme, to make it emerge, peep forth or work itself out, now so boldly and crisply, now so supplicatingly and dolefully, here so drolly, there so solemnly, that he could do what he wished with his audience—even had an unkind fate saddled him with the veriest crosspatches, so long as they had *some* musical education. It was precisely this gift that no pianist before or after him has ever possessed to the same extent. I have heard all the most celebrated virtuosi since Mozart play on this instrument (with the exception of Beethoven); I have heard much that was admirable, but nothing in the least comparable to his inexhaustible wit.

"But words are no medium for such wit. Far from it. Not seldom he would parody, though without malice, those composers, virtuosi and singers of repute whom he considered to be corrupters of art and of public taste; but when he came to certain Italian singers and to composers who had written for these latter, and in their style, and who were at that time held in high esteem, his musical satire went rather beyond mere badinage. Some of them certainly deserved ill of him. He would improvise whole opera scenes on the piano in the manner of one or other of them, and I should like to have seen the man who could have remained unmoved! Mozart did not waste time in writing such things down; but one such great bravura scene for a *prima donna*, he did write down, as I happen to know. This parody is very probably to be found amongst those of his papers which have not yet been published. It is an intricately constructed piece which at first sight seems perfectly serious and embodies the favourite ideas of Messrs. Alessandri, Gazzaniga, and the rest of them. The libretto he likewise wrote himself. It consists of a conglomeration of the bombastic and ranting phrases and exclamations with which the Italian librettist so freely overloads his text, and these gaudy beads are now strung together in the most comical fashion. '*Dove, ahi, dove sono io?*' exclaims the noble Princess, or something very like it. '*0 Dio! questa pena! 0 principe—or sorte—io tremo—io manco—io moro—o dolce morte!*' Then, like a bomb dropped into the house a deep booming chord bursts in upon this, the fair lady gives a start, and continues, '*Ah, quel contrasto—barbare stelle—traditore—carnifice!*' And so it goes on over the tottering bridges of the *imponendo, colla parte, vibrando, rinforzando, smorzando*, and so on with their profusion of gracenotes and festoons . . . "

On May 17th, the day of his departure—from now on Mozart travelled alone and at his own expense, for the Prince had gone back to Vienna—he wrote the enchanting Gigue (K.574) for the piano in the album of Engel, the Court organist. By the 19th he was in Berlin. He lodged in the Gendarmenmarkt close by the National Theatre, where on the evening of his arrival *Die Entführung* was given in his honour. A well-known anecdote is related in connection with this performance. Mozart, who was standing in the stalls, kept approaching nearer and nearer the orchestra and exclaiming under his breath. When, during Pedrillo's air in D major, the second violin played a D sharp instead of D, he was unable to restrain himself and shouted at the violinist: "Play D, damn you!" Up to that moment he had not been recognised, but now, amid the general excitement, there were murmurs of "Mozart is here", and at the end of the act he was dragged on to the stage. It was during this incident that he made the acquaintance of the beautiful twenty-two-year-old actress who was taking the part of Blondchen, the elegant and much-fêted Henriette Baranius, the King's mistress. He promised her to go through her part with her before the next performance, which was to be on May 28th. And so he came to see a great deal of this new pupil of his, and was caught in her toils, while she for her part succumbed so completely to Mozart's charm that their friends had their work cut out to separate them.

It was at this time, too, that the meeting, already mentioned, took place between Mozart and Ludwig Tieck, who was at the time sixteen years old.

"While Mozart was in Berlin," records an eyewitness, "little Hummel, his pupil, performed at a concert there without having the faintest idea that his teacher was in the audience. When he caught sight of him, however, he could scarcely contain himself, and, when he had finished playing, he pushed his way through the audience and flung himself on him most affectionately."

For all the King's goodwill towards Mozart, the usual jealousies and intrigues at Court turned the scales against him, and an appointment at Berlin was not forthcoming. Ultimately even the leading musicians and conductors aired their dissatisfaction and displeasure of Mozart, who, it must be admitted, was never slow to pass judgment. According to Rochlitz he is said to have replied to the King, when asked what he thought of his orchestra: "It is an assemblage of the finest performers in the world, but if the gentlemen kept together, they might do better."

On May 26th he played before the Queen. The open-handed and splendour-loving Friedrich Wilhelm sent him 100 Friedrichs d'or (about 900 florins), with the request that he should compose a quartet for him. But he was not to remain there much longer and on the 28th he took his departure, travelling via Dresden to Prague, where he arrived on the 31st and stayed until the morning of June 3rd. By midday on June 4th he was back in Vienna.

Innumerable were the letters that he wrote to Constanze during his absence. Several of them having gone astray, he himself gives a precise catalogue of them. We can tell from them how much loving kindness and devotion he lavished on her, how bound he was to her by the ties of habit and of affection. She had no part in him, yet he loved her truly, and to the end. Not until the very last days does their utter incompatibility seem to stand out in relief, does it seem as though she no longer occupies his thoughts. Constanze is said to have been ill herself at the time, to have lost her head and to have resigned her place at the sick bed to her sister Sophie. Is it conceivable that that day is so near? She is still a young, coquettish and not unattractive woman. Mozart, who himself so lightly deceives her, is a jealous young husband. He does not trust her farther than he can see her, and in many ways da Ponte's next libretto, *Così fan tutte,* will echo his sentiments. His Dorabella is Constanze herself. On her and her like he makes Fernando pour out his resentment, wrath, wit, satire and passion.

Unfortunately we do not possess Constanze's letters. They would help us the more easily to "fix"the flickering picture we have of her, and give us greater insight into the relationship between her and Mozart.

All that we possess is a diary which she kept in her early sixties and which reveals her in all her emptiness; a woman utterly bound up in the material things of life, and in consequence completely senile and utterly smug, for she has everything she can wish for.

Soon Mozart's sky was overcast afresh; Constanze fell seriously ill, and he was profoundly shaken. Scarcely five weeks after his return he had to apply to Puchberg again.

"July 12th, 1789.

"Dearest, best of Friends, and esteemed O.B.,

"Oh God! I am in a position in which I could not wish my worst enemy, and if you, my best friend and Brother, forsake me now, I and my poor sick wife and children, through my misfortune and not my fault, are lost. When I was with you lately I longed to pour out my heart to you, but still had not the courage! And it is only with the greatest trepidation that I venture to do so in writing, nor should I venture thus far did I not know that you know me and my circumstances and know that I am not to blame for my most unhappy, most desperate situation. Oh God! instead of thanking you for past favours here I am coming to you with fresh requests—instead of with payments with fresh demands! If you know me truly, you must feel what agony this is to me. I am sure I need not tell you again how impossible this unfortunate illness makes it for me to earn anything; but I must tell you that, despite my wretched situation, I had resolved to give subscription concerts at my house, to enable me to meet my present great and increasing expenses, for I counted on your kindness and patience; but even this proved a failure. Fate is unfortunately so against me—although only in Vienna—that I cannot earn anything however much I try. I sent round the list a fortnight ago and the only name upon it is that of van Swieten.

" . . . Dearest, best of friends and Brother, you know my present circumstances, but you also know my prospects. And our arrangement still stands; thus or thus—you understand me. Meanwhile I am writing six easy pianoforte sonatas for the Princess Frederika and six quartets for the King, which I am having engraved by Kozeluch at my own expense; moreover, the two dedications will bring me in something. In a few months' time my fate must be decided down to the smallest detail, and therefore, my dear friend, you will be risking nothing by assisting me. It is merely a question of whether you can and will lend me 500 florins. I should like, until my affairs are settled, to pay you back 10 florins every month; then, within a few months at the most, I shall repay the whole sum with whatever interest you may propose, and moreover, acknowledge myself my whole life long your debtor, which, alas, I must always remain, since I shall never be in a position to thank you sufficiently for your friendship and affection. Now, thank God! that is over. You know all. I entreat you not to take my confidence in you amiss, and remember that without your assistance, the honour, peace of mind, and perhaps the very life, of your friend and Brother are lost. Ever your most beholden servant, true friend and Brother,

"W. A. Mozart."

"At home, July 14th, 1789."

"Oh God! I can scarce resolve to send this letter—and yet I must! Had this illness not come upon me, I should not be compelled to apply so shamelessly to my only friend. And yet I hope for your forgiveness, for you know both the good and ill of my situation. The ill is only temporary, the good will certainly endure when the temporary ill has been removed. Adieu. Forgive me, for God's sake, do forgive me, and—adieu. . . ."

"Latter half of July, 1789.

"Dearest Friend and Brother,

"Since you did me so great a service I have lived in such misery that I have not only been unable to go out, but for very grief have been unable to write!

"If you can, dearest friend, do pay us a visit, and, if you can, lend me your advice and assistance in the matter you know of.

"Mozart."

Puchberg sent him 150 florins, thus enabling Constanze to embark on a series of visits to Baden. Her health, moreover, so far improved that before long she was always to be seen at the casino and the concerts.

By the middle of August the faithful and solicitous husband found himself obliged to write to the patient as follows:

"... I am glad that you are in good spirits—indeed I am, but I could wish that you would not make yourself so cheap at times. To my mind you are too free with—as you were also with—when he was in Baden. Remember that—and—are by no means as familiar with other women, whom they may know better than they do you, as they are with you. Even—,who is in general a well-bred man, and particularly respectful towards women—even he must have been misled by your behaviour, to have permitted himself to indulge in such disgusting and coarse *sottises* in his letter. A woman should always command respect or else people talk about her. My dear, forgive me for being so frank, but my peace of mind and our common happiness necessitate it. Remember that you once admitted to me that you were apt to be too complaisant! You know the consequences of such behaviour. Remember, too, the promise you gave me. Oh God! do but try, my dear. Be jolly and happy and kind to me; do not torture yourself and me with needless jealousy; trust in my love—you have proof enough of it—and you will see how happy we shall be. Believe me, it is only by prudent behaviour that a wife can hold her husband. Adieu—to-morrow I shall kiss you with all my heart.

"Mozart."

Never do these letters betray the faintest shadow of a complaint or misgiving with regard to this very expensive sojourn at a watering-place, never the faintest shadow of doubt that it is indispensable, never a hint of his appalling pecuniary difficulties! The depression, the wearing anxiety, the rushing hither and thither in search of money, the humiliations, he bears alone.

"Vienna, August, 1789.

"Dearest Little Wife,

"I arrived here safely at a quarter to eight,—and as I knocked on the door—Hofer, who is here, wrote that, and wishes to be remembered to you—I found it locked, for the servant was not at home. I waited in vain for close on a quarter of an hour; then I went to Hofer's and pretended I was at home, and dressed there. The little air that I have written for Ferraresi should, I fancy, please, if she is capable of rendering it naïvely, which, however, I very much doubt. True, she was very pleased with it. I dined there. I believe *Figaro* is sure to be given on Sunday, but I shall let you know beforehand. How I look forward to our hearing it together! I am going this very moment to see if there has not perhaps been some change in the arrangements. If it is not to be given till Saturday, I shall be with you to-day. Adieu, my love! and don't go out alone—I am appalled at the idea.

"Always your loving

"Mozart."

The revival of *Figaro* on August 29th was a great success. He added the big aria for Ferraresi, da Ponte's *femme fatale*; and in the next few months he also wrote the air, *Alma grande e nobil core*, for interpolation in Cimarosa's *Due Baroni*; the D major Sonata for piano (K.576), the quintet for clarinet, two violins, viola and 'cello, in A major (K.581), and in December twelve minuets.

Figaro was given twelve more times in that same year, fifteen times in the year 1790 and three times in the year 1791. The Emperor Joseph, who never declared himself a wholehearted admirer of Mozart's, and yet was never able entirely to forget him, at length commissioned him to write a new opera. The honorarium was to be 200 ducats; the libretto was once more by da Ponte. This was *Così fan tutte.*

Our attitude to this opera with its much-censured libretto is at variance with that of every generation before us. As a result of the Great War, which undermined so much, left so little intact, our point of view has changed. Without the experiences that it inflicted upon us, we should not to-day take the delight we do in unreality and farce. The cynicism which finds expression in *Così fan tutte* does not disturb us. Had it not been composed, the circle would be incomplete, and there would be a gap in Mozart's world. In the renunciation of a more exalted standpoint we perceive a whim, a gay caprice. For, high above the icy blast that blows upon it, what halcyon blue! Not a breath stirs. We are far from the heroic *élan*, the wonderful resonance of *Idomeneo*. The air is utterly still, even though events pile helter-skelter upon one another in complete defiance of probability, even of possibility. Within a few hours, the most inconceivable things happen: the parting from the lovers who are allegedly going to the war, paroxysms of grief, followed by the wooing of new lovers, poison phials, double suicides, conflicts, weakening resistance, Dorabella's roguish *Prenderò quel brunettino*, Fiordiligi's *Ed intanto io col biondino*, her vain apostrophising of her absent lover, her love duet with the lover of the moment, who is once more feigning to fall upon his sword, and into whose arms she sinks—all to end in precipitate marriage, not with the new, but the old, lovers, who have allegedly returned home from the wars, and finding they have lost their bet, first rage, then in the end forgive, for in this opera masculine fidelity stands firm as a rock against feminine fickleness; and as an accompaniment to all this nonsense and confusion, to the absurdities of a downright farce, the noble, almost insubstantial music, for it is its very insubstantiality that gives it its perfume-laden, its eternal loveliness.

In his boyhood Mozart had seen Naples, its gulf, its haze-covered sea. They now floated before his eyes. In the morning glow of this southern clime, such conceptions as fidelity and infidelity melt away like phantasmagoria, and it sparkles and smiles on both alike. We may be sure that Mozart took no exception to the libretto. It was on Dorabella that he vented his anger, scorn and jealousy, while Constanze, who was not to be trusted out of his sight, enjoyed herself to the full. Marvellous is the delicacy, the clear-cut line of the passion that springs to life between Fiordiligi and Guglielmo; he and not Fernando the rightful lover of the finer Fiordiligi.

This opera has been termed the sheerest rococo, but is it not rather *fin de siècle?* Is it not overlaid with that air of unreality, that highly varnished surface, which we find in certain pictures of the romantic school, in, for instance, Caspar David Friedrich's best paintings with that play of heightened and evanescent light that we so much admire.

Moreover, we can no longer really understand how it was ever possible to moralise with regard to *Così fan tutte*. Before the great turning point of our epoch we were more naïve, but also more dogmatic. It is not morality but moralising that we have unlearned.

Così fan tutte was not Mozart's last word. He was yet to pluck at golden strings to celebrate the timeless moments of love between two people; another kind of love, indeed, than that he felt for Constanze.

As honorarium for the new opera he was to receive 900 ducats, that is to say, twice as much as hitherto. On this security Puchberg lent him a further 300 florins. Inspired by fresh hopes, Mozart celebrated the New Year by holding a little rehearsal of the opera at his house for Haydn and for Puchberg, who had, of course, become an inevitable guest.

❧

1790

AT FIRST IT SEEMED THAT THE YEAR 1790 WAS NOT opening too badly. The première of *Così fan tutte* took place on January 26th, in the Burgtheater, and the reception was favourable.

We know nothing more of it beyond the fact that Fiordiligi was sung by Mlle. Ferraresi, whom Mozart did not rate particularly highly, Guglielmo by that elegant actor and excellent singer Benucci, and Despina by Mlle. Bussani, the original Cherubino. Rumour had it that the libretto had been suggested by the Emperor himself, and hence, no less than because of its frivolous nature, met with a good reception.

On February 20th, a few weeks after this première, Joseph II died. He had been, if lukewarm and vacillating, yet to an increasing extent a patron of Mozart's. It was only under his successor, the Emperor Leopold II, that Mozart was to find himself finally neglected and disregarded by the Viennese Court. Once more he built castles in the air. He applied for the posts of second *Kapellmeister* and of piano teacher to the princes, and at the end of March he wrote to Puchberg, who vouchsafed no reply.

(To Michael Puchberg, merchant, of Vienna; Vienna, end of March or beginning of April, 1790.)

" . . . I now stand on the threshold of success, but I shall lose all hope of it for ever, if I do not make use of my opportunity this time. My present circumstances, however, are such that for all my agreeable prospects, I shall be obliged, without the assistance of a loyal friend, to abandon all hope of an improvement in my fortune. For some time now you will have constantly remarked in me a note of gloom, and it is only the thought of the far too frequent favours you have already shown me that has caused me to hold my peace. But just once more, and that for the very last time, at this most vital moment, which is to decide my whole future fortunes, do I call upon you, with full confidence in your unfailing friendship and brotherly love, to assist me to the very best of your ability. You know how much my present circumstances, were they to become known, would prejudice my application to the Court, and how essential it is that they should remain a secret; for at Court they do not judge by circumstances but, alas, merely by appearances. You know, I am sure must be convinced, that if, as at present I certainly have reason to hope, I am successful in my application, you will have lost nothing. With what pleasure shall I then repay all my debts to you, with what pleasure thank you, and, moreover, acknowledge myself eternally your debtor! What an agreeable feeling it is to have at last reached one's goal, what a blissful feeling to have helped another towards that end! Tears prevent me from completing the picture. In short, my entire future is in your hands. Follow the promptings of your noble heart, do what you can for me and remember that you have to do with an upright, eternally grateful man, who finds his position painful far more on your account than on his own.

"Mozart."

On April 8th he writes to him again.

(To Michael Puchberg, merchant, of Vienna; Vienna, April 8th, 1790.)

"You are right, my dearest friend, in not deeming me worthy of an answer. My importunity is too great. But I entreat you to consider my position in all its aspects, to be touched by my warm friendship for, and trust in, you and to pardon me. But if you will and can extricate me from a temporary embarrassment, then do so for the love of God. Whatever you can easily spare, I shall be grateful for. Pray forget, if possible, my importunity, and forgive me . . .

"I should have come in person to speak to you, but my head is bandaged up because of rheumatic pains, and this makes me all the more acutely conscious of my position. Once again, assist me to the best of your ability, only this *once*, and forgive me.

"Ever your

"Mozart."

"Vienna, April 23rd, 1790.

"Dearest Friend and Brother,

"If you can but send me what you sent the last time, you will be doing a very great service to your eternally grateful friend and Brother,

"Mozart."

Puchberg sent him twenty-five florins. For what security had he now? But Constanze had to go off to Baden again for a cure.

The twenty-five florins, of course, did not go very far, and Mozart had recourse to money-lenders. What else was he to do? The fact that Constanze, whose condition shortly ceased to give cause for anxiety, should, despite Mozart's desperate situation, have treated herself to another sixty baths, would be past our comprehension, did we not live on a planet on which we are perpetually faced with the most glaring and kaleidoscopic incongruities. It is our modern world which allowed Mozart to come to grief in the eighteenth century, and Richard Wagner in the nineteenth century barely escaped death by starvation. The whole gamut of human suffering; there is no escaping it. Do but consider the resigned, the hopeless expression, as of a man weighed down by knowledge, in the eye of the laurel-crowned master, the genius so successfully "managed" by Cosima. In no other of his portraits do we encounter such sadness.

(To Michael Puchberg, merchant, of Vienna; Vienna, beginning of May, 1790.)

"Dearest, Best of Friends and Brother,

"I am very sorry to be unable to come and speak to you in person, but my toothache and headache are still too severe, and in general I feel very unwell. I agree with you as to the desirability of procuring a few good pupils, but I preferred to wait until I had moved to my new quarters, because I propose to give lessons at home. In the meantime, I beg you to make this idea of mine known. I also intend to give subscription concerts at my house during the months of June, July and August, hence it is only my present position that is so irksome. When I move, I shall have to pay 275 florins for the new lodgings, and I have also to live until my concerts are arranged and until the quartets on which I am working have been sent to be engraved. If, therefore, I could but lay hands at this moment on at least 600 florins, I should be able to apply myself to composing in a fairly peaceful frame of mind, for oh, how essential for that is peace of mind . . . "

"Vienna, May 17th, 1790.

". . . As to my debt to you, which has been so long outstanding, I must unfortunately beg you to have patience. If you only knew the worry and distress all this causes me. It has prevented me all this time from finishing my quartets. I now have very great hopes of the Court, for I know from a reliable source that the Emperor has not sent back my petition as he has those of the others, either granted or rejected, but has kept it, which is a good sign. On Saturday next I intend to give a performance of the quartets at my own house, and have great pleasure in inviting you and your wife. My dearest, best friend and Brother, do not let my importunity rob me of your friendship, but lend me your assistance. I rely entirely on you, and am ever

"Your most grateful

"Mozart."

"PS. I now have two pupils; I should like to increase the number to eight, so pray make it known that I take pupils."

"Vienna, August 14th, 1790.

"Dearest Friend and Brother,

"I feel as unwell to-day as yesterday. I was unable to sleep the whole night for pain. I must have been over-heated yesterday from so much walking and then inadvertently caught a chill. Picture my situation—ill and beset by worries and cares. Such a situation very considerably retards recovery. In a week or a fortnight things are sure to be better with me, but at present I am in serious want. Could you not help me out with a small sum? Anything at all would be a help at the moment. You would at least be for the moment relieving

"Your true friend, servant and Brother,

" W. A. Mozart."

To avoid the expenses of a double household, and also, no doubt, from motives of jealousy, Mozart was living for the most part in Baden. Who had need of him in Vienna? He had two pupils left. *Così fan tutte* was repeated ten times in the course of year, and then finally dropped out of the repertory; there could be no question of its having been a signal success. Mozart, as is clear from the letters he wrote at this period, was ailing and in low spirits. Wherever he looked, the prospect was bleak; he had come to the end of all things. A feeling that there was nothing more to be gained from the world often crept over him; it had turned its back on him, this world; the facts were so cruel that they spoke for themselves. This year and the year 1778 were the hardest of his life, the one being as unproductive as the other. Apart from the quartets for Frederick William II and the arrangement of Handel's *Ode for St. Cecilia's Day* and *Alexander's Feast*, there were no additions to the catalogue of his works. There was not the remotest prospect of further commissions, for he was completely forgotten in Vienna. When, in the autumn, King Ferdinand of Naples stayed there on a visit, Salieri's *Azur* was chosen as the opera to be given at a gala performance for him and the Emperor. Indeed, it never entered anyone's head at this period to ask Mozart, the "Imperial Chamber Composer"—for this had been his title since Gluck's death—to take part in the Court concerts; Haydn was presented to the two rulers and honoured by them, Mozart was passed over. This neglect cut him to the heart, not least because of what Constanze might think. Once more we glimpse the alternating flush and pallor on the features of the poor master.

On October 9th Leopold II was to be crowned in Frankfurt. Salieri and fifteen Court musicians travelled thither in advance. Mozart, who by virtue of his official post was a member of the Imperial suite, received no command to join it. He resolved, nevertheless, to go to Frankfurt, and to try his luck on his own and at his own risk. For the atmosphere at home was once more becoming too restricted for him; he had nothing to do, and, what was more, he did not care to remain behind and to figure in Constanze's eyes as a man who had been passed over, a failure. He preferred to pawn his silver table service.

In order to purchase a carriage—he intended to hire horses and drivers from at the various post-stations en route—he raised 800 florins on a note of hand for 1,000 florins. His brother-in-law, the violinist Hofer, who was even poorer than he, was thus able to accompany him. A fine thing indeed! But it was not to be expected that Mozart would, in his present situation, place any more restraint on his generosity than before. Quite the contrary. The two travellers set out on September 23rd, going by way of Linz, Efferding, Passau, Regensburg, Nuremberg and Aschaffenburg, and arrived in Frankfurt on September 28th.

The journey had been a very agreeable one, he wrote that same day to Constanze.

> "Frankfurt-on-Main, September 28th, 1790.
>
> " . . . The journey was very agreeable. We had fine weather except for one day, and this one day caused us no discomfort, for my carriage (I could almost give it a kiss) is admirable. We had a capital meal at mid-day in Regensburg, divine music, positively English hospitality, and a splendid Moselle. We breakfasted in Nuremberg, an ugly town. We fortified our precious stomachs with coffee in Würzburg—a fine, magnificent city. The charges were everywhere reasonable except in Aschaffenburg, but two and a half hours from here by diligence, where the landlord of the inn thought fit to overcharge us famously. I look forward eagerly to news from you, of your health, our affairs, etc. I am quite determined to make the most of my opportunities here, and look forward then to returning to you. What a glorious life we shall lead! I shall work, and work in such a manner that I may never again be reduced by unforeseen circumstances to so distressing a position . . . "

How significant it is that he should find Nuremberg ugly and Würzburg beautiful.

"Frankfurt-on-Main, September 30th, 1790.

" . . . My love, I shall without doubt achieve something here—but certainly not as much as you and some of my friends imagine. Well, we shall see. But I always like to play a safe game, hence I am very anxious to settle the business with H——, for I shall thereby get some money, and shall have no need to pay it back, but merely to work, and that I shall gladly do for the sake of my little wife. Where do you think I am staying? In the same house as the Böhms; Hofer is here too. We pay thirty florins a month, which is remarkably cheap. We also eat with them.

"As I do not know whether you are in Vienna or Baden, I am addressing this letter also to the Hofers. I am looking forward like a child to being with you again. If people could see into my heart, I should be almost ashamed. All within is cold, icy cold. If you were with me, I should perhaps derive some pleasure from the kindly manner in which I am treated here, but as it is, everything seems so empty. Adieu, my love, I am ever

"Your husband who loves you with his whole heart,

"Mozart."

But he is once more in good spirits.

"Frankfurt-on-Main, October 3rd, 1790.

" . . . I have been living here in complete retirement up till now, do not go out the whole morning, but stay in my hole of a room and write. The theatre provides me with my only relaxation, and there I meet with acquaintances in plenty, from Vienna, Munich, Mannheim and even Salzburg. Franz Lange and Gres, the Secretary of the Treasury, are here, also old Wendling, with his Dorothea . . . I should like to go on living thus, but I fear it will end soon enough, and a disturbed life begin. I am in great demand everywhere, and unpleasant as I find it to let myself be seen everywhere, I realise the necessity of doing so, and must bear with it in God's name. There is reason to suppose that my concert will not go off so badly. I wish it were over, if only in order to be nearer the time when I may hold my dear one in my arms again. On Tuesday the Elector of Mainz's company is to perform my *Don Giovanni* in my honour. Farewell, my love. My regards to the few friends who mean well by me, take care of your precious health and be ever my Constanze, as I shall ever be

"Your

"Mozart."

If only the money-lenders had not been in the background with their expectant countenances! Constanze had by now been taken into his confidence with regard to his difficulties, and she must at times have been anxious. In his letter of October 8th there are once again a great many references to sums of 800 and 1,000 and 1,600 and 2,000 florins:

" . . . I shall certainly not make so much here that I shall be in a position to pay 800 or 1,000 florins immediately on my return; but if at least the Hofmeister business is so far advanced that only my presence is required to settle it, I shall lay hands immediately (reckoning the interest at 20 per cent) on 2,000 to 1,600 florins, and still have 600 florins in hand. In Advent I shall in any case give a few small subscription quartet concerts, and also take some pupils (I need never repay the capital since I write for H.) and so all will be well. But I entreat you to settle the H. business if you wish me to return. If you could only see into my heart, in which the desire, the longing, to see you and hold you in my arms again battles with the desire to bring home a considerable sum of money. I have often toyed with the thought of travelling farther afield, but whenever I have brought myself to the point of making such a resolve, it has come over me how dearly I should rue it, were I to part for so long from my dear wife and set out on a possibly fruitless journey, with no certain prospects. I feel as though I had been away from you years already. Believe me, my dear, if you were with me I might perhaps more easily make up my mind to such a course, but I am too used to your presence and love you too much to endure separation from you for long. And besides, people talk a great deal of nonsense about the German cities. I am, it is true, famous, popular and admired here; for the rest the people are even more close-fisted than the Viennese. If my concert turns out moderately well it will be thanks to my reputation, and to the Countess Hatzfeldt and the Schweitzers, who have taken endless pains on my behalf. Incidentally I shall be glad when it is over. If I work hard in Vienna and take pupils, we shall be able to live really well; and nothing but a good engagement at one or other of the Courts will dissuade me from this plan. But try to settle the business with Hofmeister. . . and to make known my intention to take pupils, and then we shall certainly not fare ill. Adieu, my love, you will receive further letters from me, but I unfortunately can get no more from you.

"Ever love your
"Mozart."

He was once more living in the whirl of activity that he really liked. On October 15th—the coronation celebrations were then over—he gave his concert in the Stadttheater. The programme consisted solely of works by himself. He played two piano concertos, presumably those in F and D major (K. 459 and 537). He was enchanted by the performance of the young Frau Margarethe Schick, who, with Ceccarelli of Salzburg, sang airs and duets from his operas. In addition he played a concerto for two pianos with old Beecké, whom he had met again in Frankfurt; and of course his poor brother-in-law, Hofer, in whom we may be sure no one was interested, was one of the performers and played a Duo Concertante for piano and violin with him. The double bass player, Ludwig, a member of the orchestra, had some interesting things to say about the rehearsal.

He related how the agile and restless little composer frequently jumped up from the piano, which stood on the stage, leaped over the prompter's box into the orchestra, and then after an animated discussion with the musicians clambered back just as swiftly on to the stage.

From the handbills of the concert it is clear that Mozart eventually moved to Kahlbechergasse 167, in the neighbourhood of the theatre.

The proceeds of the concert were inconsiderable.

> " . . . my concert took place to-day at eleven o'clock; so far as honour went it was a great success, from the monetary point of view pretty wretched. Unfortunately a certain Prince was giving a *grand déjeuner*, and the Hessian troops were holding grand manoeuvres. But then all the time I have been here there has always been something to interfere with my concerts, you cannot conceive what it has been like. All this notwithstanding I was in such good spirits and so delighted my audience that I was entreated to give another concert next Sunday . . . "

The second concert never took place. On October 16th or 17th he set out on his homeward journey.

> "Mannheim, October 23rd, 1790.
>
> " . . . to-morrow we are going to Schwetzingen to see the garden. This evening *Figaro* is being given here for the first time, and the day after tomorrow we leave. It is on account of Figaro that I am still here, for the whole company entreated me to stay on until the performance and to give them my support at the rehearsal. That is also the reason for my being unable to write as long a letter as I should like, for the dress rehearsal has begun. Indeed, the first act at least must be over by now. I hope you have safely received my letter of the 17th from Mainz.
>
> "The day before my departure I played before the Elector, and received but a miserly 15 Carolin. Do but set on foot the

business with H . . ."

In Mannheim, during the dress rehearsal of *Figaro*, which Mozart mentions in the letter of October 23rd, there occurred that scene which is described by the actor Backhaus: "I found myself in a very embarrassing situation with regard to Mozart. I took him for a little journeyman tailor. I was standing by the door during the rehearsal. He came up to me and asked me whether he might listen. I turned him away.—'Surely you will let Kapellmeister Mozart listen? '—At this I was as embarrassed as it is possible to be."[1]

Where is now the elegant young Mozart the people of Leipzig and Berlin had seen in him the year before. The expensive lace-cuffs, the jabots, the trinkets and buttons, the fine coats even—had they too been either sold or pawned?

Mozart's journey home took him via Heidelberg, Augsburg, and, on October 29th, to Munich. There he stayed with his old friend Albert, the host of the "Schwarze Adler", a tavern in the Kaufingerstrasse. His stay was prolonged until November 6th, because he had been commanded by the Elector of Bavaria to play at a concert in honour of the King of Naples, who, on his way home from Frankfurt, stayed two days in Munich.

" . . . I intended (apart from the fact that I should like to spend some time with my old Mannheim friends) to stay here only for one day, but I shall now have to stay until the 5th or 6th because the Elector has requested me to give a concert in honour of the King of Naples. This is really a distinction. A

[1] Ludwig Nohl, 'Musikalisches Skizzenbuch'

fine honour for the Viennese Court that the King is obliged to hear me outside Vienna . . .

"I look forward eagerly to seeing you, for I have a great deal to discuss with you. I have in mind to make this same tour with you at the end of next summer, my love, so that you may try some other waters; the distraction, the travelling, and change of scene will do you good, for it has agreed with me famously. I am really delighted with this plan, and so are all my friends.

"Forgive me for not writing as long a letter as I could wish, but you cannot conceive how much I am sought after here . . ."

It would have been only natural for him to have met his sister again either in St. Gilgen or Salzburg, but since Leopold's death there had been some sort of breach with her. Here there is no mistaking Constanze's influence on Mozart—and of course matters connected with the inheritance played no small part—and at this time, in particular, her influence was very considerable. Mozart's letters to her were full of devotion and love, the undertones were franker; his affection for her was much more unqualified than in the previous year. A premonition of death was already casting a sombre shadow on him. He would not admit this, for he loved life, he was still so young, and Constanze personified for him "the dear familiar things of life"; she was the element that bound him more firmly than all else to the terrestrial; he clung to her, she was to him a harbour of refuge, the dam that held back the illimitable, the palpable negation of all the terrors that lay beyond. In the midst of all his oppressive cares, his acute anxiety and distress, he yearned to make of her his confidante, his helpmeet, his true comrade. But in reality Constanze's affection for him had cooled. And to substantiate this we have no need of her letters. It is self-evident, if only from the way in which Mozart dwells in *his* letters on everything favourable or flattering that happens to him, perhaps even exaggerating a trifle here and there, in order to appear to advantage in her eyes.

For what was Constanze if not an ever-recurring wave that gradually ebbed far away from the unsuccessful Mozart, a fly that danced in the sun? It was not the incomparable musical genius—for what did that mean to her in the absence of outward splendour ?—that she beheld in him, but the musician who had achieved no success, half of whose household goods and chattels had found their way to the pawnbrokers, and who had now fallen out of popular favour. Others, after all, composed better than he . . .

So she accepted without question all his self-abnegation, all his chivalry, all the sacrifices he made for her; she had come to expect nothing else from him. Very nice too, he was a dear. But what about the thing that mattered most of all? With her cupidity we are sufficiently familiar. And this was not the first time that Mozart had begged her in his letters not to set too great hopes on the financial gain of a tour. She was used to being told this. In other words, he was once more coming home with empty pockets. Their misery would continue and become worse and worse. What attraction could he still have for her? She now preferred to stay in Baden, away from him. Life there, free from household cares and the worry of the children, was more amusing. And, pester him though she might with her jealousy, was it not after all more agreeable to take her baths, to enjoy gossiping and listening to the band, rather than to have him at her side—at one moment so near to her and ready for all sorts of fun, the next withdrawing himself completely from her, plunged into a mood of hopeless depression? How could she have had any inkling of his greatness! She did not even rate him particularly highly. Questioned about him after his death, all she could find to say was: "One had to be kind to him; he was such a kind person."

By the beginning of November Mozart was home again. A few weeks later, on December 15th, Joseph Haydn set out for London, there to compose some works for Salomon. Mozart, who was to have been engaged on the same terms for a later date, had, moreover, received a letter from O'Reilly, dated October 26th, 1790, containing a proposal couched in the following terms:

> *"Par une personne attachée à S.A.R. le Prince de Galle j'apprends votre dessein de faire un voyage en Angleterre, et comme je souhaite de connaître personellement des gens de talent, et que je suis actuellement en état de contribuer à leurs avantages, je vous offre Monsieur, la place de Compositeur en Angleterre. Si vous êtes donc en état de vous trouver à Londres vers la fin du mois de Décembre prochain 1790 pour y rester jusqu'à la fin de Juin 1791 et dans cet espace de temps de composer aux moins deux Opéras ou serieux ou comiques, selon le choix de la Direction, je voue offre trois cents livres Sterling avec l'avantage d'écrire pour le concert de la proposition, ou toute autre salle de concert, à l'exclusion seulement des autres théatres. Si cette proposition peut vous être agreable et vous êtes en etat de l'accepter, faites moi la grâce de me donner une réponse à vue, et cette lettre vous servira pour un Contrat."*

Here was the munificent offer he had so often dreamed of. It is strange enough that in view of his desperate straits he should have turned it down. But his thoughts were no longer on concert tours; perhaps, too, he no longer had the determination and the energy to undertake them. He vainly attempted to dissuade Haydn from accepting the engagement, and it was with a heavy heart that he saw him depart.

An unproductive year drew to a close. In December he composed the quintet in D major (K.593) for two violins, two violas and violoncello. This work and the Quintet in E flat major (K.614) which was not completed until April—Mozart's last chamber compositions—we owe, according to the publisher's announcement, to the "very active encouragement of a music-lover", by which he no doubt meant financial assistance; and we may perhaps presume that Gottfried von Jacquin, whose name crops up again after a long interval, is the person referred to.

❧

1791

MOZART'S LAST PIANO CONCERTO (K.595) WITH ITS interesting harmonies dates from December 5th of this year. No more trace of concessions, but once more an almost orchestral rush of lovely cadences and a larghetto the melancholy of which is traced in such pure lines that it only finds very restrained, almost subdued, expression.

January and February were filled with works that had been commissioned: an adagio with rondo in C minor for accordion, flute, oboe, violin and 'cello (K.6 17), songs, cantatas, all kinds of dances for Court and other festivities, dance music of moving abandon, sublime gaiety and arrogant grace. Yes, both his gaiety and grace were now arrogant. Mozart's affairs were at their lowest ebb. All of his possessions that were not fixtures had found their way to the pawnbrokers; even pawn-tickets had been pawned. He was obliged to accept the most beggarly commissions to keep the wolf from the door. There seemed to be no further prospect of his ever writing again for the theatre, and he found himself forgotten, a back number, in Vienna.

Then all of a sudden fortune once more smiled on him; and such creative energy was released in him that he soon made up for lost time, and his output was greater than ever it had been.

At the beginning of March Emanuel Schikaneder, whom Mozart knew from the Salzburg days, approached him with the suggestion that he should write a German "magic" opera. Schikaneder, a courageous, indeed, inspired impresario, was a man who had done much for the German theatre. Himself a famous Hamlet, he was responsible for productions not only of Shakespeare and Lessing, but of Goethe's and Schiller's first plays, of operas by Gluck, Haydn and Mozart and a whole string of German *Singspiel*e, and his company stood in high repute. It has become a tradition, however, for all biographers of Mozart to cast a slur on his name, and we are all too apt to take over uncritically so-called closed records. In September, 1857, the following account of the circumstances in which *Die Zauberflöte* came to be written appeared in the "Wiener Monatsschrift für Theater und Musik":

"It was on March 7th, 1791, that Emanuel Schikaneder, the Director of the Theater auf der Wieden, called at eight o'clock in the morning on Mozart, who was still in bed, and addressed him thus: 'Friend and brother, unless you help me, I am lost!' Mozart, still drunk with sleep, sat up, and said: 'How can I help you? I am a poor devil myself.'—Schikaneder: 'I need money—my affairs are in a wretched state; the Leopoldstadt is ruining me.' Mozart (bursting out laughing): 'And you come to me, brother? You are knocking on the wrong door.' Schikaneder: 'Not at all! Only you can save me. H—— has promised me a loan of 2,000 florins if you will write an opera for me. Out of this loan I should be able to pay the expenses, settle the rest of my debts, and give new life to my theatre. Mozart, you will save me from ruin and prove yourself before the world to be the most magnanimous man that has ever lived. Moreover, I shall remunerate you handsomely, and the opera, which will, without doubt, be a great success, is sure to bring you in a considerable sum. People say of me: Schikaneder is reckless, but ungrateful he certainly is not.' Mozart: 'Have you got a libretto?' Schikaneder: 'I am working on one. It is a magic tale, taken from Wieland's "Lulu" in the "Dschinnistan," and, I flatter myself, truly poetical. The prose is by me, but as I fear you will not approve of my verses, I am having them written by my friend Cantes, who, as you know, takes a very active interest in me and my theatre. So you can rely on him. In a few days' time the whole thing will be ready, and I shall bring it to you to read. Well, my dear friend, what do you say—will you say yes?' Mozart: 'I shall say neither yes nor no; I must think it over. I will give you a definite answer in a day or so.'

"Repeating over and over again that he was leaving his fate in Mozart's hands, Schikaneder took his departure. On the stairs he had a brilliant inspiration, and ran panting, as fast as was possible for a man of his bulk, from the Rauhensteingasse to the Wieden, to the so-called 'Kapäundl' in the Kapaunergasse, that stood there at that time. There lived Madame Gerl, who, with her husband, the bass-singer, belonged to Schikaneder's company, and who, people said, exerted a great influence on Mozart. The wily Schikaneder enlisted her interest in his plan, and the very next evening Mozart came to Schikaneder on the stage and said to him: 'Well then, see to it that I get the libretto soon, and I'll write the opera for you. If we come to grief I can't help it, for I have never yet composed a magic opera.' Within about a week Mozart had received the libretto, which he liked tolerably well, for it really did contain poetic, or, to be more precise, romantic ideas, which, owing to Schikaneder's complete lack of technical skill, were not fully worked out, but were nevertheless there.

". . . The opera was given in October, 1791, and, despite the limited size of the theatre and the cheapness of admission at that time, brought in by November 1st the sum of 8,443 florins, which seemed an almost fabulous sum. From then on it was put on frequently; but the master, who was growing weaker and weaker, who had been ill several times since his journey to Prague, and who was already worn out by incessant mental exertion (he wrote *La Clemenza di Tito, Die Zauberflöte,* and his *Requiem* all at about the same time), learned of his triumphs only by hearsay. At this time he seldom left his bed, and no longer ventured out at all.

". . . Mozart made very little out of *Die Zauberflöte*, for Schikaneder paid him very poorly for it and, moreover, sold the score to several theatres, without giving its great composer a share of the proceeds. When the attention of the good and noble man was drawn to this injustice, which was all the more flagrant in view of the fact that he had saved Schikaneder from ruin, all he said was: 'What am I to do about it? He is a wretch!' and there was an end of the matter. Obviously, apart from the already delicate state of his health, the work he got through, which was far beyond his physical strength, the sitting-up all through the night, and the resorting to stimulants to drive away sleep, all contributed to bring about his early death. The day before his death he said to his wife, the future Frau von Nissen, from whom Schreiber himself had it: 'I should so like to hear my *Zauberflöte* once more,' and proceeded to hum in a voice that was scarcely audible: '*Der Vogelfänger bin ich ja*.'"

The source of this whole story, then, was Constanze. Arthur Schurig, in the biography he published in 1923, challenges this version of the matter:

"Mozart gladly assented to Schikaneder's proposal. A German opera! For years this had been the master's great wish, apart from the fact that Schikaneder promised him the usual honorarium and certainly paid him an advance. The story that Schikaneder was himself in pecuniary straits at the time does not correspond with the actual facts. Equally base and untrue is the generally accepted story that Schikaneder cheated Mozart of his honorarium. According to the custom of those days a composer received a fixed honorarium, usually a hundred ducats, irrespective of whether his opera were a success or not. Royalties were only known at the time in France. There is not the slightest reason for supposing that Mozart did not receive his honorarium, particularly since Schikaneder's motto (put into practice in a thousand and one ways) was 'Live and let live'.

"It is highly probable that when, after Mozart's death, Constanze Mozart saw what a splendid profit Schikaneder was making out of *Die Zauberflöte*, she put forward claims which Schikaneder repudiated. She accused him of having illegally sold the score to other German theatres. What there may have actually been in this it is no longer possible to determine. In any case, Nissen's vague suspicions are merely based on the biased statements of the covetous Constanze. Schikaneder, in the years 1792–1804, was in such an extremely good financial position that an action at law based on genuine claims would have been well worth while. But most probably no such claims existed. Moreover, at that time in Vienna anyone who was successful laid himself open to the most monstrous and incredible accusations. Kormorzynski, Schikaneder's biographer, is convinced that it is doing Schikaneder an injustice to accept as historical truth the idle gossip spread abroad by Frau Constanze and Nissen."

There is food for thought in the fact that at this very time Mozart addressed the following lines to the faithful Puchberg:

> "Esteemed Friend and Brother,
>
> "On the 20th of this month, that is to say, in a week's time, I draw my quarter's salary. Until then if you can and will lend me some twenty florins, you will, my dear friend, render me greatly obliged to you and on the 20th (so soon as I receive my money) you shall have it back again with all my thanks. Till then I am ever
>
> "Your most beholden friend,
>
> "Mozart."
>
> "April 13th, 1791."

The advance, therefore, cannot have been considerable. And if actually, as Constanze knew so precisely, *Die Zauberflöte* had already brought in 8,443 florins by November, how did it come about that by December 5th, the day of his death, his total worldly wealth consisted of 60 florins? How do we know, however, that everything was not mortgaged in advance, that the usurers did not at once pounce upon whatever money came in? What is all that to us to-day? What we *do* know is the most essential thing of all, namely that, thanks to Schikaneder's offer, Mozart once more found himself in his true element, that a heaven opened out before him comparable only to that of the year 1776 and profoundly akin to it. Nothing of the light and bliss of that summer is lost or buried in the past; the first love of youth has not faded. But the ecstasies, the raptures, of this year are born of memories. The breezes of this year are wafted along in the light of *immaterial* suns. A new spring—alas, how far from his actual life is its blossoming!

For his life was now but a feverish zig-zagging between exuberance, exhaustion, battling against hopeless odds, ultimate success and ultimate collapse: a wild chase, himself the hunted prey.

May, June and July he devoted to *Die Zauberflöte*. In June Constanze once more betook herself to Baden for a cure, this time taking with her their seven-year-old son. Funds were non-existent, and Mozart had to find them. In order to reduce housekeeping expenses, the cook, who was also maid-of-all-work, was dismissed. The ailing, seriously overworked Mozart, himself so sorely in need of care and attention, remained neglected and alone at home. For the first few days he slept at the Leitgebs', old friends from the time of the Italian tours.

"June 6th, 1791.

"*Ma très chère épouse,*

"*J' écris cette lettre dans la petite chambre au jardin chez Leitgeb où j'ai couché cette nuit excellement-et j'espère que ma chère épouse aura passé cette nuit aussi bien que moi. J'y passerai cette nuit aussi, puisque j'ai congédié Léonore, et je serais tout seul à la maison, ce qui n'est pas agréable*—

" . . . I have this moment received your dear letter, and am delighted to learn that you are well and cheerful. Madame Leitgeb tied my neckcloth for me, but how? My God! I kept telling her how to do it, but it was of no use . . . "

"Baden, June 7th, 1791.

> "Since you wrote Vienna, I must write Baden!
> "I received your last letter of the 6th with indescribable pleasure, and see from it that you are happy and well. (We thought as much!) . . . Yesterday I ate at midday with Süssmayr at the *Ungarische Krone*, because at one o'clock I still had business in the town . . . To-day I am dining with Schikaneder, as you will know, since you also were invited . . ."

Mozart's profound dejection did not, however, escape Schikaneder's notice. To keep him in the cheerful frame of mind which was so essential for the composition of *Die Zauberflöte*, he invited him frequently to dine at his house, where there was feasting and carousing and revelry, and Mozart willingly let himself be drawn into this circle; it was only tedious people that he could not endure. He became caught in the toils of the captivating Frau Gerl, a member of Schikaneder's company. Franz Gerl, her husband, was the original Sarastro. In a courtyard, next door to the theatre, was a small pavilion—the one that now stands on the Kapuzinerberg in Salzburg and to which hordes of foreigners make pilgrimages every summer. This pavilion was fitted up as a work-room for Mozart, and there he spent many hours of the day; there too Schikaneder often visited him, bringing along young actresses to raise the composer's s spirits. Many a night, we are told, he spent there dancing. For Mozart not only worked hard, he also lived hard. In his eyes Constanze's absence was not an unmixed evil. His letters to her were as tender and solicitous as ever; sometimes he wrote to her twice a day, but the bond that held them together had long since slackened; nothing was left of their infatuation, nothing but jealousy. And never was there a word in his letters to her about the state of his work—his real life. On the other hand, he never made her suffer for the fact that his nerves were strained to breaking-point. Everyone else was made to feel his irritability; his temper was uncertain. Constanze alone was spared. She had made all kinds of undesirable acquaintances at Baden, of whom he disapproved. What did that matter? For the lazy Constanze, who was incapable of reading between the lines, who was utterly outside his real life, he found no sacrifice too great. The problem now arose of finding the money for her trip. Once more typical "negotiations" were entered into by poor Mozart with a certain ——. The humiliating chasing hither and thither was indescribable, the disturbance to his work unspeakable.

How characteristic of the composer is the disparaging tone that he adopts when writing of his favourite pupil, Süssmayr! Süssmayr, whom he deemed worthy of being his collaborator, with whom he talked over all his problems, whom he took so fully into his confidence with regard to his work. He would make game of him in and out of season—that same Süssmayr whom he kept at his side until the very last, who was the principal figure at his death-bed, and to whom he entrusted the completion of his Requiem.

"Vienna, July 12th, 1791.

"Dearest, sweetest little Wife,

"Why did I receive no letter yesterday evening, to relieve my anxiety with regard to the baths? This and one or two other things ruined the whole of yesterday for me. I went to see —— in the afternoon, and he promised me on his word of honour to come to me between twelve and one o'clock, to settle everything. I could not, therefore, dine with Puchberg, but was obliged to wait. I waited until it struck half-past two, and as he did not come I wrote a note and sent the girl to his father's house. I then went to the *Ungarische Krone*, because it was too late anywhere else, and even there I had to eat alone, for everyone had already left. You can imagine what my meal was like, what with my anxiety on your account and my vexation at ——'s behaviour. If only I had had a soul with me to afford me some small consolation! It is not good for me to be alone when I have anything on my mind. At half-past three I was back at home. The girl had not yet returned. I waited, waited—and at half-past six she arrived with a note. Waiting is disagreeable at any time, but much more so when the results do not come up to one's expectations. The note contained nothing but excuses, regrets, that he had not yet learned anything definite, and assurances that he would not forget me and would quite certainly keep his word. I then went, in order to cheer myself up, to the Kasperltheater, to hear the new opera, *Der Fagottist*, which has made such a stir, but there's nothing to it. As I went by I looked in at the café to see if Lobel were there, but he wasn't there either. In the evening I dined again at the 'Krone' (so as not to be alone), for there I at least had an opportunity of talking to someone; then I went straight to bed. At five o'clock this morning I was up again, dressed immediately, called on Montecuculi, whom I found at home, then went on to ——'s, but he had already flown! I am only sorry that because the business had not been settled I was unable to write to you early this morning. I did so want to write to you!"

"June 12th, 1791 (?)

"*Ma très chère épouse,*

" —— has this moment left for Baden. It is nine o'clock in the evening and I have been at his house ever since three o'clock. I think he will keep his word. He promised me to visit you; I beg you also to do your best with him. But I entreat you not to go to the Casino. In the first place, because of the company there—*you must know what I mean*—and in the second, you cannot dance in any case, and as for looking on—you can do that better when your husband is there. I must close, for I have still to go to Montecuculi's—I just wanted to send you these hurried lines—a proper letter from me will arrive to-morrow. Adieu.Do what I have asked you in my letters with regard to the baths and love me as I do and always will love you.

"Always your

"Mozart."

"My regards to your Court Jester!"

"Vienna, June 25th, 1791.

" . . . You ask me where I slept? At home, of course. I slept capitally, except that the mice bore me very good company—I had a regular discussion with them. I was up before five o'clock. A propos, I advise you not to go to Mass tomorrow—the peasant oafs are too rough for my liking. True, you have a burly companion, but the peasants have no respect for him—*perdent respectum*, for they can see at a glance that he is a great booby. Snai !—

"I will answer Süssmayr by word of mouth—I grudge wasting paper on him . . . "

"Vienna, Saturday, July 2nd, 1791.

" . . . Please tell that bungler Süssmayr to send me my first act, from the introduction to the finale (of *Die Zauberflöte*), so that I can orchestrate it. It would be a good thing if he could get it ready to-day, so that it can go off by the first coach to-morrow, and then I shall get it by midday. Some Englishmen have just called; they were anxious not to leave Vienna without making my acquaintance. But no, this is not true! They really wished to meet the great Süssmayr, and came to me to ask where he lived, having heard that I had the good fortune to have some standing with him. I told them to go to the 'Ungarische Krone'; and wait there till he returns from Baden. Snai! They are going to offer him a post as lamp cleaner . . . "

"Vienna, July 4th, 1791.

" . . . I must be brief, for it is half-past one, and I have not yet dined. For the present here are three florins. I wish I could send you more. To-morrow at midday you shall have more. Be merry, keep your heart up, everything will be well yet. I send you 1,000 kisses. I am faint for lack of food. Adieu.

"Ever your

"Mozart.

"I have waited until now, as I hoped to be able to send you more money."

"Vienna, July 5th, 1791.

"Here are 25 florins. Settle your account in Baden. Then when I come we can settle up everything. —— really must send me Nos. 4 and 5 of my score, also the other thing that I have asked for, and must . . . I must rush off to Wetzlar's, or else I shall not find him in. Adieu. I send you 2,000 kisses and am always

"Your

"Mozart.

"P.S. Did you not laugh when you received three florins? I thought, however, it would be better than nothing. Enjoy yourself, my little precious; and be always my Stanzi M."

"Vienna, July 5th, 1791.

" . . . Do not be melancholy, I beg you! I hope you have received the money. It is really better for your foot that you should remain in Baden, as you can get out more easily there. I hope to hold you in my arms on Saturday, perhaps sooner; as soon as my business is settled I shall be with you. I intend now to take a real rest in your arms, and I shall need it too. For all the worry and trouble and all the rushing hither and thither in connection with it, is, after all, somewhat wearing. I received the last packet, and thank you for it. I cannot tell you how glad I am that you are no longer taking the baths. In a word, the only thing I lack is your presence, I do not think I can wait for it; I could, of course, have you back for good when all this business is settled, but—I so much want to spend a few more happy days with you in Baden . . ."

"Wednesday, July 6th, 1791.

"I cannot tell you how pleased I was to hear that you had received the money safely. I do not remember having written to you that you were to settle *everything*. How could I, as a reasonable creature, have written such a thing? If so, my wits must have been wandering. At the moment, when I have so many weighty matters on my mind, it is very possible. I only meant to refer to the account for the baths. The rest is for your own use, and as to anything else there is to pay, which I have included in my reckoning, I shall settle it myself on my arrival. At this very moment Blanchard is either going up in his balloon or fooling the Viennese for the third time. This Blanchard business is not at all to my liking to-day. It is preventing me from settling my affairs. —— promised me before he went off there to call on me, but he did not come. Perhaps he will come when the fun is over. I shall wait until two o'clock; then I shall swallow a little food, and go in search of him everywhere. Our life is not exactly a pleasant one. Patience, it will soon mend, and I shall rest in your arms!

"I thank you for your counsel not to rely entirely on —, but in a case of this kind one must only do business with *one* person. If one gets into touch with several, one appears to the others, with whom one cannot close, to be either a fool or unreliable. Well, you can give me no greater pleasure than to be happy and jolly, for if I am but assured that you want for nothing all the pains I am taking will be pleasant and agreeable, for the most desperate and most preposterous situation in which I could find myself would be a mere trifle if I knew that you were well and happy. And now farewell, make use of your Court Jester, think and talk of me often, love me always as I love you, and be always my Stanzi Marini, as I am ever

"Your

"*Stul !—Knaller paller*
Schnip—schnap—schnur
Schnepeperl—
Snai!—"

"Vienna, July 7th, 1791.

". . . There is something I cannot read in your letter and something I don't understand. You write: 'To-day my little husband will also, no doubt, be in the great com. in the Prater,' etc. etc. The adjective before 'little husband' I cannot read. 'Com', I take it, means 'company', but what '*great company*' you mean, I do not know.

" Tell Sauermayr (Süssmayr) that I have had no time to keep running to his servant, and whenever I have gone there he was never at home. For pity's sake give him the three florins to stop him from blubbering—

"The only thing I long for now is for this business to be settled, if only so that I may be with you again. You cannot conceive how long a time it seems since I was with you! I cannot explain what I feel to you—it is a certain emptiness that positively hurts, a certain longing that is never appeased and, therefore, never abates, but persists, nay, grows from day to day. When I think how childishly merry we were together in Baden, and what gloomy, tedious hours I spend here! Even my work gives me no pleasure, for I have grown accustomed to break off from time to time and exchange a few words with you, and that pleasure is now, alas, an impossibility. If I go to the piano and sing something from my opera, I am obliged to break off; for I am overcome. Basta! The very moment this business is settled, I shall be gone from here . . . "

Here we have alas! our only quotation from Constanze's letters to Mozart. She saw in him her "little husband" who belonged exclusively to her and was at her service—no more.

"Vienna, July 9th, 1791.

" . . . I hope you received my letter of yesterday. Well, the time, the happy time, of our being together again draws near. Be patient, and keep up your spirits. Your letter of yesterday made me so downhearted that once more I almost resolved to come out to you without settling my affairs, and then where would we be? I should have to return at once, or else, instead of being happy, live in a state of anxiety. In a few days the whole thing is sure to be settled. Z. made me too serious and solemn a promise to fail me now, and I shall be with you immediately. If you like, however, I will send you the necessary money, so that you can settle up everything, and come home! That would suit me, although I fancy that in this fine weather you may still find Baden very agreeable, and salutary for your health, because of the lovely walks. You will know best. If you think that the air and the distractions are doing you good, then stay, and I will come and fetch you, or, if you like, stay on a few days; or, as I have said, if you would prefer, come home tomorrow; write to me frankly. And now adieu, dearest Stanzi Marini. I send you a million kisses and am ever

"Your
"Mozart."

Constanze's anxiety to return home this time was due to the fact that she was shortly expecting her confinement; their youngest son, Franz Xavier Wolfgang, was born on July 26th. But the expenses of her stay in Baden had first of all to be met, and we have seen from Mozart's letters how much rushing hither and thither this meant for him. On the 9th he travelled to Baden, on the 10th conducted his Mass in B major, and by the 11th was already back in Vienna with his family.

In June, too, he had paid visits of several days' duration to Baden; he was, we see, always glad to be with his Stanzi when she was in a good mood. But whereas she spent her time with chance acquaintances, he formed a close friendship with one of the most enthusiastic admirers of his work, Stoll, schoolteacher and choirmaster. Mozart took Stoll seriously, and therefore treated him as he treated Süssmayr, venting his high spirits on him and making a butt of him. The first letter he ever wrote him contains the following post-script: "This is the silliest letter I have ever written, but it's just suitable for you." On the other hand, he lent him his Masses, and on one occasion, when a soprano soloist refused to follow his instructions, he dismissed her out of hand and replaced her by Stoll's eleven-year-old niece, Antonia Hüber, devoting a week to going through the part with her. On the day of the performance the child sang to his entire satisfaction, and in his delight he made her a present of a ducat. "Tonerl," he said to her, "see that you grow up quickly into a big girl, so that I can take you to Vienna with me!" He was now composing uninterruptedly. And suddenly this incalculable Mozart turned his attention afresh to the composition of religious music.[1] His *Ave, verum corpus,* that gem from our treasury of Church music, composed at Stoll's instigation for the feast of Corpus Christi, was completed on June 17th. In this composition, too, there was a meeting between the Mozart of today and the Mozart of long ago, the pupil and disciple of Padre Martini.

Things have been thrown out of their normal course. Is there any security left for the landmarks of our European cities, their cathedrals, their cupolas, their steeples? Are we not being despoiled right and left of our old churches? How few have remained entirely immune from the universal desolation? We do not allude to the saints on the portals, whose heads were struck off by an inflamed mob—stone is merciful, it weathers !—but to the ruin or destruction of secular stained-glass—it too is music, impassioned diapasons! In their place we are perpetually confronted with shrieking disharmonies in the colours of the substituted windows, in the inset doors, which resemble those of com-

[1] Upon application he had been appointed assistant to the *Kapellmeister* of the Stefanskirche, with the prospect of succeeding him.

mon lodging-houses, in lighting fixtures which are like those to be found in multiple shops, in the whole ghastly paraphernalia of coloured statues and restorations.

Because this had to be, the great masters, who never die out on this planet, of ours, took thought for us. Ships, ready fitted out, are always waiting to sail the seas of our forlornness from any quarter of the heavens. We have Haydn's and Mozart's masses, Beethoven's *Missa Solemnis*; they too are cathedrals; ecclesiastics too the creators of these *Credo*, these *Incarnatus est*, these *Gloria*. We have the *Sancta Maria*, that Sainte Chapelle, Palestrina and Johann Sebastian Bach.

After the return from Baden, commissions all of a sudden came pouring in. Da Ponte suggested that Mozart should go with him to London and there compose for the Italian Opera. Mozart was not averse to the plan, but wanted first to finish *Die Zauberflöte*, and asked for six months' grace. Da Ponte was unable to wait so long, and set off alone.

Shortly afterwards came the mysterious commission for the *Requiem*, received in a flattering but anonymous letter, containing enquiries both as to terms and as to the time within which the work could be completed. The bearer was a sinister-looking, lean man dressed in mourning. Mozart discussed the matter with Constanze, and on her advice named a sum of 100 ducats (according to others 50), but did not undertake to complete the work within a fixed time. A few days afterwards the messenger turned up again, bringing the required sum, and holding out hopes of a further sum on delivery of the work, but cautioning Mozart against trying to discover the identity of the man who was giving him the commission, whose name he was never to learn.

This incident proved—though too late for Mozart—to have a more than prosaic explanation, and turned out to be a ruse resorted to by a certain Count Walsegg. This man, at once megalomaniac and plagiarist, was in the habit of procuring quartets, which he copied out in his own hand and then had performed. This invariably aroused a great deal of conjecture as to the authorship of the work, and the audience always paid the Count the compliment of ascribing it to him. A short time previously his wife had died, and he surreptitiously set about obtaining a beautiful requiem in her honour. His was no isolated case at that time. Those who have, always want to have everything. It is the well-known envy of the possessing classes. How preposterous it was that people who were nothing, and had nothing, composed music, wrote poetry or painted?

Mozart was at first unable to give any attention whatever to this new work. *Die Zauberflöte* was not yet completed, and at the beginning of August he was given the much more urgent commission to write an opera for the celebrations in connection with the coronation of the Emperor Leopold as King of Bohemia. The libretto, which had been adapted by Mazzola, poet to the Dresden court, and had been set to music innumerable times already by, amongst others, Jomelli, Hasse, Guiseppe Scarlatti and Holzbauer, was *La Clemenza di Tito*. An *opera seria*, therefore, a form with which Mozart had not concerned himself since his *Idomeneo*, and which he regarded as something that he had put behind him. But how could he refuse such an honourable task, which, moreover, was to carry with it a fee of 200 ducats? The offer came from Guardasoni. No one in Prague could compare in popularity with Mozart. The coronation, however, had long since been fixed for September 6th, and, because opposition had made itself felt in certain quarters at Court, Mozart received the commission so late that he had only a few weeks in which to get through the enormous amount of work involved. His days were now one long incessant chase, and he himself, far more than he knew, was the creature hunted. *Tito* consists of 50 numbers; to tackle them single-handed in such a short space of time was an impossibility. He therefore drew in the trusted and talented Süssmayr as collaborator. We know nothing definite of Süssmayr's share in the work, beyond the fact that all the secco recitatives are by him, and that Mozart took him with him to Prague, so that they might work together on the journey. Just as he was about to step into the chaise, the sinister messenger once more appeared, plucking at Constanze's dress and enquiring after the Requiem. Mozart excused himself by referring to the commitments that had hitherto prevented him from working on it, but promised, so soon as he should return, to make a start on it.

Constanze? Was she also going to Prague? Why, of course. Whenever there was a question of her enjoying herself, she was forthwith in the pink of health. If the children stood in the way, they were speedily boarded out: the seven-year-old at Perchtoldsdorf, near Vienna, and the babe in arms elsewhere. One would like to be able to attribute this to anxiety for her sick husband. But she knew that in the Villa Bertramka, where his visits were always eagerly looked forward to, he would be well looked after. Far better than in Vienna, where, on their return, she immediately left him on his own again, and went off to Baden for another cure. Her visit was anything but welcome to the Duscheks, and she could only have had an acutely disturbing effect on her over-worked husband. That he had not counted on her coming, for, after all, there were so many duties to keep her at home, we may gather from the fact that he had asked Süssmayr to accompany him. The carriage that he had secured for himself was surely far less roomy than the one in which he had travelled to Prague as the guest of Lichnowsky. It is unlikely also, that they all three found accommodation in the Villa Bertramka, and probable that Mozart had to pay for Süssmayr's board and lodging in Prague at a time when it was over-crowded and all prices had been raised. How much more expensive must the journey of several days' duration and the stay of several weeks in Prague have been rendered by Constanze's irresponsible behaviour, how many of the 200 ducats must have been swallowed up! It was all one to her, she was not going to miss the festivities in Prague; Mozart was always fêted and made much of there; she wanted to have her share in it all, and he was not the man to deny her. She was to have her way, but she was not often again to see Mozart in cheerful mood, and she, too, was to be disappointed. Not only was *La Clemenza di Tito* a failure at Court, where the Empress gave a lead by terming it a *sporcheria tedesca*, but it also failed to rouse enthusiasm among his friends and admirers. Although its reception at the numerous repetitions during September was warmer, it was given for the last time on the 30th, the day of the première of the *Zauberflöte*, and then disappeared from the stage, only to be resurrected in the year 1795, at a benefit performance for Mozart's widow, at which Aloysia Lange took the role of Sextus. Even the approval of posterity was denied it. It shared the fate of Mozart's other *opera seria, Idomeneo*. We can only regret it.

In the remote past, the comfortable pre-war days in Munich, an abundance of major and minor works held the stage at the Royal Hof- and Nationaltheater: *Der Wild-*

schütz, Stradella, Malawika, Der Evangelimann, Das Nachtlager von Granada, Undine, Lobetanz, Der Corregidor, Ingwelde, Tiefland—and interspersed among all these the *Puppenfee* ballet drew packed audiences, and also in carnival time, sold out weeks beforehand, *Der Staberl auf Reisen*. There was no end of first-nights, of works by Thuille and Klose, Gräner and even Grieg; and under the musical dictatorship of Cosima Wagner the works of Siegfried Wagner, of the tedious and pretentious Max Schilling and the uneven Eugene d'Albert. Unable to withstand the great change, they have all been swept away by the tide.

Tito, too, was given once or twice in those old Munich days. How long ago it seems! But the flow of the music, for all the wooden lifelessness of the drama itself, its compelling charm, the passion that, like an inner tempest, impels Sextus across the stage, all this has not died away; they are impressions as of yesterday, though one may never again, even at concerts, have heard arias or other selections from *Tito* and may therefore have had no opportunity of revising one's first impressions. For how much can anyone, unless he happens to be a conductor, reconstruct from piano scores? And what wretched substitutes they are!

We know from the case of *Cosí fan tutte* that the light in which we view a work is susceptible of change. Why not at least try out *Idomeneo* and *Tito* from this standpoint? One would rather have them with amendments, or even cuts, than not at all. Even on gramophone records very little of *Idomeneo*, and nothing of *Tito* except the overture, has been recorded.

The high-water mark of Mozart's stay in Prague, his one compensation, was again a performance of *Don Giovanni*, which on September 2nd he himself, "a little man in a green coat", conducted in the presence of the Emperor and heard for the last time.

He was no longer the gay cavalier, who had had such a way with the women. They had been the light of his life, but the gathering shadows were now dimming that light.

Niemetschek relates that he "was ailing the whole time and was for ever taking medicine. His countenance was pallid and his expression melancholy, although in the company of his friends his spirits would revive and he would often bubble over with gaiety and fun".

In the middle of September he returned to Vienna. The failure of *Tito* was a great blow to him, and, as a result of over-work and disappointment, his health had deteriorated. He was overcome with emotion on taking leave of those true friends of his, the Duscheks. He knew that it was for ever. It is said that as he drove out through the gates of Prague he burst into a flood of tears. He was lamenting his hard fate, his early end, which he knew was near. In addition he was haunted by the thought of the man who had commissioned the *Requiem*, who had now sent a messenger to him three times, and whose name he did not know. The haggard, tall, sinister-looking fellow, who was nothing but a servant in mourning livery, became in his imagination a messenger from the other world. It was Death who had commissioned the *Requiem*, and he had been given the task of writing the Mass for his own obsequies.

Mozart's unstable state of mind at this time is perfectly explicable. He was worn out not only by the feverish amount of work he was getting through, but also probably by the feverish state of his health; kept restored temporarily by the various stimulants to which he resorted from time to time in order to keep himself awake, he was left all the more exhausted when their effects wore off. He felt himself to be weary unto death, and in this he was not mistaken.

True, he had called Death his friend. But what dreary abysses loomed in sight at His approach! Towards what yawning gulfs of horror was this Orpheus turning his steps? What depths of affliction was he penetrating? All the solemnity of death was upon him, who was only too apt to he aware of things about him. And yet how blessèd was he! How soothingly his last work was to open, in strains that suggest an end of all suffering:

Requiem aeternam dona eis.
(Give them eternal peace)

Much as it was already occupying his thoughts, he had still not had time to set to work on it. *Die Zauberflöte* had first to be brought to its gay conclusion. There was but little lacking now: the Men in Armour perhaps. Perhaps Papagena had not yet spread her wings. Perhaps the bird-call, which he put into the mouth of Pamina, had not yet been uttered—that love call of yearning assuaged, of ultimate, of overflowing bliss, an anguished cry of such universal appeal as has never been wrung from the breast of any other musician or poet—neither Bach nor Schubert, neither Walther van der Vogelweide nor Goethe, nor Eickendorff.

So wird Ruhe, so wird Ruh im Tode sein
(Peace shall come with death)

According to Constanze, Mozart very much feared death. Fear it he certainly did. But in the scale of his being this fear was only one key, a key it is true which was in itself a whole orchestra, but which was only to be struck and boom forth above all the others when he had only strength enough left to see himself being slowly submerged.

Numbered as were his days now, we recognise him clearly from the meteoric changes of his moods. And nowhere are they expressed in such wild fulness as in *Die Zauberflöte*. While he was putting the finishing touches to it, he wrote this letter to da Ponte:

> "My dear Sir,
>
> "I should like to follow your advice, but how am I to do so? . . . I cannot shake off the vision of this unknown man. I see him continually, he entreats me, he exhorts me, and impatiently bids me set to work. I go on working because composing is less tiring than resting. Moreover I have nothing more to fear. I can tell from my condition that the hour is striking; I am about to breathe my last; I have come to the end of my life before having had the full enjoyment of my talent. And yet life has been so beautiful, my career began under such happy auspices. But one cannot, after all, change one's own destiny. No one can measure the length of his own days; one must resign oneself, all will be as Providence wills. I must conclude, here before me is my death song; I must not leave it unfinished.
>
> "Vienna, September 7th, 1791.
>
> "Mozart."

Die Zauberflöte is not a mere segment of life like *Figaro* and *Don Giovanni*, or an episode like *Fidelio*; it is not a page torn out of life like *Die Meistersinger*, a classical piece such as Gluck's *Alceste*, a myth or a legend like Wagner's *Ring*, a reverie like Schumann's *Manfred*, a romance like *Der Freischütz*, a dream like Handel's *Acis and Galatea* or Richard Strauss's *Ariadne auf Naxos*—to bring this vast survey to an end in our own times. It is a fairy tale presenting the world in all its baffling entirety; it mirrors the perpetual struggle of the forces of the spirit against the lawless and the brutal; it anticipates the victory, won step by step, along mysteriously remote and devious paths, of the sublime over the base. And it is at the same time a popular Viennese "magic" extravaganza.

"The German," wrote Richard Wagner, "cannot exhaustively enough appreciate the significance of this work." Its deeper meaning, however, has in the course of time gradually revealed itself to us. And at last we have the key to the Queen of the Night, to the baroque *colloratura* passages in her airs. They are scintillating embellishments of a demonic sphere which is one with the resplendent figure of the Queen herself, who is in her turn one with the starless darkness which closes round her and her doings. And yet it is from her hands that comes the magic flute — that magic light !—which her attendant ladies—witches, then !—convey to Tamino. She is the principle that always desires evil . . . it is her own downfall that she encompasses in selecting Tamino as the instrument of her vengeance—light and darkness in their mysterious implications. Does not even Sarastro, who fulfils all that Plato demanded of a ruler, keep the sinister monster Monostatos in his service?

We should not let the naïve quality of the verse deceive us as to the content and fullness of the libretto. Goethe, who possessed so many of the traits of Sarastro, began work on a continuation of *Die Zauberflöte*, which was intended as a kind of study for Faust and remained a fragment. Schikaneder had borrowed the idea of this opera from a little tale of Wieland's called "Lulu oder die Zauberflöte". Schurig remarks in this connection: "In view of the daily interchange of ideas between Mozart and Schikaneder it is hardly singular that the libretto also should contain fleeting inspirations of Mozart's."

As a matter of fact they are discernible in all sorts of places, for Mozart felt in his element as never before. His own double life, his own apotheosis, is reflected in the opera. And yet no words can express the tragedy of his fate. Young, at the zenith of his creative powers, the Shakespeare of music, Mozart, in full awareness of his fate, bring his career to an end with *Die Zauberflöte.*

For nowhere else but in Shakespeare do we find young women of such extreme purity and yet possessed of such passion. And who is Monostatos if not a Caliban with a spice of the comic in his make-up, no less dangerous because his mode of expression is buffoonery. The German, too, of the Queen of the Night is of the village. This does not worry Mozart, for he is well able to make up for such shortcomings. And is she not, thanks to her music, as regal as though clad in a coronation robe of splendour and majesty?

Not infrequently in this opera verse and prose meet on the same level:

> Zu Hilfe! zu Hilfe, sonst bin ich verloren,
> Der listigen Schlange zum Opfer erkoren,
> Barmherzige Götter, schon nahet sie sich!
> *(Help me, O help me! I'm lost–*
> *Chosen as a sacrifice to the deceitful serpent*
> *O! merciful gods, it's getting nearer!)*

And a little further on:

> Ha! eine männliche Gestalt nahert sich dem Tal.
> *(Ha – a male figure is approaching the valley)*

In Mozart's opinion, however, a libretto should be no more than an "obedient handmaid" of the music. He drew it through the gold of his melodies. He freed it of all its inadequacies by the nobility of the music.

And what, forsooth, does the vagueness or not of the words matter when they are suffused with the first crimson flush of dawn as in Tamino's air:

Dies Bildnis ist bezaubernd schön, wie noch kein Auge je gesehn!
(This portrait is so enchantingly beautiful, no eye has ever seen)

And in his cry of yearning:

O, wenn ich sie nur finden könnte! O wenn sie doch schon vor mir stände!
(If only I could find her, that she, so beautiful, could stand before me)

And in Pamina's impatience:

Führt mich hin, ich mocht ihn sehn.
(Lead me there, I must see him . . .)

Richard Wagner, whose views on the role and importance of the words in music-drama were so widely divergent from those of Mozart, abandoned all his theories in his enthusiasm for *Die Zauberflöte*. "What an unconstrained and at the same time nobly popular appeal there is in every melody, from the simplest to the most overpowering," he exclaimed. "Indeed, Mozart took almost too enormous a stride in this opera, for by creating German opera, he produced at the same time the most finished example of that form of art, a masterpiece which it would be impossible to surpass, indeed, the brilliance of which can never be heightened or carried further."

On September 28th Mozart wrote the overture, and on the 30th the première took place in the "Theater auf der Wieden", a somewhat long, rectangular building resembling an enormous chest. Mozart conducted from the piano. Süssmayr sat beside him and turned over the pages. Nothing happened on this evening to give any hint of the enormous response which the *Die Zauberflöte* was to call forth so soon afterwards. The applause was so half-hearted that after the first act, Mozart, pale and agitated, rushed up to Schikaneder behind the scenes, and the latter had to bid him take heart. During the second act the audience warmed up somewhat, and at the conclusion of the opera there were calls for the two authors. But Mozart had hidden himself and it was only with the greatest difficulty that he was persuaded to appear before the footlights, so deeply hurt was he by the lukewarm reception of the work into which he had given of his best.

The next day he conducted the second performance and then, in accordance with custom, handed over the baton to another conductor. *Die Zauberflöte* was now performed hundreds of times in succession to vaster and vaster audiences. This, his greatest success, was also his last consolation.

Again Prague was the first town after Vienna to give a performance, and this took place on October 25th, 1792. It began its triumphal progress through Germany in Frankfurt in the year 1793. This is what the wife of Goethe has to say of its reception:

> "There is no news here except that *Die Zauberflöte* has been given eighteen times and that the house has always been cram-full. No one will have it said of him that he has not seen it—all the artisans, gardeners, indeed, even the *Sachsenhäusser*, whose boys play the lions and apes, go to it. Such a specta-

cle has never been witnessed here before. The house has to be opened for each performance before four o'clock and withal hundreds who are unable to obtain a seat have to return home again, and this has brought in a great deal of money. The king, when he was last here, paid 100 Carolin for the three times he visited it, and that only for Willemer's little box." ". . . Last week *Die Zauberflöte* was given for the twenty-fourth time to a house that was cram-full, and has already brought in 22,000 florins. How was it performed with you? Are your apes as good as our *Sachsenhäusser?*"

Thus Mozart repaid in full and overflowing measure all the money he had borrowed, as Wagner was also to do later, although in both cases it was others than their creditors who profited thereby!

The Italians called *Die Zauberflöte 'musica scellerata'*. The éclat it evoked remained for a long time, simply because of the German libretto, confined to Germany. It was regarded as too German. The best production was considered to be that put on in Berlin in May, 1794. The Berliners, indeed, were not sparing of their criticism of the Viennese production. And generally speaking even in our own day one hears more frequently of good performances of *Die Entführung, Figaro,* and *Don Giovanni*. The singer who played the title role of the latter used to go from one theatre to another, for it is hardly likely that there could have existed two famous Don Giovannis at one and the same time.

It was only during the war that many of us were privileged for the first time to hear perfect performances of *Die Zauberflöte*. The libretto had fallen into disrepute, and was treated with scant respect. In the year 1917 an entirely new production was put on under the direction of Richard Strauss, who brought out to the full all the magnificent features of the opera. The whole thing was presented to us with such creative taste, such consummate delicacy, that it left behind an indelible impression, and we were carried away by it: we had seen love, understanding, and wisdom triumph, and when, after the fall of the curtain, we dispersed and went our several ways, out into the dark nocturnal streets, there rose up in many of us that cry with which we awake to a new day after a terrible nightmare, except that in this case reality was the nightmare, the horror, and not the dream, which was so charged with the fragrance of Mozartian warmth and kindness. Oh how dark and nocturnal were our days at that period!

Very soon after the première, on October 7th, Constanze, accompanied by Süssmayr and her youngest sister Sophie, went to Baden again to take a second course of baths. Mozart himself had encouraged her to do so. He was once more the owner of a horse. Schikaneder had obviously fulfilled his obligations, for there was no question of rushing hither and thither to find the money for this stay. The children, now as ever, were boarded out, and Mozart was able to resume his bachelor existence in peace. Primus, the janitor, acted as his valet. He no longer missed Constanze. But he had begun to slip not only out of *her* reach but out of that of all his circle. *Die Zauberflöte* now lay behind him, and his thoughts were turned solely upon the *Requiem*. He refused to touch anything else until he had finished it; nor would he take any pupils; he even refused one recommended by Jacquin. He was wrapped in quiet—he who as a rule avoided being alone. And who could have roused him from his dejection? Even while he had been finishing *Die Zauberflöte* he had had fainting fits; less than ever now did he spare himself, for he felt weary unto death and the *Requiem* had to be brought safely into harbour; it must not be left unfinished. Now abandoned to boundless melancholy, now plucking up courage, often overcome by fits of weeping—this was the state in which he worked. A lamentable death it was, indeed, that he lamented as his own mourner. His genius was in full flower, now at last he saw himself on the threshold of success and fame, but he no longer had the strength to cross it.

His letters to Constanze—there are only three more of them—betray not the least hint of overstrain or weariness of spirit. He does not summon her to his side, and the letters read much as usual.

"Vienna, October 7th and 8th, 1791.
"Friday, half-past ten at night.

" . . . I am just come from the opera" (*Die Zauberflöte)*, "it was as full as ever. The duet '*Mann und Weib*, etc.' and the glockenspiel in the first act were encored as usual; also the boys' trio in the second act. What pleases me most of all, however, is the *silent applause*. One can clearly see that the opera is becoming more and more popular. Now as to how I have been spending my time: after you left I played two games of billiards with Herr v. Mozart (the man who wrote the opera at Schikaneder's theatre). Then I sold my nag for fourteen ducats. Then I got Joseph to tell Primus to bring me a cup of black coffee, and while I was drinking it I puffed away at a famous pipe of tobacco; then I orchestrated almost the whole of Stadler's rondo. Meanwhile a letter arrived from Stadler in Prague. The Duscheks are all well; it seems to me they cannot have received a letter from you—and yet I can hardly credit this. Enough! They have all heard of the splendid reception given to my German opera. The strangest thing of all is that on the very evening that my new opera was given for the first time and received with such applause *Tito* was given for the last time in Prague and was also received with immense applause. Bedini sang better than ever . . . at half past five I went out through the Stubenthor and took my favourite walk by way of the *Glacis* to the theatre. What do I see? What do I smell? Don Primus with the cutlets! *Che gusto!* Now I am eating your health; it has just struck eleven. Perhaps you are already asleep? Hush! Sh! Sh! I don't want to wake you!

"Saturday, the 8th.—You should have seen me at supper last night. I could not find the old tablecloth and so I got out a snowy-white one, and set the two-branched candlestick before me . . . Get Süssmayr to write something for Stadler for he has implored me to urge him to do so. You will no doubt be enjoying the baths as I write this. The barber came punctually at six o'clock, and Primus had lit the fire by half-past five and waked me by quarter to six. Why must it rain just now? I was hoping that you would have good weather. Do wrap up well to avoid taking cold. I hope that the baths will set you up for the winter, for it was only my wish that you should remain well that made me urge you to go to Baden. Time passes slowly without you—I knew it would. Had I had nothing to do, I would without hesitation have gone with you to Baden for a week. But I have no facilities for working out there, and I am very anxious to avoid, as far as possible, getting into difficulties. Nothing is more agreeable than to live in some sort of peace, and to this end one must work hard, and that I am doing with a will. Give Süssmayr a few good boxes on the ear from me, and please ask Sophie A. (whom I send 1,000 kisses) to give him a few as well. For heaven's sake do not let him go in want of them. I would not for anything in the world have him complain that you had not waited on him and looked after him fittingly. So give him rather too many slaps than too few.

"It might be well if you were to tweak his nose, knock out an eye or inflict some other visible injury on the fellow, so that he will be unable to deny what he has received at your hands. Adieu, my dear little wife. The coach is just about to leave. I hope for certain to have a few lines from you to-day and in this sweet hope I send you a thousand kisses and am ever

"Your loving husband,
"W. A. Mozart."

"Vienna, October 8th and 9th, 1791.
"Saturday night, at half-past ten.

"Dearest little wife,

"It was with great joy and delight that I found your letter on my return from the opera. The opera *(Die Zauberflöte)* was given to-day to a full house and received with the usual applause and encores, although Saturday, being post day, is always a bad day. It is to be repeated to-morrow, but suspended on Monday, so Stoll will have to come on Tuesday when there will be another opening performance; I say opening performance because it will probably be given again several times in succession. I have just eaten a delicious meal of hare brought me by Don Primus (my trusty henchman) and since my appetite is fairly hearty to-day, I have sent him out again to see whether he cannot get me something more, and in the meantime I am continuing my letter to you. I wrote so hard this morning that I went on without being aware of it until half-past one, and then rushed off in great haste to Hofer's (merely to avoid dining alone), where I also met Mamma. Immediately after dinner I came back and went on writing until it was time to go to the opera. Leitgeb asked me to take him again, and I did so. I am taking Mamma tomorrow; Hofer has given her the libretto to read beforehand. In Mamma's case, no doubt, it will be a question of her seeing, rather than hearing, the opera . . . I went behind the scenes during Papageno's air to the glockenspiel, for I had a strong impulse to play it myself to-day. Just for a joke I played an arpeggio during one of Schikaneder's pauses. He started, looked in the wings, caught sight of me, and would not proceed. I could guess what he was thinking and once more I played a chord. At that he struck the glockenspiel, saying 'Stop that!' The whole audience laughed; I fancy that many of them realised for the first timed that he does not play the instrument himself. By the way, you cannot imagine how much more delightful the music sounds from a box near the orchestra than from the gallery. When you come back you must try it for yourself.

"Sunday morning, seven o'clock. I slept capitally, and hope that you have too. I thoroughly enjoyed half a capon brought me by friend Primus. At ten o'clock I am going to Mass at the Piarists' chapel, for Leitgeb tells me that I can then speak to the Director. I shall stay there for dinner.

"Primus told me yesterday evening that a number of people are ill in Baden. Is this true? Take care of yourself in this treacherous weather. Primus has just come back with the tiresome news that the mail-coach left before seven this morning, and that no other leaves until the afternoon, so that all my writing last night and early this morning has been to no purpose. You will not get the letter until this evening, which vexes me very much. I shall most certainly come out next Sunday, and then we can all visit the Casino together and return together on Monday.

"Lechleitner has been to the opera again; if not exactly a connoisseur he is at least a true music-lover, which — most certainly is not. He is a real monster; he much prefers a good dinner. Farewell, my dear, I send you a million kisses and am ever

"Your

"Mozart.

"PS. Kiss Sophie for me. I send Siesmay (probably Süssmayr) a few punches on the nose and a good hair-pull. A thousand compliments to Stoll. Adieu. The hour is striking—farewell—we shall meet again . . ."

"October 14th, 1791.

"Dearest, sweetest little wife,

"Hofer drove with me yesterday, the 13th, to see Carl. We dined there, and then drove home together. At six o'clock I called for Salieri and Cavalieri in the carriage, took them to my box, and then went quickly back to fetch Mamma and Carl, whom we had left at Hofer's. You cannot conceive how kind they both were, and how delighted not only with my music, but the libretto and the whole thing. They said it was an opera worthy of being performed on the most festive occasion before the greatest monarch, and that they would go very often to hear it, for they have never seen a finer or a more charming spectacle. Salieri listened and gazed with rapt attention and from the symphony to the final chorus there was not a single number that did not call forth from him a 'bravo' or a 'bello'; it seemed as if they would never be done with thanking me for the favour I had done them. They had in any case intended to go to the opera yesterday. But they would have had to be in their seats by four o'clock, whereas in my box they heard and saw the performance in peace and quiet. After the performance I arranged for them to be driven home in my carriage and then supped with Carl at Hofer's, after which we drove home together, and both slept soundly. Carl was overjoyed at being taken to the opera. He looks splendid; in so far as his health is concerned he could not be in a better place, but everything else, unfortunately, is wretched. They may succeed in turning out a good peasant! But enough! Since his great studies (God save the mark!) do not begin until Monday I have asked if I may keep him till next Sunday after dinner; I said that you were very anxious to see him. To-morrow, Sunday, I shall drive out with him to you, when you can either keep him with you or I will take him back to Hecker's after dinner. Think this over, I do not think a month can do him any harm. . . . At any rate he is no worse, though not a scrap better, than he always was; he is as unruly as ever, chatters away as usual, and is even less anxious to work than before, for all he does at this school is to run about the garden for five hours in the morning and five in the afternoon, as he himself admitted to me. In a word, the children there do nothing but eat, drink, sleep and go for walks . . . I have just sent my faithful comrade Primus to get me some dinner from the Bürgerspital. I am highly pleased with the fellow. Only once has he left me in the lurch, and then I was obliged to spend the night with the Hofers, which I found very provoking, for they do not rise early enough for me. I prefer being at home, because I have settled down to a regular routine, and this one occasion put me in a very bad humour. Yesterday was wholly taken up with going to Bernsdorf; so I could not write to you, but there is no excuse for your not having written to me for two days. But I definitely hope to hear from you to-day, and to see you myself to-morrow and to embrace you with all my heart.

"Farewell, ever your
"Mozart."

We do not know whether Mozart's intention to visit

Baden was ever carried out, whether Constanze's return took place according to plan, whether she stayed away longer or whether she was given some warning and hastened home earlier than she had intended. We only know that when she saw her husband again and all the ominous signs of utter collapse stared her in the face, she was rudely brought down to earth. She was seized with panic; and he no longer hid his distress from her. She was with him again; he opened his heart to her. Salieri, he thought, had poisoned him. For had he not, since the production of *Die Zauberflöte,* which was proving a greater and greater success, become a dangerous rival to Salieri? Constanze called in the family doctor, a certain Dr. Closset, hardly a worthy successor to the late Dr. Barisani; and she took the *Requiem* from her husband and locked it away. In her eyes it was the *Requiem* that was to blame for everything. She would have liked to tear it to pieces—as she had once torn up Mozart's promise of marriage We know her to have been an emotional woman. But the care she now lavished on the invalid, who had been left far too long to fend for himself, proved so efficacious that he recovered. He went for a drive with her; once more they were able to show themselves in the Prater as in the old days. She was his Stanzi of their happiest days. And he now regarded. his fear of having been poisoned as a delusion. His condition had so far improved that he was able to complete the unfinished Masonic Cantata; this was on November 15th. He conducted it himself. He plucked up courage, and was inspired with hope. He insisted that Constanze should get out the *Requiem* for him, and applied himself afresh to the exhausting task.

"Tell Mamma that I am getting well, and that I shall come during the octave of her name day to offer her my congratulations" was a message he gave to his sister-in-law

Sophie. According to her he had latterly grown fonder of the old lady. He frequently visited her house in the Wieden "and never came to us empty-handed"[1]

This happiness was of short duration. His illness once more returned, to gain a firmer hold of him than ever, and with it returned the shadows, the old despondency, the conviction that he had been poisoned and that all was lost. "Primus", the janitor Deiner, has left us an account of how, one cold, unfriendly November day, Mozart ventured forth for the last time. He saw him enter the tavern "zur silbernen Schlange", which was situated in the Kärtnerstrasse and bore the number 1112. Finding strangers sitting in the first parlour, he went straight into the smaller one adjoining it, threw himself wearily into an armchair and let his head sink on to his right hand. He ordered wine, but when the waiter had brought it remained sitting there quite motionless without touching it. Joseph Deiner, who had entered through another door, was transfixed by the sight, and could not take his eyes off him. Mozart's extreme pallor appalled him. His powdered fair hair was in disorder, the queue negligently tied. Suddenly he looked up, and seeing Deiner, "Well, Joseph, how are you?" he asked. "It is I who should be asking you that," said Deiner, and assuming that Mozart's digestion was upset, he remarked: "That's nothing to worry about, *Herr Musikmeister.*" "My digestion is better than you think," said Mozart. "I have learned to digest a good many things." And he sighed. "I suppose I must not tell you the story of the Turkish music," Deiner now asked, "over which you have so often laughed?" "No," replied Mozart, "I feel there will soon be an end for me of music-making. I feel an icy chill upon me which I cannot explain. Deiner, drink my

[1] Letter to Nissen.

wine and take this coin. Winter is upon us, and we need some wood. My wife will go with you to buy it. I shall have the stove lit to-day."

Next morning at seven o'clock, Deiner put in an appearance at Mozart's lodging in the Rauhensteingasse. The maid told him that the *Herr Kapellmeister* had been very ill in the night; but Constanze called to him to come in. Mozart lay in a white-draped bed, which stood in a corner. Hearing Deiner' s voice, he opened his eyes and whispered: " There will be nothing today, Joseph, our business to-day is with doctors and apothecaries."

It was this same Deiner who had come to Mozart's house at the same time the year before, the period of his greatest want, to see if he required any wood. On that occasion Deiner had seen him dancing very gaily round his study with Constanze. On his asking him whether he were teaching his wife to dance, Mozart had laughed. "We're only warming ourselves up," he said, "because we're freezing and can't afford to buy any wood." Deiner had rushed off immediately and brought some of his own. Mozart had promised to pay him well for it the moment he was in funds.

This time he had no difficulty in paying for the wood, but he never rose from his bed again. His hands and feet swelled. And at this stage Constanze lost her head and broke down completely. What was to happen to her if he were to leave her? It was her sister Sophie who stepped into the foreground in the sick-room. Mozart was to linger on for another two whole weeks, fully conscious the whole time and with death always before his eyes. He paid no heed to the doctor's reassurances. Whence came this certainty?

The one thing that held him more than ever in its spell

was the *Requiem*. He would have each number sung to him the moment it was completed, and, as long as he was still able, would accompany it himself on the piano.[1]

The friends who visited him during these days found him quite composed and as charming as ever. Watch in hand, he would follow the course of the performances of *Die Zauberflöte*. Now the first act would be over, and he would hum to himself the bird-catcher's song. And now the interval would be over, Sarastro would be singing his emerald song. Pamina would be lying in her rose bower; the nimble Moor would be skipping across the stage, the Queen of the Night descending. The audience would fill the circles and the stalls . . . And he, Mozart, was to leave all this—arrived at his goal, assured by his fame of a carefree existence, borne aloft to the heights, liberated at last from the petty struggle for daily bread, dedicated, as was fitting, free and unimpeded, to his creative work, and spared the trials of poverty. For not only was he assured from now on of 1,000 florins annually from the Hungarian nobility; an even more splendid offer had come from Holland, and da Ponte was able to hold out the most tempting prospects for him in London. All these riches fell into his hands when they no longer had the strength to grasp them.

Thus the ties that anchored him to the earth were richly and closely woven, and nothing could be more tragic than their severance. At last the lovely summer of life was approaching and wafting his way its genial breezes—too late. As his strength ebbed, the torturing realisation of all this increased. We know that he spoke of it to his sister-in-law Sophie. His farewell from life was that of a martyr; but his death was that of a conqueror. The *Requiem* affords

[1] Contemporaries spoke highly of his soft tenor voice; when conducting however, he would sometimes speak loudly in his excitement.

proof of this: that graceful elegy is pervaded with the security, the confidence, the indestructible peace of his spirit, far removed from the terrors that pervade the *Qui Tollis* of his Mass in C minor. The shadows lift, a new morning dawns upon this death-bed. It is not without a certain timidity that we speak today of the religious feelings of a human being. But those of Mozart cannot be passed over. He was, although he did not probe into the matter, for self-analysis was a thing utterly alien to him, the timeless human being *par excellence,* the eternal pioneer. In taking up his stand against Italian music, which had already degenerated, he had acknowledged himself a German composer. His later incidental remarks on this theme were unconscious reservations. There are widely differing conceptions of what is meant by German, but both he and Goethe were typical Germans, if in a class apart. We know how far Goethe felt himself to be a citizen of the world and how he advocated an unprejudiced attitude in national matters; and we know also what Mozart felt about militarism even before such a thing can be said to have been known.

He was a pacifist before ever the term pacifism existed. And we have already said what a worthy exponent the watchwords of the French revolution, before they were even coined, before the Terror debased them, had found in him.

His Catholicism was of a quite special nature, and in this connection we must challenge the view of Henri Ghéon, who represents Mozart as a man of naïvely pious temperament. That he certainly was not. He took things *cum grano salis* and certainly did not swallow them whole. Nothing was novel to him and there was, a great deal he discounted; indeed, his simplicity did not extend beyond a certain point. His best friends were two priests, the musical Abbé Bullinger and the great teacher of music, Padre Martini. Otherwise his attitude towards the clergy was not untinged with scepticism. His experiences with the Archbishop had not been without their effect. He had no great knowledge of people, it is true. The study of human nature takes time which he could not afford to devote to it; but in all essential matters he evinced at a very early age exceptional powers of discrimination. He looked beyond the dross, his concern was with what the passage of time could never shatter or destroy.

His Church compositions, by which we mean, not those composed in the course of his duties and thrown off from time to time more or less according to formula and in deference to the taste of Archbishop Colloredo, but the Masses, which came from his heart, all the lovely motets, dating in part from the days of his adolescence, the *Litany of the Sacrament*, the *Sancta Maria*, the *Ave verum corpus*, the unfinished *Requiem*—all these, like Beethoven's *Missa Solemnis*, Haydn's *Seven Words* are just as much syntheses of genuine catholicism as is Strasbourg Cathedral, as is many a baroque church in Bavaria and Austria, as are the loggie of Raphael. Let us contemplate the cathedral of Chartres, let us enter it. Even more powerful than the aesthetic, is the ethical impression we get of a truth formulated out of stone, marble and glass, of a *verité intrinsèque*, the function of which lies beyond anything that can be expressed in words. What is the purpose of art if not to imply and suggest? Debating with God? Oh no—at most wrestling with the angel; at the best the gilded meshes of the net mercifully outspread to break the fall into the last abyss of perplexity and confusion.

Johann Sebastian Bach's Passion music, his Christmas

Oratorio, almost all his ariosos, without doubt, derive their inspiration from the purest sources of Christianity, and we all love him—that goes without saying. He is never so impelling as when he begins to cry out, as when his spirit raises its voice to God or the heavens in joy or in lamentation. It is only from his explicitness, from that alone, from invocations such as "Jesu mine" that we shrink back. For us these two words do not go together. At this point our spirit takes refuge in the ceremonial of a language that admits of no first person singular—the universal, aloof and reticent Latin, which, without variant, without fervour, in the same level tone throughout the ages, identifies itself with the immensity it proclaims; which, in spite of or because of this, is so constructed as to convey inward communion, nay, ecstasy.

Any other starting point than this for Mozart's devotional music is unthinkable. As for Bach, he was too close in point of time to our common past strictly to be called a Protestant composer. Protestantism as such had not yet attained its full growth. It had already given proof of its achievements for our spiritual life, but what other possibilities did it offer? . . . In this respect the Reformation Symphony of that noble composer, Mendelssohn, is vastly instructive. In it, to be sure, we find a gallant fighter facing the Lord, giving battle, nay, making an onslaught. But the wretched architecture of Luther's "Rock and Fortress" compared with that of the "Eternal City" is also apparent in it. Even the churches that had been left standing, the expropriated churches—into what tedious lecture halls had they not been turned! Instead of candlelight and soft shadows, what a cold, prosaic light! What bare pews! In such a chill atmosphere how could the unfathomable ceremonial of the Mass, in all its insubstantiality, fail to be thrust aside, to be driven away like the ghost of a ghost. Here was the ultimate source of the deplorable and yet inevitable breach, for as to the necessity of reforms there was unanimity. Here lay the kernel of the dissensions to which ignorance on the part of this world stood sponsor; that world which is so constituted that the most preposterous absurdities can bear witness both for and against a cause, that success affords no proof of its truth, that ultimate verities can be misapplied and nullified, that ultimate latitude can be misconstrued as dire restriction. So many of us are Catholics without being aware of it, and vice versa. And here is the bridge that joins us brothers in the shadow of the mills that grind slowly.

Wherefore then the bickering? "Man does not go back," is a saying of Goethe's, and, "a true Catholic is really a Protestant. For he wishes to be so." For Catholicism too a new hour will strike; the 'Reformation' so ardently longed for by Catherine of Siena has still not been achieved. But the artists and the poets have never failed to appreciate the mildness of its watchwords, its concealed elasticity.

That ultra-Catholic, Francis Jammes, would like to include in his heaven the gods and demi-gods of classical mythology, and Pan especially is dear to him. His faith drives him to the point of acknowledging the eternal and transcendental element underlying the earthly. Hence we find in him those traces of latent serenity in face of the ups and downs of life; it is as though he could detect an element of escape even in the inevitable, in what is past and done with. Such Catholics, however, indulge, within the fold really of their *credo quia absurdum,* in "free-thinking", and they would be the last to object to the fact that Mozart, when he "already had the taste of death on his tongue"[1]—what a grim realisation for a sick man!—had no thought of summoning a priest. His sister-in-law did so for him. The priest wanted to know whether she had been asked by the dying man to call him in, and when she replied in the negative, he declined to visit him, for which he was reviled by the family. But we prefer to assume that he was an enlightened man who realised that in special cases his consolations might only prove an intrusion, nay, might be construed as meddling . . . The thing that occupied Mozart solely and exclusively during the last day of his life was his *Requiem.* All his fevered thoughts turned on the unfinished *Requiem.* At two o'clock he had the score brought to his bedside, and a death-bed rehearsal took place. Benedikt Schack sang the soprano, Hofer the tenor, Franz Gerl, the original Sarastro, the bass; Mozart himself sang the alto. After a few bars of the *Lacrimosa* he burst into such a passion of weeping that he was unable to continue.

Lacrimosa dies illa
qua resurget ex favilla
judicandus homo reus.

At this point the *Requiem* breaks off. Later in the day he gave his favourite pupil instructions as to how it should be concluded, no doubt raising his hand from the coverlet, and conducting with his fingers. It grew dark. The night of sorrow had set in which Mozart was not to survive.

In the evening, while he was discussing with Süssmayr the conclusion of the *Lacrimosa,* he enjoined upon Constanze and his sister-in-law to keep his death a secret from everybody until Albrechtsberger[1] had first been informed. "That," he declared to them, "is my duty before God and

[1] Remark made by Sophie, his sister-in-law, in a letter to Nissen.

the world." So certain was he that he would not live until the morrow.

Someone was now sent for the doctor, but found him only after a long search in the theatre. He sent a message to say that he would come as soon as the performance was over. When he arrived Mozart lay in a burning fever. He was past help now. Süssmayr was informed secretly of the hopelessness of his condition. Nevertheless cold compresses were applied to the dying man. Shuddering from head to foot, he soon lost consciousness. His sufferings were at an end. But his imagination obviously still revolved round the unfinished composition. "The last movement of his lips was an endeavour to indicate where the kettledrums should be used in his *Requiem*. I still seem to hear the sound."[2]

Towards midnight he sat up suddenly and stared out of large fever-wearied eyes into space, fell back again, turned his face to the wall, and sinking gradually into a deep sleep, breathed away his spirit without a struggle. It was five minutes to one in the morning of December 5th, 1791.

Thus died this glory of Catholicism.

The night had been stormy. Snow and rain over Vienna. In her unbridled despair, Constanze, utterly forgetful of her children, wanted to lie down by the side of her husband and to die with him. Yet did she even carry out her husband's strict injunctions to keep his death a secret until Albrechtsberger had been informed of it? She sent word, if not first at any rate simultaneously, to Baron van Swieten. And it is the latter, not the former, whom we find taking charge of things both as mourner and counsellor. He was

[1] Johann Georg Albrechtsberger expected to be appointed to the post of assistant *Kapellmeister* at the Stefanskirche after Mozart's death.
[2] Letter of his sister-in-law to Nissen.

only too willing to let himself be regarded as a friend and patron of Mozart's. Did Constanze hope to touch his heart by the admission that she only had 60 florins in hand? How many kindnesses Mozart must have shown him, how many priceless pages of music from the hand of the master had not the rich baron in his possession! But he was not to be trapped in this way; in view of the family's position, he considered a pauper's funeral to be indicated. Later on a memorial to the Emperor. Condolences, hand-shakes. Exit Baron van Swieten.

Albrechtsberger was eliminated. And so things took their inevitable course.

The appearance before daybreak of a certain Count Deyn, the Director of the Cabinet of Arts, to take a plaster cast of Mozart's features, remains unexplained. How revealing this death mask would have been! It was not to be. It was allowed, as all the world knows, to crumble to pieces.

Sixty florins is a small sum. But for a third-class funeral it more than sufficed. The expenses of the interment amounted to eight florins, thirty-six kreutzer, the hearse cost three florins. A total of eleven florins thirty-six kreutzer.

Benediction was pronounced on the corpse at three o'clock on December 6th, in the Chapel of the Holy Cross in St. Stephen's. That is to say, not even in the main body of the Church. Very few candles, of course. No honours of any kind.

Süssmayr had followed the coffin from the house of mourning, and at the church he was joined by Salieri, *Kapellmeister* Roser, Dasler the 'cellist, Deiner the janitor, and Baron van Swieten; presumably also Hofer, Albrechtsberger, Lange, Schack, Schikaneder and Anton Stadler.

But we have no proof of the presence of these latter. There were also three women present; Constanze was not among them.

The way led along the Schulerstrasse to the churchyard of St. Mark's. Arrived at the Stubentor, the little cortège allowed itself to be daunted by the inclemency of the weather. A consultation was held, and in the end not a single mourner continued to the graveside. Only the two bearers went on to the end to deposit the coffin in the funeral chapel, whence it was removed on the following day and lowered into the grave. According to contemporary accounts, Josef Deiner was the only person who took the trouble to look for the grave. He went to Constanze and asked her if she was not going to have a cross put up for her husband's grave. Her answer was: "That is sure to be seen to."

Six days after Mozart's death she handed her memorial in person to the Emperor. With the payments that subsequently came in she had a total of 200 florins in hand. (Two loans were entered among Mozart's assets as bad debts: one of 300 florins to Gilowsky and one of 500 florins to the clarinettist, Stadler.) The proceeds of the benefit concert which took place on December 28th covered all the most pressing debts, particularly as the faithful Puchberg, who proved himself as loyal a friend now as ever, waived his claims until "better times". One wonders whether Constanze remembered him when they did come?

Aroused from her fleeting grief, this woman who had hitherto shown herself to be so happy-go-lucky now developed an uncommonly good business sense, and busied herself in every direction. It has been proved that she did all she could to wrest from Süssmayr the *Requiem* which Mozart had so expressly entrusted to him, and that it was only when one conductor after another had refused it that she returned it to him.

She also tried to gain possession of "two interesting letters on music" which Mozart had written to Frau von Trattner. Presumably there were a good many more than two of them. Frau von Trattner refused to give them up. Probably one of Mozart's dearest friends, his junior by two years, she died as early as 1794 and preserved the secret of her relations with him.

Constanze continued to show no interest in her husband's grave. Sixteen years after his death, at the prompting of Haydn's biographer, she paid, in his company, her first visit to the cemetery of St. Mark's. No one there knew anything of the grave. It had been lost sight of ever since 1799. All she managed to discover was that the grave-digger employed at the time of her husband's death had recently died.

In the year 1832 King Ludwig I of Bavaria, an admirer of Mozart, paid a visit to Salzburg, where Constanze, hardly to the delight of poor Nannerl, had settled upon the death of her second husband, Nissen. The King, from whom she received a pension as Mozart's widow, looked her up and asked her how it was that she had never had a monumental tablet erected over her husband's grave. Whereupon she answered: "I have often visited cemeteries, both in the country and in large towns, and everywhere, particularly in Vienna, I have seen a great many crosses in the cemeteries. I was therefore under the impression that the parish where the burial took place saw to the crosses too."

This is the drivelling style of her diary. She left a fortune of 250,000 florins, of which, according to her own account, only six or seven thousand came from her second husband's estate. She would, then, have been quite capable of looking after Mozart's affairs and relieving him of the cares and worries of daily life.

. . . . .

"In solcher feierlicher Pracht
Wirst du nun bald der ganzen Welt erscheinen,
Ins Reich der Sonne wirket deine Macht,
Pamina and Tamino weinen,
Ihr höchstes Glück leigt in des Grabes Nacht."[1]

The "tomb's darkness "—as Goethe's lines indicate to us—is our portion, and it is against us that the sting of this death is turned. Pamina and Tamino weep. Nothing more was to follow on those arias, those *divertimenti,* nothing more on the breath-taking beauty of those pieces of chamber-music, nothing more on the bewildering magic of those dances. The G minor Symphony was his last, and from the stage he had nothing more to say to us.

It is highly improbable that Salieri poisoned him, even if, as some maintain and others deny, he accused himself of the crime when in a delirium. There are no grounds whatever, moreover, for referring to Mozart's vast output as a reason for his premature death. He got through an enormous quantity of work, it is true, this "little man in the green coat", but work was at once his pleasure and his elixir. All the more wide of the mark is it to ascribe his death to a constitution weakened by illnesses in childhood

[1] "In such resplendent majesty
To all the world will you 'ere long appear,
Your power reaches ev'n to the realm of the sun,
Pamina and Tamino weep,
In the tomb's darkness lies their highest bliss."

or even to his mode of life.

Oh no! but the *conditions* under which he had to produce his masterpieces—it was they that wore him out.

We have seen how mental sufferings wore him down, how he collapsed after the mysterious experiences of the year 1776 and how he was racked by fever after the violent abuse levelled at him by Archbishop Colloredo and his suite.

For in Mozart the world possessed not only a musical miracle, but the most sensitive and vulnerable instrument that has perhaps ever existed. And yet to him was given the lot of a common, humble mortal, and whilst he enriched the world to a degree of which he was quite aware, it abandoned him to dire poverty, to its bondage, its privations and hardships. He had not the good fortune to encounter, like Leonardo, a Medici and a King of France, or like Goethe a German prince, themselves noble enough to appreciate the nobility of genius and to know that it required to be quite specially fostered and cherished. Such understanding, such comprehension, is in all circumstances rare. It was the first care of the eighteen-year-old Ludwig II of Bavaria, his coronation scarcely over, to send someone in search of Richard Wagner in order to reach out to him the hand of a brother. Wagner, haunted by creditors, was at his lowest ebb. Philistines to this day hold him up to censure for not having been more circumspect in financial matters. Peace, peace, he returned everything in full and overflowing measure. For Mozart salvation came too late. He too had no idea of how to deal with money, how to manage his affairs. Granted, granted. Was that his business? He was far too fine to swagger, far too genuine to try to impress, far too noble not to take his neighbour seriously. How could so tender a soul have withstood any longer the atmosphere to which it was exposed? Its golden strings were taut like those of a harp and life seized hold of them with all too ungentle and importunate a hand. He should never have been subjected to the necessity of having to haggle with money-lenders. It was insupportable for the proudest of all givers to continue in the role of a beggar, to compose begging letters . . . His world killed him. The way in which it suffered him to depart is merely a symbol of the fate it meted out to him. Has the world grown any better? What security would it offer him now? What would he be to-day? A war cripple perhaps. And to-morrow? Things, it is true, turn towards the light, but this world knows no awakening. Let us seek salvation in beauty, in goodness, in the spirit. Let us take refuge in these suns that shine upon us.

Index

BOCA RATON PUBLIC LIBRARY, FLORIDA
3 3656 0290087 3